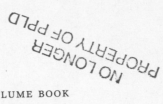
A PLUME BOOK

THE ART OF DOING

CAMILLE SWEENEY has known she wanted to be a writer since she was five years old. She is a frequent contributor to the *New York Times* and other publications. As a project editor for the *New York Times Sunday Magazine*, she worked on numerous special issues and features and won a New York Times Publishers Award. She is a MacDowell Arts Colony Fellow and in her spare time writes fiction.

JOSH GOSFIELD has worked on farms and as a carpenter and cartoonist. He was the art director of *New York Magazine*. He has won numerous awards for illustrations and photographs he produced for major magazines, record companies and book publishers. He has had several one-man shows of paintings in New York and Los Angeles and has art directed music videos and written and directed short films. For his latest fine-art project, *GIGI, the Black Flower*, Gosfield was both author and creator of a critically acclaimed, multimedia archive of a fictional celebrity.

The Art of

DOING

How Superachievers
Do What They Do and
How They Do It So Well

**Camille Sweeney
and Josh Gosfield**

A PLUME BOOK

PLUME
Published by Penguin Group
Penguin Group (USA) Inc., 375 Hudson Street, New York, New York 10014, U.S.A. •
Penguin Group (Canada), 90 Eglinton Avenue East, Suite 700, Toronto, Ontario, Canada M4P
2Y3 (a division of Pearson Penguin Canada Inc.) • Penguin Books Ltd., 80 Strand, London
WC2R 0RL, England • Penguin Ireland, 25 St. Stephen's Green, Dublin 2, Ireland (a division
of Penguin Books Ltd.) • Penguin Group (Australia), 707 Collins Street, Melbourne, Victoria
3008, Australia (a division of Pearson Australia Group Pty. Ltd.) • Penguin Books India Pvt.
Ltd., 11 Community Centre, Panchsheel Park, New Delhi – 110 017, India • Penguin Books
(NZ), 67 Apollo Drive, Rosedale, Auckland 0632, New Zealand (a division of Pearson New
Zealand Ltd.) • Penguin Books, Rosebank Office Park, 181 Jan Smuts Avenue, Parktown North
2193, South Africa • Penguin China, B7 Jaiming Center, 27 East Third Ring Road North,
Chaoyang District, Beijing 100020, China

Penguin Books Ltd., Registered Offices: 80 Strand, London WC2R 0RL, England

First published by Plume, a member of Penguin Group (USA) Inc.

First Printing, February 2013
10 9 8 7 6 5 4 3 2 1

Photograph credits appear on pages 271–272.

LIBRARY OF CONGRESS CATALOGING-IN-PUBLICATION DATA

Sweeney, Camille.
  The art of doing : how superachievers do what they do and how they do it so well / Camille
Sweeney and Josh Gosfield.
    p. cm.
  "A Plume book."
  ISBN 978-0-452-29817-0 (pbk).
  1. Success—Case studies. 2. Success in business—Case studies. 3. Achievement motivation—Case studies. 4. Successful people—Case studies. I. Gosfield, Josh. II. Title.
  BF637.S8S837 2013
  650.1—dc23   2012032177

Printed in the United States of America
Set in ITC Esprit Book

ALWAYS LEARNING   PEARSON

To Roxie

Who's Who in
THE ART OF DOING

How to Act
Laura Linney

How to Be a Diva
Anna Netrebko

How to Be a Dog Whisperer
Cesar Millan

How to Be a Game Show
Champion
Ken Jennings

How to Be a Major Leaguer
Yogi Berra

How to Be a Tennis Champion
Martina Navratilova

How to Be Funny (on TV)
Alec Baldwin and Robert
Carlock

How to Be the Most
Fabulous You
Simon Doonan

How to Build a Beautiful
Baseball Park
Joseph Spear

How to Create a Great
Company Culture
Tony Hsieh

How to Create a Mind-Bending
Crossword Puzzle
Will Shortz

How to Create One of the
World's Most Popular Blogs
Mark Frauenfelder

How to Cultivate an
Exceptional Wine
Randall Grahm

How to Fight for Justice
Constance Rice

How to Find
Extraterrestrial Life
Jill Tarter

How to Find Love Online
OkCupid Founders

How to Get the Funk
George Clinton

How to Get the Inside Scoop
Barry Levine

How to Grow Killer Weed
Ed Rosenthal

How to Hunt Big Game
Chad Schearer

How to Inspire a Student
Erin Gruwell

How to Live Life
on the High Wire
Philippe Petit

How to Live Life on the Road
Ray Benson

How to Make Erotica That
Turns Women On
Candida Royalle

How to Make It as a Rock Band
in the Digital Era
OK Go

How to Negotiate a
Hostage Crisis
Gary Noesner

How to Open a Great Restaurant
(and Stay in Business)
David Chang

How to Optimize Your Brain
Richard Restak

How to Produce a
Smash Hit on Broadway
Marc Routh

How to Rehabilitate
a Bad Reputation
Michael Sitrick

How to Sail Around the World
Jessica Watson

How to Shoot a Great War Shot
Without Getting Shot
Lynsey Addario

How to Start a Start-up
Bill Gross

How to Win Friends and
Influence People (in the
Twenty-First Century)
Guy Kawasaki

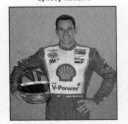

How to Win the Indy 500
Helio Castroneves

How to Write a
Runaway Bestseller
Stephen J. Dubner

Contents

Nothing succeeds like success.

—Alexandre Dumas

Express yourself! Whatever you do, uh, do it good.

—Charles Wright & the Watts 103rd Street Rhythm

AUTHORS' NOTE

How This Book Came to Be

The inspiration for this book came from an unusual person, unusual because she doesn't exist. Gigi Gaston, '60s French pop star, was invented by coauthor and fine artist Josh Gosfield, who documented her fictional career with everything from meticulously created LP covers to music videos. The art project prompted the questions, "What is success?" and "Who gets it?" and "Why do people care about it?" Armed with these queries and an insatiable curiosity about the lives of other people we came up with the very simple idea for this book. Instead of theorizing on success Gladwellian-style or offering up some easily digestible, quick-tip formulae, why not go straight to the source? Why not simply ask successful people how they do what they do?

We dreamed that this book could be a version of the world's most fabulous dinner party. "Your guests should be remarkable for something—either beauty, wit, talent, money," wrote Lady Constance Howard in her 1885 book on etiquette. "You should be certain of such a flow of bright conversation that no one can be bored or feel in any way neglected." Although a bit dated, Lady Constance's advice summed up our own philosophy about our fantasy guest list for this book. We wanted brilliant, accomplished people at the top of their field, and of course a mix that would include people in business and art, media and sports, the young and old, the high-brow and low and the revered as well as some rogues.

Take a look at our table of contents—the world's most famous dog whisperer, Cesar Millan, is sandwiched between an opera diva and the winningest game show champ in history. A vintner is next to a civil rights lawyer who is next to an extraterrestrial hunter. Alec Baldwin has tennis champion Martina Navratilova on one side and cultural gadfly Simon Doonan on the other. And after all, what's a dinner party without a big game hunter, a rock band, a hostage negotiator, a bestselling author and Will Shortz, the cross-word puzzle editor of the *New York Times*?

Many people asked us, "How did you get to all of those people?" Our strategy: *Never say never.* Successful people are busy people. We hit dead ends. But we never took "No!" from a handler for an answer. (At least not until we heard it for the fifth or sixth time.) We employed a vast network of family, friends, semi-acquaintances, insta-pals, colleagues, even exes, chasing down every lead, including one example of six degrees of separation when we got in touch with Camille's sister's high school friend's daughter's speech therapist whose best friend was married to a Zen billionaire whom we desperately wanted for the book. Did he say, "Yes"? No, he didn't. But maybe we'll get him next time. Meanwhile, we're still waiting to hear back from Hillary Clinton and Lady Gaga!

Since we had no preconceived notions of what our participants would say, our conversations with them were often part tango, part wrestling match. We tried to both draw out our interviewees and challenge them on their beliefs of what led to their success—their work habits, turning points, experiences, insights and goals. As we accumulated interviews about these amazing people's vocational lives, the book began to feel like Studs Terkel on steroids. And then we did our best to distill their thoughts, experiences and principles into 10 concise strategies—written in their own words—to reveal not only how they do what they do, but how they do it so well.

And since a collaboration is a lot like a marriage, we'd find ourselves saying, "I do" all the time—*I do* like that idea, or *I do* like that suggestion, or *I do* like that turn of phrase. Except when one of us would say, *I don't.* Then, just as in a marriage, we'd have to compromise. But because we actually *are* married, we had the advantage of already knowing (at least in theory) how to do that. We also had the pleasure of sharing the thrilling and mind-altering moments of speaking with some of the world's superachievers. And then discussing it afterward, at home, over dinner, often so excessively that our six-year-old would plead, "Could we please stop talking about *The Art of Doing?*"

Reading about how to produce a smash hit on Broadway, write a runaway bestseller or start a start-up, you may feel inspired and think: *I'm going to get off this couch and go do one of these things!*

Or, you may think: *Actually, I'm not likely to do any of these things, but I can use some of these strategies in my own work.*

Or, you may simply flip through these pages, delighted to be entertained by the achievements of others.

Whatever your motivation, whether you are a college student, middle manager, entrepreneur or retiree, we hope you enjoy the opportunity as much as we did of hearing directly from these extraordinary people and peeling back the layers of their vocational and life experiences to discover their *Art of Doing.*

Introduction

What Superachievers Have in Common

In the beginning, our goal was to uncover what was unique about each one of the dozens of superachievers we interviewed for this book—what were the particular qualities or approaches that vaulted them above others in their fields? But after months of research and over 100 hours of conversations, we were often surprised to discover how much a tennis champion, for instance, and a rock band think alike, or how a race car driver and an extraterrestrial hunter share similar traits. Our participants' vocations, goals, philosophical perspectives and personalities could not have been more different, but as their responses to our questions accumulated, we began to see patterns. We came to realize that these extraordinary people shared many core principles and practices that had led to their great successes.

Here you will read about the 10 most important strategies we discovered. Perhaps learning about what our superachievers have in common will inspire you to reflect on your own work habits and approaches—it certainly did with us.

1. Dedication

What does a young Frenchman leafing through a magazine in his dentist's office have in common with an African-American teen ironing her family's clothes as she watches the Watergate Hearings on TV in the basement of her home?

The Frenchman and the African-American teen, now grown up, told us of experiences in which they'd had visions of their vocational futures. Philippe Petit (Chapter 22), reading the magazine, came across a rendering of the not-yet-constructed World Trade Center that inspired him to embark on his six-year odyssey to walk on a wire 110 stories high across the void between the towers. Constance Rice (Chapter 14), the teen at the ironing board watching the Watergate Hearings, was transfixed by the black congresswoman Barbara Jordan who rose up and in a booming voice addressed the Senate Committee and the nation. At that moment Rice not only burned a hole through her father's shirt, but she knew what she was meant to do—fight for justice.

In the aftermath of their visions, Petit and Rice could not have imagined all that would be required of them. Neither Petit's dream of crossing the towers nor Rice's of fighting for justice came with an instruction manual. To accomplish their feats they'd have to overcome fear, test their plans against reality and maintain an unwavering focus on what their visions had revealed to them about their future selves.

Others that we spoke with were similarly inspired by visions, as varied as the individuals themselves. They received messages about their future selves encoded in natural phenomena, great societal events, chance encounters, books, movies, inner voices—one was even inspired by a humble bowl of soup. Some of their inspirations were instantaneous flashes; others occurred in phases or as a series of ephemeral nudges. They came at different stages of life—from childhood to middle age.

By their very nature, these visions are so mercurial and mysterious that there may be no satisfactory way to define them. But what we wanted to know was, what does one do when called to fight for justice or to walk a wire 110 stories in the sky? Once you've devoted yourself to a calling, can anything else matter? Accumulation of wealth, material goods or fame? Even daily life? What we found in our conversations with these superachievers was that success did not come to them in the thunderclap of their *Eureka!* moments. Talent was just the beginning. Their sustained success depended on many factors—some in their control, and some not—but the first steps of these superachievers were to know themselves and to assess what they had to work with. Then, their progress toward their goals was furthered by their fierce dedication to the day-to-day struggle for achievement.

Beyond venturing into the desert for forty days and nights, popping peyote or donning a "God Helmet" (designed by a neuroscientist in Ontario to induce mystical experiences), there is no surefire way to *call* a calling.

But, when you *do* have glimmerings of something that you might like to do one day—if you only had more time on your hands or more money, or were in the right place at the right time—you can take heart from the people you will read about in this book. Just like any one of us, they started with no road map or guarantee of success. But they went out and picked up the ball or the pen, the guitar or the kitchen knife, and took the first step. And then, the next.

2. Intelligent Persistence

In the early '90s a beautiful young Russian soprano who loved music was studying opera at the St. Petersburg Conservatory. She told us how despite her single-minded focus on developing her voice, her teachers thought that perhaps, at best, one day she could sing in a chorus somewhere.

But the soprano wasn't going to let her teachers' low opinion of her stop her from achieving her goal. While becoming a part-time janitor may not seem like a brilliant career move for an aspiring opera star, she took a job mopping floors at St. Petersburg's Kirov Opera, the greatest opera company in Russia. Still working hard in the conservatory, she earned the chance to audition for the Kirov and was accepted into the ensemble. During rehearsals, when the lead singer became ill, the stage director asked the soprano if she knew the part. "Of course I knew it," she told us. "I knew all the parts. I was ready." She had worked hard; she had worked smart by putting herself in the right place at the right time. And she peformed well. Her once-skeptical teachers never could have imagined the career that the soprano, Anna Netrebko (Chapter 2), would go on to have, becoming an operatic superstar and the reigning diva of the twenty-first century.

Anyone pursuing a goal is likely to be given the conflicting advice to "Hang in there and persevere" on the one hand and "Always be ready to shift gears" on the other. Reid Hoffman, the CEO of LinkedIn, and others have discussed this strategic dilemma, suggesting that a key factor in success is having the flexibility and intelligence—as Anna Netrebko did—to be able to follow both pieces of advice; to know when to pivot, to rethink your plan, while still maintaining the mission.

David Chang (Chapter 27), who had trained in New York City's best kitchens, was persistent, too. He worked insane hours to realize his dream of opening up a restaurant in which he served a humble meal—noodle soup—prepared with four-star technique. But not enough people came. On the verge of going out of business, Chang could have kept working just as hard at the same thing, but instead he "pivoted." Deciding to go for broke, he and his partner began to cook as if it were their last days on earth—throwing everything they had ever learned and anything they had ever loved about being chefs into creating dishes *they'd* want to eat. The critics came and customers followed. Now, Chang is an award-winning food star who owns 11 critically acclaimed Momofuku restaurants and bakeries on two continents.

We have all known the doggedly persistent types who work hard but not smart—the Wile E. Coyotes of the workforce. In fact Wile E.— for those who have never watched Saturday morning cartoons, the foil of the Road Runner whom he was never able to catch—operated under a set of rules that determined the laws of his universe, made up by his creator, animator Chuck Jones. Theoretically, Coyote could stop his futile pursuit of the Road Runner at any time; only his own ineptitude (or the faulty strategies he employs) can harm him; and he is never allowed to achieve his ultimate goal—to catch the Road Runner. It is a fair description of many people who persist unthinkingly.

Every one of the people we interviewed practices a resolute persistence, but what distinguishes them from the Wile E. Coyotes of the world is an intelligent application of persistence. In other words, if the Road Runner can't be caught, go chase an armadillo.

3. Community

In 1992, when the Baltimore Orioles' ballpark, Camden Yards, was built, the typical sports stadium was a multipurpose, hulking, generic concrete mass that owners, players and fans took little pride in. But Camden Yards was the first of the so-called neo-retro ballparks, an eclectic, intimate park that was so fan-friendly that the *Baltimore Sun* wrote, "No matter where they sit fans will benefit from design ideas that sprang from the goal of building a paradise for baseball lovers."

Joseph Spear (Chapter 9), the architect of Camden Yards (and many other MLB parks), is too humble to call the millions of fans who visit his ballparks his *partners*, but even though only a tiny fraction of them would know him or his firm by name, in a sense they are. They have voted overwhelmingly for the Spear-designed ballparks with their dollars spent on tickets, hot dogs and beer, radically increasing attendance and bringing such positive attention to the teams that all but a few MLB owners who have built or renovated a park in the last 30 years have hired Spear's firm, Populous (formerly HOK Sport), to do the job—a staggering 19 (of a total 30 MLB parks) that host over 60 million fans annually.

With his satisfied baseball fans and team owners, Spear has built an analog version of what business guru Guy Kawasaki (Chapter 34) calls an *ecosystem*—a community of people whose "success is intertwined with yours." Kawasaki, a sort of digital age Dale Carnegie, explains: "An ecosystem is a community of people—partners, friends, allies, evangelists—who work with you and align themselves with your cause's success. You can apply this to a rock band, a muffin store or a billion-dollar start-up. First you have to create something worthy of an ecosystem. Then pick your evangelists.

Give people something meaningful to do. And create a dialogue with blogs, Web sites or social media."

Our participants cited teamwork—in the traditional sense of a group working together for a common goal—as an important criterion of success. But many have expanded their vision of what teamwork can mean beyond the traditional *us vs. them* version practiced within the confines of an organization. They have actively sought community with as large a network as possible, including customers, investors, bloggers, advertisers, fans, fellow enthusiasts, critics and even perceived competitors.

One of the pluckiest examples of someone who used this new paradigm of community was an 11-year-old Australian, Jessica Watson (Chapter 31). Watson spent five years of her life bringing together experts and mentors and veteran solo circumnavigators who both taught her how to become sea-ready and bought her the boat to help launch her plan. They also kept her informed and inspired during her solo, nonstop, seven-month voyage around the world at the age of 16. Watson told us she was overwhelmed with how many friends and strangers donated time, labor, education and sponsorship to her cause. And with a satellite dome and cameras donated by Panasonic, the young sailor kept in touch with the community she had formed via video blog as she sailed around the world.

4. Listening

One day, Erin Gruwell (Chapter 21), an idealistic white student teacher hoping to make a difference with her mixed-race class of remedial students at a school in Long Beach, California, went ballistic. As she faced a roomful of hostile teens she had been unable to reach, let alone control, Gruwell intercepted a racist caricature of an

African-American student that was being passed around. The caricature reminded her of anti-Semitic images of Jews in Nazi propaganda. When she found out that her students had never heard of the Holocaust, she was so angry, she challenged them for the first time: "How many of you have been shot?" In response, the students pulled up their shirts, showing their scars—bullet wounds and stitches. They began to talk. As Gruwell listened to their harrowing stories of gang-related violence, she felt something inside her shift. Her anger turned to empathy. She began to see their lives from *their* perspective.

Without having heard the term, what Gruwell was practicing that day was *active listening*, a concept pioneered by psychologists Thomas Gordon and Carl Rogers. Active listening is not at all the passive pursuit we may associate with listening. It requires one to listen without judgment, to hear from the speaker's point of view and to let the speaker know you understand the content of what he or she is saying as well as the feeling behind it. Rogers explains that active listening not only builds "deep, positive relationships," but changes the attitude of the listener.

What Gruwell heard that day convinced her that to reach her class, she would have to become "a student of the students." And she was not the only one to change. "One of those simple but beautiful paradoxes of life," Thomas Gordon wrote about the result of active listening, "is when a person feels that he is truly accepted by another . . . he is freed to move from there and to begin to think about how he wants to change . . . how he might become more of what he is capable of being."

No one could have guessed from Gruwell's simple act of listening that her students, who had entered school believing that no authority figure would have any interest in their points of view, would not only go on to academic success but would collectively author a bestselling book that was made into a movie based on the stories they wrote about their lives.

"Enough about me. Let's talk about you. What do *you* think of me?" is the classic line of a conversation hijacker. It's just one of the many habits of poor listeners along with interrupting, ambushing, glazing over and pseudo-listening. Although all of our participants are so highly focused and hardworking that you may think they have little time to listen, every one of them credits listening as an important aspect of their work. Some use it to validate others, but they all listen to learn.

Zappos CEO Tony Hsieh (Chapter 10), for example, created a listening experience in his company's digital space. Rather than hole up with top executives to formulate a list of company values for the online shoe store, Hsieh sent out an email to all of the Zappos employees asking, "What should Zappos' values be?" Knowing that their points of view were valued, the employees responded with a deluge of ideas. Through a year-long back-and-forth, the responses were eventually shaped into the list of company values. And now, because Hsieh "listened," Zappos' company culture is a true reflection of *all* the employees, resulting in a company that is not only perennially on lists of the "best companies to work for," but has grown into a billion-dollar business.

Some of our superachievers practice surprising forms of listening. What they *hear* does not necessarily involve actual sound, but just the same, it requires an active receptiveness and open-mindedness.

They describe how these alternate forms of listening have been key to performing well in their fields. The visionary vintner Randall Grahm (Chapter 13) told us that to cultivate the wine of his dreams, he actually *listens* to the land to divine which varieties of grapes to grow so that his wines will reflect and embody a sense of place.

Award-winning actress Laura Linney (Chapter 1) described her unique process of preparing for roles—how she pores over and immerses herself in scripts, waiting and listening for a moment when a "magical line" will "ring" in her brain, unlocking the story.

5. Telling a Story

The wife of a hugely successful rock star came to Michael Sitrick (Chapter 30), a crisis manager and reputation rehabilitator for entertainers, sports figures, CEOs and other high-profile clients. She told Sitrick how she had been drugged and beaten and was left convulsing on the floor by her husband and how she was trying to negotiate a divorce—but his lawyers wouldn't even return her lawyers' calls. After listening, Sitrick picked up the phone and offered *People* magazine her story. The editors put her on the cover. The impact was predictably huge.

Sitrick, who has been a lifelong student of the press, broke down this process for us. It was not a legal fight over the facts with her lawyers that he believed would achieve his client's goals, but her *story*. First he chose the ideal venue, the celebrity-focused, mass-market *People* magazine. Even though the magazine readership was not the target audience, the story would influence public opinion of the rock star. And when that public opinion reached Sitrick's actual target audience, the rock star's record company executives, they would take action to protect their financial investment in their recording artist. After the story broke and became a media sensation, that's exactly what happened. The record company immediately put pressure on the rock star's lawyers to settle. The divorce was negotiated soon thereafter.

Richard Gerrig, an author and professor of psycholinguistics at Stony Brook University who has researched the cognitive effects of narrative, explained to us how one can be "transported" by a story. "You are so immersed in the narrative and involved with the characters that you are not just identifying with them, you become part of their world and have a stake in the story." Gerrig cites studies that demonstrate how, in the grip of a story, we encode the narrative contents in the same way we would if we were actual participants in that story. As a result, our rational powers of cognition and reason can be so weakened that an effectively told story, as Gerrig describes it, can seem to become proof of its own content.

But stories can be told in ways that might not be as obvious. We found an unusual example of this when we spoke to the founders of the online dating site OkCupid (Chapter 16), four math nerds from Harvard who told us that the most important piece of advice they can give to anyone trying to find a partner online is to "create a conversation." In essence, to start a narrative or *tell a story*. "If a profile picture is a close-up of someone's beautiful face, the viewer knows that person is attractive," one of the founders, Sam Yagan, told us. They "can say something like, 'Nice glasses . . . I wear glasses, too.' But . . . if you're playing a guitar up on stage, then we know something about you. You're in a band. Now, we have a conversation: 'Oh, you play guitar? I do, too.' If you're standing in front of the pyramids of Egypt, someone can say, 'Oh, I've been there.' Now you've got something started." And, in fact, evaluating the site's statistics, OkCupid's founders have determined that the profile pictures that tell a story lead to a much higher quality of contacts.

Gerrig discusses these alternative forms of storytelling, such as a user of a dating site creating an online profile to attract potential partners. "There's no *fictional* narrative involved as there would be if created by a writer or filmmaker. But it is a similar experience. The only difference is in these cases someone is trying to get you to believe that if you enter their story, your *actual* life will change in a material way."

No matter what the people interviewed aspire to do—create a brand, sell a product, promote a cause or increase their visibility—they understand that shaping their message into a believable and compelling story will help them communicate with their target audience, whether it be their customers, investors, fans, colleagues or potential dates. As Michael Sitrick puts it bluntly, "If you don't tell your story, someone else will tell it for you."

6. Testing

In 1998, Bill Gross (Chapter 33) had an idea—to sell cars online. This was "back when people were still nervous about giving credit card information to Web sites," said Gross, founder of Idealab, an incubator for start-ups. "People said, 'You're crazy! Who's going to buy a car online?'" Gross hated going to the auto mall and haggling with a car dealer, so he knew that he, for one, would buy a car online. What he didn't know was, would anybody else? "Let's put up a site and see what happens," he told his colleague, an entrepreneur who was working with him on the idea. The morning after the site went up, the entrepreneur called Gross in a panic: "We sold four cars last night!" Gross shouted, "Turn the site off! Now!" He had done the minimum to test if the premise was right. Then he went ahead and built the site, CarsDirect.com. And after some ups and down, the company went on to become Internet Brands, one of the largest online retailers.

Gross, who has started nearly a hundred companies, explains his philosophy of testing: "You're biased toward your company's ideas and success, so test your idea as soon as you possibly can—before you invest too much time or money to find out if people will open their wallets and give you their cash." Gross and anyone else who tests their ideas are simply trying to resolve the gap between what they *think* will happen and what *will* happen. Testing is a way to close that gap by letting reality speak for itself.

We couldn't have predicted the varied forms of testing our interviewees practiced to improve their skills and learn more about their products or services or the environment in which they would be used. When big game hunter Chad Schearer (Chapter 20) practices for a hunt, he doesn't just stand and shoot. He throws down his weapon, runs forty yards to get his heart pumping and adrenaline flowing as they would during an actual hunt, then picks up his weapon, tries to control his breath, steadies himself and shoots.

Stephen Dubner (Chapter 36), the bestselling author of *Freakonomics*, told us, "Writing was originally a way to preserve oral speech, and I've never forgotten that." Dubner has written five books and hundreds of articles, most of which will be read silently by his readers, but after writing every sentence he reads it out loud, personally testing every phrase for how it sounds as spoken word.

7. Managing Emotions

Gary Noesner (Chapter 26), a former FBI hostage negotiator who has spent much of his adult life interacting with right-wing zealots, armed militias, murderous cult leaders, cold-blooded killers and terrorists, told us, "The most important trait of a hostage negotiator is self-control. . . . Even when lives are on the line, I have to think clearly. . . . If someone is yelling and screaming at me and I overreact to everything he says, how can I expect to be a positive influence?"

For Noesner to successfully negotiate a crisis situation he must also help others around him keep their cool. But the SWAT teams and tactical forces he partnered with did not always see things the same way. Noesner told us that he'd seen commanders of these operations lose patience and get angry. "So when a negotiation takes time, sometimes their viewpoint is, 'Why should we let this despicable character control the situation? I've trained my guys. They're ready to go. This guy's a problem. Let's go in and get him.'"

Dr. Richard Restak, a neuropsychiatrist (Chapter 28), explained to us how every event we experience is accompanied by what psychiatrists call an "emotional valance," a positive or negative reaction based on the event that occurs in the brain's emotional processing area, the limbic system. Even in a highly stressful situation, Noesner, who has what Restak would describe as a well-developed "observing ego," can both recognize and regulate the emotions he feels. This enables him to view the perpetrator objectively as a man in distress who could do harm to others, but if handled well, could be coaxed out of violent acts. A less accomplished negotiator or an overly gung ho SWAT team commander may experience the hostage taker as someone who is disobedient, disrespectful or embarrassing to them. That negotiator's or commander's highly emotional response to the perpetrator will likely create a situation where others on the scene will respond to the emotion itself and not the crisis. If anger is unexamined, Restak explains, "our limbic system can override the rational alternatives suggested in our prefrontal lobes." In life-and-death circumstances like Noesner's, the stakes are so high that a loss of self-control can lead to needless loss of life, but all of us, even in our much less dramatic lives, have experienced the sort of overwrought situations that can spin out of control.

Restak urges us to train our observing ego, explaining, "Eventually you will recognize the first stirrings of emotion and be able to not only recognize your emotions but to use them as personal inquiry, asking yourself, 'Why am I responding with such anger to this situation?' And then you can begin to determine if there are actions you can take to clear up situations. Your ability to observe your emotions objectively puts you at a tremendous advantage in emotionally charged situations."

The emotional struggles described by our interviewees—overcoming fear, dealing with disillusionment, controlling anxiety, gaining confidence, avoiding hubris, learning acceptance and keeping a sense of humor (the list goes on)—were as varied as the people themselves. But what they shared was an awareness of the powerful emotions they felt. And then, when these emotions compromised their goals, they had the commitment and the skills to examine those emotions and figure out effective ways to cope with them.

8. Evolving

One spring, at 24, Martina Navratilova (Chapter 6), the Czech-born tennis player, had a nightmare about her upcoming match. It was the night before she was to play Chris Evert. The match was as bad as the dream. She lost to Evert 0-6, 0-6. Sportswriters called it "a career worst." Only two years earlier, she had been ranked number one in the world, but since then her play had become inconsistent and she faced the distinct possibility of a steady slide down the ranking ladder. Navratilova wondered if she would ever be the champion she'd hoped to become.

In the 1970s, Harvard University Business School professor Chris Argyris studied how people (and organizations) react when blocked from achieving their goals—just the sort of situation that Navratilova found herself in. Argyris discovered that those unable to reach their goals first try to detect what the problem is. Next they attempt to correct the problem based on that information. But people go about this in two very distinct ways. The most common response is an insular, self-protective process Argyris called *single-loop learning*—a process where only external or technical causes are questioned and none of the underlying assumptions are examined. For example, if Navratilova was *not* becoming a champion, perhaps she believed it was due to a technical glitch or that she just needed an attitude adjustment. The second response, a deeper and much rarer form of the questioning process, Argyris labeled *double-loop learning*, a method that requires self-awareness to recognize deeply held assumptions, brutal honesty to assess what is or isn't working, and accountability to take action on what is learned.

Shortly after her match with Evert, Navratilova began working with a new, aggressive trainer. At a workout session, after only five wind sprints, Navratilova collapsed on the ground in pain and tears. Recognizing her physical limitations for the first time, she became aware of her hidden assumption that she could become a champion based on instinct and talent alone. Navratilova saw that her problem was *not* a technical glitch or needing a minor attitude adjustment. Her problem was that she had not made training a critical part of her game. When Navratilova made this realization, she became the first tennis player to create what was at the time a revolutionary cross-training regimen to improve her strength, endurance and speed. With this physical advantage over others she began to win consistently. She applied this same intensity to evolving the tactical aspect of her game, as well as her diet, leading to a full-scale transformation in which she became the most successful female tennis player of her time and the champion she wanted to be.

OK Go (Chapter 25), a band hoping to live out their rock star dreams, underwent a similar transformation. Operating under the late twentieth-century paradigm of rock band success, they signed with a major label, toured, made music videos and promoted themselves. But with the collapse of record sales and altercations with their record company, their assumptions about what would make them successful were failing them. What distinguished OK Go from other bands was their ability to confront these assumptions and adapt. YouTube was still in its infancy when they circumvented their record company and reached out directly to their fan base by uploading a DIY video of themselves doing a dance routine on treadmills for the song "Here It Goes Again." It exploded, with 700,000 views on in its first day, catapulting them into the public consciousness and inspiring them to invent a new business model for a rock band.

"In the struggle for survival, the fittest win out at the expense of their rivals," wrote Charles Darwin, over 150 years ago, "because they succeed in adapting themselves best to their environment." When the high achievers we spoke to for this book were confronted with setbacks as they worked to fulfill their goals, they could have defaulted to those strategies that hadn't worked in the first place with minor tweaks and adjustments. But because they possess a willingness to challenge their deeply held assumptions and the courage to act on that information, they have been able to overcome obstacles by discarding what doesn't work and evolving entirely new ways of thinking about their lives and goals.

9. Patience

A young Brazilian boy who began racing when he received his first go-kart on his 11th birthday wanted to lead every single lap of every single race. His father tried to break him of the habit, telling him, "You don't have to win on the first lap." A few years later, for the first time, the racer found himself cruising in the middle of the pack. He waited. He surveyed the situation. It wasn't until he suddenly saw an opening—a strategic moment to go full throttle—that he floored the accelerator to pass the three cars in front of him to win the race. He had finally understood his father's advice to take a longer-term view. But more important, he had developed the ability to take action—or, as in this case, to *not* take action—based on that insight.

Evolutionary psychologists describe this kind of decision as a choice between a short-term reward (the pleasurable high of being in front of the pack) and the more valuable, long-term reward (increasing one's chances of winning the race). Race car driver Helio Castroneves (Chapter 35) came in second that year in the Brazilian Karting Championship, and although he faced many obstacles in life, he went on to become one of the world's most celebrated race car drivers, winning the Indy 500 three times.

Castroneves' story tells us that one important milestone on his road to long-term success was his ability to overcome the natural inclination to take actions that favor short-term rewards. To be sure, many other factors entered into his achievements, but drivers who lacked this strategic insight were at a distinct disadvantage to drivers like him.

Many of our superachievers cited *patience* as a critical skill. But their practice of patience took place over varying durations of time, from fractions of seconds in a competitive sport to days, months, years or even decades for other endeavors.

Jill Tarter (Chapter 15) is our poster child of patience. For almost half a century, Tarter, an astronomer, has been searching for extraterrestrial intelligent life in an expanse so large that if it were the equivalent of all the world's oceans, what she and her team have examined so far amounts to only a single glass of water. And she has done this in the face of having no certainty of what she is searching for or how long the search will take—decades, even centuries—with no guarantee of success. Individuals such as Tarter with visions much larger than themselves must have the extraordinary patience to forego the short-term reward of achieving conventional success in their lifetimes for the much longer-term reward of furthering a cause they believe in—in her case, a deeper understanding of the universe. Tarter, a leader at the SETI (Search for Extraterrestrial Intelligence) Institute in Mountain View, CA, told us, "Fifty years of silence doesn't mean SETI is a failure; it means we're just getting started."

10. Happiness

George Clinton's career as the front man of one of the most important and influential funk collectives of all time, Parliament-Funkadelic and the P-Funk All Stars, has been anything but smooth going. Clinton (Chapter 17) has spent decades handling scores of headstrong musicians who came and went, would come back, mutiny and go again; record companies that reneged on deals; and bands that fell apart while he produced and performed at a hectic pace. He's had to fight for publishing rights to his music, some of his band names and compensation for the samples of his music on hundreds of hip-hop tracks. And yet he loves the struggle of trying to make great music. "It's easy to get tired at 70 years old, but I'm not successful yet," he told us. "If you get to the top and catch up with happy, you got a real problem because you'll get bored. I'm not trying to catch up with being happy—because it's the *pursuit* of happiness I'm after. I want to be so close behind it I can almost touch it. That's what keeps me looking forward to moving ahead."

Sonja Lyubomirsky, who conducted a meta-analysis of 225 studies on well-being, describes what Clinton is experiencing as "upward spirals," the more successful someone is at their job, the happier they will be—and that happiness will create even more vocational success and further enhance happiness, and so on. Clinton has an iconoclastic definition of happiness as not a fixed state but the actual *pursuit of* happiness—in his case, his work.

Lyubomirsky goes on to explain, "It's not work per se that makes people happy; it's rewarding and successful work. It's up to you to change how you perceive your work. Do you think of it as a job? Or do you think of it as a true calling?"

This experience of the upward spiral, or positive feedback loop, was echoed by many of the people we spoke with who believe that happiness is not just a personal goal but something that has been integral to their success. For Ken Jennings (Chapter 4), the winningest game show champion in history, the upward spiral of winning gave him confidence to pursue another life dream. "Once I was a contestant, playing on the show [*Jeopardy!*] I became someone who loved his job," he said. "The passion that came from that contributed to my winning, and helped me see for the first time that doing something you love really *can* change your life. I leveraged that to quit my old job and become a writer. And now I love what I do every day."

. . . .

In writing this book we assimilated dozens of life lessons, tactics and tips—from the macro to the micro—that changed the way we do things and how we think about our work and lives.

From Philippe Petit, the high wire artist, we learned that to be great at something you have to let life be your teacher and be willing to do the dirty work, "like washing dishes and shoveling horseshit."

From Stephen Dubner, bestselling author of *Freakonomics*, we learned that good writing is not about impressing people with how smart you are but about explaining your subject as simply as possible.

From Jessica Watson, the 16-year-old sailor who had to contend with a capsized boat, mechanical failures and heartbreaking loneliness on her 210-day solo journey around the globe, we learned that no matter how arduous the process, we need to remember to pause for a moment and enjoy the experience.

From Simon Doonan, cultural critic, we learned that dressing down is a crime against humanity and that if you always dress in what you'd wear to a Gaga concert, your life will *always* be more fun. (This actually works!)

As you enter these pages we hope you will not only be entertained but will discover some useful strategies that you can apply to your own work and life.

The Art of

DOING

Chapter 1

How to Act

. . . .

Laura Linney

Three-time Oscar- and Tony-nominated actor, winner of
three Emmy Awards and, most recently, winner of a
Golden Globe Award for her television role in *The Big C*

When Laura Linney takes on a role, she immerses herself in the script. In a process in which she is part alchemist, part detective, she opens herself up to let the story work on her as she digs through the text asking, Why?, searching for hints and glimmers to reveal the core of the character. Her goal then is to so thoroughly internalize her role that once she steps on set or stage, she can "throw all the preparation away and let the work bleed through." This practice has enabled Linney to elicit extraordinary performances from often ordinary characters. Linney dreamed of being an actor from a very young age. Her father, an off-Broadway playwright, and her mother, a nurse, who encouraged her to trust her instincts, divorced when Linney was six months old. It was from her early childhood exposure to the theater—seeing her father Romulus Linney's plays, working backstage and acting in summer stock—that Linney intuited she would have to work hard to earn a place on stage. After completing formal training, Linney did not know whether she'd land on her feet or "just go splat." Not only has Linney built a career, but she has been described by the *New York*

Times as "an actress of peerless emotional transparency, capable of conveying a multitude of conflicting feelings through minimal means." Her choices of nuanced roles—a conflicted wife accused of witchcraft in the Broadway production of *The Crucible*, a harried playwright in the film *The Savages*, a middle-aged woman delivered a cancer death sentence in Showtime's *The Big C*—are ultimately motivated by her belief in the story. "As a kid, getting lost in stories was so primal," says Linney. "As I developed an awareness of psychology and human behavior, stories only became more complicated and exciting. When I am on stage or set, I'm not acting for a director or producer. I'm not even acting for the audience or for myself. I'm acting for the story."

Takeaway: *"Trust acting. If you put everything in its place and don't skip steps along the way, the right result will come."*

1. Get training. When I traveled with my father to the regional theaters I'd see these ingenues in his plays. They were wonderful, like gorgeous flowers. But when they reached a certain age they'd just fall apart. They would get to the more complicated roles, and because they were only acting on instinct, they didn't know what to do. I said to myself, "Get yourself trained," because I wanted a long life in the theater. I thought, "When I'm older, I want to be able to play the Nurse in *Romeo and Juliet*."

2. A good script is hard to find. Most scripts aren't written to be acted. They're written to appeal to an executive who doesn't know how to read a script but has the power to get a film made. But when a good script does come along something happens. If your actor brain turns on and starts working before you've finished reading it for the first time, pay attention. It will awaken your senses. Your imagination comes alive. You can feel it in your body. Every once in a while a script like *You Can Count on Me* or *The Savages* comes along that is so well written, so film ready, that I'll see the character's emotional life and their physicality almost in 3-D. When you get that feeling, don't listen to advice. Just take the role.

3. Audition the director. When I go on audition I think, "Do I want to spend three months of my life with this person?" You can learn a lot about a director by the way they talk about their work—or anything that they care about. You look for red flags. If you're at a table with someone who treats a waiter like shit—that's basic. Sometimes you'll just take a liking to someone. But there is a lot to look for. What are their strengths? Weaknesses? Do they have talent? Experience? And, what do they need from me? Film is a director's medium, so you need to find out if you share a point of view so you can help them make the movie they want to make. A first-time director—and I've worked with a lot of them—may have talent but not experience. They might not know how to work with actors, and that might piss you off at times. But that's okay if they're willing to learn and you're willing to work with them. On the first day of shooting *You Can Count on Me* I had to teach the director, Kenny Lonergan—who had never been on a film set—how to read a call sheet. But he understood his own material better than any other first-time director I've ever worked with.

4. Unlock the story. After taking a part I read the script and ask, "Why?" I ask "Why?" until there's no more "Why?" to ask. I read a script, and it'll say, "INTERIOR: Chicago tenement." I stop and ask, "Why is it a tenement? Why is it Chicago?" Some actors will skip steps, just breezing over the script and getting a quick picture in their mind. But you have to saturate yourself with the text to lead you to the core of the story. When you sit quietly with a script reading it for clues, sometimes there will be a magical line that will ring in your brain. All of a sudden, everything falls into place. It's a wild moment, an epiphany, an intense chemical understanding of what's going on. There was a moment when I was reading Chekhov's *The Seagull* for an infamously bad production I was to appear in. Nina tells Treplev that he can't come to her house because "Papa has his gun." I wondered why she would be upset since probably everybody has a gun in the Russian countryside. But something reverberated inside of me. All of a sudden I understood Nina. She came from a violent home, which would explain her naïveté and feeling trapped by an overprotective parent, her need to become someone else to escape. That one line just gave me an ocean of information on the entire narrative of the story.

5. Find the physicality. They say talent is in the choices an actor makes. I become like a mad scientist when I'm researching for a role. For *The Truman Show*, I developed the character's physicality—the poses, the cock of the head, the hand positions—from the silhouettes of the models in a 1940s Sears and Roebuck catalog. For *Kinsey* I listened to tape recordings of Kinsey's family to hear the way my character sounded when she interacted and spoke with her husband and the others. For *John Adams*, I devoured American history and consulted with scholars on every aspect of the Adams' lives in a hunt for clues. I found out that Abigail Adams was pigeon-toed. Walking that way was not very graceful. I didn't feel very elegant. It made me focus on other things. Even though I knew the camera might not pick up on the walk, I hoped it would communicate something about her character.

6. Let go. You can't play an idea, a quality or emotion. You've done all the preparation for a role, but once you walk on set you have to throw it all away. And then it gets a little magical. You've done all your work on the story—and now the story is working on *you*. You're so prepared that whatever you do is going to be within the bounds of what that character should be. And if you work with like-minded actors, the cameras roll and you just get on with it. It's like having a great dance partner. And it's *fun*. Such as with Liam Neeson. He and I have done a lot of work together. We never talk about the work. Ever. We just fall into it.

7. Fight for the story. My loyalty is not to a director or a producer—it's to the story. Sometimes it takes a director a while to see that I'm not trying to do anything other than illuminate the story. When they realize, "Oh, she's really trying to make the movie better," you have a chance to figure it out together. Other times it just pisses people off because they want you to be more *likable* to help sell the film. But what if that doesn't accurately reflect the story? If it's not about the story, it's no fun. When people come up to me and say, "You're so *brave*, letting yourself look that way," I think, "Well, what was I supposed to do when I was playing Abigail Adams, who had rotten teeth?"

8. Look behind the camera. The fact that I work in film and TV cracks my old friends up because I used to be terrified of cameras. That is, until I realized I should stop worrying about the camera and start connecting with the people *behind* the camera. It's an amazing group of people around a camera. They're always very quiet. I don't talk to them about it; I'll just glance up at the camera operator or the focus-puller and know what I am doing is working by the look in their eye.

9. Be kind. When things go wrong, when you're having a rough day, you have to be kind. You have to be kind to yourself. You have to be kind to the people around. Kindness can be a look that says, "It's okay. Keep going." It's almost telepathic. Your fellow actors know what you're going through and they're rooting for you. During the run of the play *Time Stands Still*, my father died. The theater was very important to him, and there were references in the play to a father. When I had to go back out on stage, it was very emotional, almost an out-of-body experience. My costar, Brian Darcy James, carried me through. We never spoke about it, but I could have shattered into a thousand pieces and he would have made sure that none of them touched the ground.

10. The play's the thing. If you want to be a famous movie star, then just go do it! But if you really want to be an actor, then you need to make different choices. Just after the success of *You Can Count on Me*, I did a few stage productions, including *The Crucible* with Liam Neeson. People said, "Why did she go *back* to the theater?" As if I were choosing something lesser than films. But I'm not going *back* to the theater; I never *left* the theater. I return to the stage every two years or so because it reminds me of why I love being an actor. Unlike film, theater has the element of time. Time works its own magic. Every night of a play is slightly different. An actor responds to a line in a new way; an emotional moment opens up. As the weeks go by, layer upon layer opens up, and a great play takes on a rhythm and a life of its own. Even in a play with great undertow and emotional depth that requires you to go places that are emotionally charged, the actors have such a wonderful sense of goodwill. It's fun. It's rigorous. When you're doing a play, the work never stops.

LAURA LINNEY FACTS

Stage fright: 1989: At Julliard, Linney is going to quit acting school because of stage fright and join the Peace Corps, but changes mind when acting teacher tells her, "Fail here."

Early paycheck: Linney "snorts nasal spray" for Dristan commercial.

Gay icon: 1993: Linney stars as Midwestern naïf Mary Ann Singleton in TV miniseries *Tales of the City*, adapted from Armistead Maupin's novels set in San Francisco's swinging '70s.

Low budget: 2000: On location in upstate New York, in *You Can Count on Me*, cast stays in "moldy summer bungalow," crew is underpaid, people are underfed and everyone shares old chicken coop as dressing room.

Diver: 2010: To prepare for role as terminally ill cancer victim in cable series *The Big C*, Linney puts up pictures of divers and watches tapes of U.S. Olympian Greg Louganis diving to see "the leap up and the beauty of the moment of suspense before you start to fall, knowing you'll finally hit the water."

Oscar-nominated: Playing sister opposite Mark Ruffalo, *You Can Count on Me*, and Philip Seymour Hoffman, *The Savages*, and wife opposite Liam Neeson, *Kinsey*.

Favorite quote: "We don't have a lot of time so we have to work very slowly." —Artistic director Josie Abady

ACTING FACTS

First actor: Sixth century BC, Greece: According to Aristotle, Thespis is first actor to appear on stage playing a character. Disasters in theater are sometimes blamed on his ghostly intervention.

No more drag: 1660: In England, men or boys play all women's roles until Margaret Hughes, believed to be first professional actress in England, plays Desdemona in *Othello*. 1662: King Charles II decrees all female roles are to be played by actresses.

Death: 1673: French actor and playwright Molière is seized by violent coughing fit while playing title role in *The Hypochondriac* and dies.

Sleeping on it: 1844–1923: French-born Sarah Bernhardt, most famous actress of her time, sleeps in coffin instead of bed to help her understand her tragic roles.

Method to his madness: 1863–1938, Russia: Constantin Stanislavski experiments in maintaining characterization in real life by disguising himself as a tramp, drunk and fortune-telling Gypsy at train stations as he pioneers new acting style of identifying with psychological core of roles. His teachings become huge influence on modern acting style often called "the Method."

Speak no more: 1929: When glamorous silent film star Norma Talmadge appears in her first talking pictures, moviegoers hear her flat Brooklyn accent. Her film career ends shortly afterward.

Most leading roles: John Wayne, 142.

Most Academy Awards: Katharine Hepburn, 4.

Chapter 2

How to Be a Diva

. . . .

Anna Netrebko

Opera's top soprano, the critically acclaimed reigning diva
of the twenty-first century

Since she was 23—an age when many opera singers are still struggling to break into the business—Anna Netrebko has been electrifying international audiences with her voice of "astonishing richness and power." Competing for attention in today's celebrity-driven entertainment culture, the opera world has pinned its hopes on the star power of the Russian-born soprano. With her sultry beauty, riveting stage presence and stunningly modernistic portrayals of traditional roles, Netrebko fills opera houses and has sold millions of records. But if you ask her about the keys to her success she is likely to answer with a mischievous shrug or a wink—as if to brush off the dedication and rigorous training required to become an operatic superstar. As a child growing up in a provincial town in Communist Russia, Netrebko felt she was born to perform. She made her way to St. Petersburg at 16 to study opera. When her teachers told her she was destined for the chorus, she went rogue and developed her own plan. She worked part-time mopping the lobby floor at the Mariinsky Theater, home to the famed Kirov Opera, to soak up the atmosphere. Her oft-told fairy-tale discovery didn't occur while she had a mop in hand, but when she won a competition that earned her an audition with Valery Gergiev, the Kirov's renowned artistic director and her future mentor. One rehearsal when the lead in *Le Nozze di Figaro* fell ill, Netrebko stepped into the role of Susanna. Netrebko has gone from one acclaimed performance to the next ever since, playing some of opera's greatest roles—Violetta, Manon, Lucia and Mimi—in the world's most illustrious opera houses. Struggling for superlatives, critics describe her performances as having "an intoxicating air of sinful glamour" and "gut-wrenching conviction," and she left one critic "shaken, stirred and still quivering at the knees." When compared to the great diva Maria Callas, Netrebko says, "Flattering, but I'd like to one day be celebrated for being myself."

> **Takeaway:** *"No matter how big you become, you can never be self-satisfied and say, 'Okay, I've made it,' because the next day you have to go back and prove yourself again."*

1. Know what you want. When I started out, I met a lot of extremely talented singers. Everybody thought, "Oh, this one or that one will be a star." But after a very short time, many of them disappeared. Talent, which is a gift from the gods, isn't enough. You have to be incredibly smart about your choices. At 18, I knew perfectly well that I didn't want to finish college. It would have been a waste of my time. Instead, I took the exam for the conservatory, chose exactly which repertoire I would sing, and of the three teachers who wanted to take me on, I knew exactly which to choose. If you don't have these smarts, this intuition, there are too many paths to follow and you may be seduced by those that seem easier or more flattering. To put it simply: Keep what you need, drop what you don't.

2. Stay focused on the music. As we say in Russia, "It's a dead soldier who doesn't dream of being a general," so of course I had hopes of being a prima donna singing on the stage—somewhere.

But my dreams never went too far. Maybe it would be in my home region of Krasnodar? When I studied, I was not thinking, "I'm going to be the one." That was not my goal. I loved the music so much that my goal was simply to sing well. That's it. That's what I wanted to do. I focused on learning the music, developing my voice and practicing very hard so I could get better.

3. Be prepared to seize the opportunity. As my voice improved, I set my sights on getting to the greatest opera company in Russia, the Kirov Opera. Eventually, I earned the chance to audition for the Kirov's director, Gergiev, and he accepted me into the ensemble, offering me a small part in *Le Nozze di Figaro*. During rehearsals, the lead singer became sick, and unexpectedly the stage director asked if I knew the part. It was the role of Susanna, the lead. Of course I knew it. I knew all the parts. I was ready. I had worked incredibly hard in anticipation of an opportunity like that. I performed the role in rehearsal, got most of the blocking right and went on as Susanna. And after that they offered me the principal role in the second cast.

4. Act your part. How can a contemporary audience relate to you if you just stand there in your old-fashioned costume and sing? Even a seventeenth-century queen or nineteenth-century courtesan needs to be interpreted with psychological depth. Take Donizetti's Anna Bolena, who is traditionally played as not much more than an angry, suffering woman. When I got the opportunity to play her, I studied the music and watched clips of the divas of the past in the part. I wanted to get under the surface to the core of the role. Yes, Anna's story is tragic, but I saw that there could be more to her. Just as an actor would, I portrayed her with the complex emotions of a real person, with hints of viciousness, envy, arrogance and ambition—even playing her with a manipulative sexuality. We have to work hard to make opera come alive for the modern age by creating complex characters the audiences can believe in.

5. Opera is teamwork. I don't think of opera as a competition between divas. I don't obsess on who can hold a note the longest. Envy can destroy your soul. Sometimes when I first come to rehearsal, colleagues whom I haven't worked with assume the worst about me. There's a wall. But I break that wall down by being friendly and funny. We need each other because opera is company work. Many things can go wrong in a live performance. Someone gets sick, gets lost or forgets the words. No matter how big or small your role, you have to be attuned to your fellow performers to hold it together for each other. You may not notice it from the audience, but sometimes when a performer is very tense a partner will come up to them and literally hold their hand to relax them and give them the support to continue.

6. You've got to have soul. Your own emotions are too small for the opera stage. The audience is too far away to catch them, so I go into myself and become absolutely cold. My brain becomes a computer running my performance like clockwork. I am absolutely concentrated on my singing. But something else has to come through to capture the audience's attention. It's soul. Callas had it. You have to find it in yourself. It took me years to find it. I couldn't even tell someone how I did it except to keep searching for it and allowing it to come out. It's very difficult to do, but performing with soul is the only way you can move an audience, stun them, shock them, make them cry.

7. Be a material girl. Opera is about more than just being a voice. We have to give pleasure to the eyes as well as the ears. It's not being a diva to ask for costumes in which you will look beautiful, because that's what the audience wants. I love playing Manon in black silk Dior lingerie during a boudoir scene or Violetta, lying in a perfect formfitting red cocktail dress, being carried on a bright red couch by a chorus in tuxedos. It's not just for the audience. *I* want to look good. It can never be too much. I need fantastic costumes and, of course, jewelry to spark on stage.

8. Be modern. It's a pity that lots of people have never been to opera because they are put off by its stuffy image. They have no idea how wonderful it can be. The opera world, like everything else, has to change to reach out to more people. Even though opera purists wish everything would remain the same forever, it's not enough to park and bark. I've made MTV-styled music videos of opera arias. I pose and give interviews to glossy magazines and TV shows. I have an interactive "ask Anna" feature on my Web site. It's not that I want to be a pop star or an official ambassador of the opera world, but I believe in opera. We do what we can to reach more people so opera will never die.

9. Age well. One of the incredible realities of singing opera is that you can actually get better with age. Like a fine wine! Your voice can get so big. It's not that the young singers are not important—of course they are. But when you are young, you have to choose your roles carefully, because there are parts that will literally wreck your voice forever if you are not ready for them. Don't sing too many *Traviata*s! And try to take at least two weeks between shows. Even be ready to walk offstage during a performance. Save your voice for later when some of the most amazing roles will become available.

10. Make it (seem like) magic. Opera training is incredibly difficult. Even if you have a naturally beautiful voice, to project onstage without microphones it has to be trained with perfect technique. You must learn to improvise words, musical phrases and the colors of emotions. All of these things have to work together perfectly to make your voice truly become *something*. I am a professional, so of course I know how it has to be done. But to add to the mystery of a performance and the magic of the art form, the audience should not know these kinds of things. To be as powerful as it can be, the diva's voice must seem like magic. How I achieve this is my business and nobody else's.

ANNA NETREBKO FACTS

Stage debut: 1988: Age 16, St. Petersburg, Russia: Netrebko is the hind legs within the costume of the Cockerel in Rimsky-Korsakov's *Le Coq d'Or.*

International debut: 1995, San Francisco Opera House: Kirov Opera director Valery Gergiev takes what he calls "an insane risk" entrusting Netrebko with "an absolutely central, extremely difficult role," Ludmila in *Ruslan and Ludmila.* And, "she was tremendous."

Big sales: 2004: Operatic DVD of MTV-styled videos, *Anna Netrebko: The Woman, the Voice,* outsells Beyoncé and Britney Spears in Europe.

Scalper's dream: 2005, Salzburg: Tickets to Verdi's *La Traviata* with Netrebko and Mexican tenor Rolando Villazón reportedly sell on black market for $7,000 a seat.

Dud: 2007: Verdi's *Rigoletto* in Munich, staged as *Planet of the Apes* in which entire cast plays monkeys except leads, who are astronauts. Audience arrives with bananas to throw. Netrebko temporarily loses voice after first performance.

Romance: 2007: Erwin Schrott, Uruguayan bass-baritone, invites Netrebko out on date offering to cook dinner for her if she'll cut the garlic and onions. 2008: Their son, Santiago, is born.

Weight loss: Netrebko can lose up to two pounds during a performance.

Honors: 2007: Netrebko is included in *Time* magazine's 100 Most Influential People in the World. 2008: She receives Russia's highest award in arts and literature, the title People's Artist of Russia, and *Playboy* names her one of the Sexiest Babes of Classical Music.

OPERA FACTS

First opera: Circa 1597, Florence, Italy: Elite circle of humanists gather to revive Greek drama, influencing Jacopo Peri to compose the now lost *Dafne*, in which the "chorus" sings the text.

High drama: 1734, England: The famous Italian castrato Senesino, playing a furious tyrant, is so moved by the performance of another famous Italian castrato, Farinelli, playing a hero in chains, that he forgets his stage-character, runs to Farinelli and embraces him onstage.

Dueling divas: 1950s: A rivalry is alleged between the dramatic and unconventional soprano Maria Callas and the angel-voiced soprano Renata Tebaldi. Tebaldi is quoted saying, "I have one thing that Callas doesn't have: a heart," while Callas is rumored to have said that comparing her with Tebaldi was like "comparing champagne with Coca-Cola."

Death in the opera: 1960: In performance at the Met of Verdi's *La forza del destino* ("The Force of Destiny"), baritone Leonard Warren falls down and dies on stage after singing an aria that begins, "To die, a momentous thing."

Opera's dirty little secret: 1990s: Opera houses begin to use electronic acoustic enhancement to compensate for flaws in acoustical architecture and boost offstage voices, child singers, onstage dialogue and sound effects.

Opera goes digital: 2011–12 season: The Metropolitan Opera Live in HD program, in which live opera performances are transmitted in HD video to theaters around the world, sells 2.6 million tickets in 47 countries.

Chapter 3

How to Be a Dog Whisperer

. . . .

Cesar Millan

Dog rehabilitator and star of the hit reality TV show
The Dog Whisperer

"I owe a lot to dogs," says Cesar Millan, who as a child had an insatiable curiosity about the farm dogs on his grandfather's small ranch in rural Mexico. He'd spend hours watching the dogs, pondering why they did what they did and marveling at their innate ability to survive and thrive. Years later, inspired by the Spanish-dubbed television reruns of *Lassie* and *Rin Tin Tin*, the teenaged Millan dreamed of becoming Hollywood's greatest dog trainer. At 21, Millan crossed the border illegally. Arriving with no money and no English skills, he became a fixture at a dog-grooming salon in San Diego. Millan's skill with the dogs enchanted his employers and their clients. Remembering the perfectly balanced dogs of his Mexican youth, he was mystified by the American owners, who were so oblivious to the true nature of dogs that they obsessively showered love on their pampered pets, creating a host of bizarre behavioral problems. On a quest to undo the damage done to dogs by their American owners, Millan moved to LA, opened the Dog Psychology Center to rehabilitate problem dogs, was discovered by celebrity dog owners and starred in his hit TV reality show, *The Dog Whisperer*, changing America one dog at a time.

Takeaway: *"Some of my clients say, 'The dog's the problem.' But the dog's not the problem. The owner is the problem. You have to retrain yourself, not the dog."*

1. Know your dog is a dog. Be honest with yourself about why you want a dog. Do you want a cute little white fluffy dog as a fashion accessory? Or a mean-looking dog to protect you? Do you need a dog because you want the baby you never had? Or a soul mate? Treating your dog like a purse, a weapon or a child can turn your home into a living hell. The dogs I grew up with on my grandfather's farm didn't have these problems, because we let them be dogs. They ran in packs. They were given jobs. They interacted with other species. They were fed when they were hungry and rested when they were tired, the way nature intended. Dogs are pure and unselfish and give us so much, so as owners we should take the time to look into their hearts and minds to discover what they need. For a dog to be truly happy and well balanced we must allow him to express his true physical and psychological nature.

2. Match your energy level. If you're a laid-back person, don't get a hyper dog that's jumping around like crazy in his cage. You'll end up saying, "This dog destroyed my house; I'm sending him back." If you're a runner, a low-energy, short-legged bulldog is not going to be a good fit. Most problems between owners and dogs are because of a mismatch in energy levels.

3. Speak your dog's language. "Sit! Stay! Come! No! Heel! Stop!" Screaming commands at a dog will only confuse him. We humans think that words are the only way to communicate, but the universal language between man and dog is energy. Dogs read your energy and emotions. They know if you are happy or sad or tired. It's not what you say; it's how you say it. I advise my clients whenever they're communicating to their dog to project what I call a "calm assertive" energy. That doesn't mean you're angry; it means you're relaxed, confident and in control. Your dog will pick up on that, and he'll react in a more balanced way.

4. Be the leader of the pack. A dog is a pack animal. From the day he is born, a dog needs leadership, first from his mother, then from his pack leader. It's in his DNA. The pack leader determines and enforces the rules, gives direction and provides protection. But so many owners in the modern world get it backward. They let their dogs run their lives. I meet CEOs of major corporations who can't control their dogs and Harvard graduates who can't walk a Chihuahua. It may sound odd, but homeless people are often the best pack leaders. Homeless people set the agenda. Their dogs walk with them for eight to ten hours a day. Their dogs follow them on their daily rounds and live a structured and simple life. At the end of the day, the homeless person leads them to food, water and a place to rest. The dog doesn't care if his owner has one dollar or a billion. Your dog will accept you if you set the direction of their lives, not the other way around.

5. Stop thinking about yesterday. One of the beautiful things about dogs is that they don't look back. Unlike a child, your dog is not going to understand if you punish him today for something he did in the past. "Yesterday you ripped up the carpet, so today I'm not bringing you to the dog park." No. Dogs understand immediate cause and effect. They live in the present, and when you are around them, you should, too.

6. Respect the breed. Of course, every dog is most importantly a dog—but he is also a breed. We humans created breeds to help us hunt or herd or guard our homes. The more purebred a dog, the more he is driven by the genetics of his breed. A border collie, for example, *needs* to herd, to bring back any animal that moves. Instead of buying your border collie new toys, take him out once a month to a place with cows or sheep or ducks where he can herd and really *be* a border collie. Or, if you think you want a Siberian husky, know that they were bred to travel over very long distances. If you don't have the kind of lifestyle to fulfill the bare minimum of a husky's needs, you will have a very frustrated dog.

7. Walk the walk. No matter how busy you are, you need to provide your dog with his most basic need: exercise. A dog needs exercise to remain balanced and burn off excess energy; otherwise, he might chew up your shoes because he's going stir-crazy. And by exercise, I don't mean opening the back door and letting your dog out in the yard. That's not exercise. Walk your dog every day. Preferably twice a day. And when you do, there are a few simple rules. It's you who should always be in control. Make sure your dog is calm before you leave the house. Walk like a pack leader, shoulders and head high, with your dog beside or behind you, never pulling you ahead. Hold the leash firmly with a relaxed arm as if you were carrying a briefcase. Alternate between a structured walk and short breaks to play and explore. It's you who decides when your dog can stop, sniff or run ahead.

8. You make the rules. In many homes the rules for dogs are unclear, but correcting a dog shouldn't be complicated. Keep the rules clear and consistent—when the dog is fed, where the dog sleeps, when playtime is, et cetera. Everyone from your toddler to your grandparents needs to enforce the same set of rules so your dog doesn't get mixed signals. Every time a dog breaks a rule there is a consequence. Be calm, firm and direct. Never discipline out of frustration or anger. You want to bring the dog's attention back on you. You can use a word, a touch, a snap of your fingers or a sound.

9. Work with what you have. Not everyone can afford a dog trainer, but if you have a neighborhood, you have a dog psychology center. Observe who has a balanced dog in your neighborhood and then reach out and ask, "Can you please help me with my dog?" Most people will be proud to share their techniques.

10. Love your dog right. A person wakes up and says, "Come on, puppy, let's get breakfast. What do you want? Bacon? Chicken?

Salmon?" Then they carry the dog to the lawn to do his business, and then back to the bed. The dog's feet haven't even touched the floor, and that's just the beginning of the day! You may mean well by putting affection first, but those good intentions will damage your dog. Give your dog the exercise she needs to create calm, the discipline to create understanding, followed by a reward of food. Only then, when the dog is in a calm, submissive state, give her affection. This is the way to show your dog honor and respect. And when they return the same to you one thousand fold, you'll experience the miracle of bonding with another living species.

CESAR MILLAN FACTS

Martial arts: At age 6, Millan is enrolled in a Judo course. By 14, he has won six championships, learning meditation, focus and how to use the power of the mind.

First purebred: At age 9, Millan sees first purebred, an Irish setter, and follows dog and owner home every day. Two years later, owner gives Millan puppy from setter's litter, Saluki, who becomes Millan's companion for next 10 years.

"El Perretro": At age 15, Millan works at local veterinarian's office, sweeping floors and cleaning up. Demonstrating his way with dogs, he becomes groomer and vet technician. Local kids call him "the Dog Boy."

Illegal crossing: At age 21, after three failed attempts to cross the border, Millan waits shivering in chest-high water, then runs through mud, a junkyard, across freeways and down a tunnel to illegally enter the United States. Eventually, Millan pays fine, gets his residency card and becomes a U.S. citizen.

Brush with fame: 1994: Jada Pinkett (now Pinkett-Smith) hires Millan to train her dog and is so impressed she refers him to other celebs, including Ridley Scott, Michael Bay and Vin Diesel.

Dog business: 1994: Millan opens Dog Psychology Center, a 2-acre facility in south LA to rehabilitate troubled dogs in packs of 30 to 40. In 2002, center moves to 43-acre site in Santa Clarita Valley.

Media empire: 2004: First episode of Millan's reality TV show, *The Dog Whisperer*, airs. Show is broadcast in over 100 countries. In addition, Millan coauthors six bestselling books, releases instructional DVDs, publishes a magazine and creates a line of dog products.

DOG FACTS

Dogs of war: Roman army had entire companies of Molossian dogs that wore ankle and neck collars spiked with curved knives and were often starved before battle.

Presidential dogs: 1789–97: George Washington owns over 20 hounds, including Mopsey, Taster, Cloe, Tipler, Forester, Captain, Lady Rover, Vulcan, Sweetlips and Searcher. 1901–9: Teddy Roosevelt's bull terrier, Pete, tears off French ambassador's pants during a White House event. 1920–29: Warren G. Harding's Airedale terrier, Laddie Boy, sits in his own hand-carved chair during cabinet meetings.

WWI hero: 1917–26: Stubby, an American pit bull terrier mix, serves in the U.S. infantry during trench warfare in France. After being gassed and wounded, he convalesces, returns to trenches, warns his unit of poison gas attacks and incoming artillery, locates wounded soldiers, captures a German spy by biting him, is promoted to sergeant, arrives home a celebrity and becomes Georgetown Hoyas' team mascot.

Man's best friend: 1923–35: Hachikō, a purebred Akita, be-comes Japanese national symbol of loyalty after waiting pa-tiently for his deceased owner at commuter train station every day for nine years. Hundreds of dog lovers turn out to honor him in an annual ceremony.

Space dog: 1957: Laika, a stray found on Moscow streets, is launched by Soviet Union in *Sputnik 2*. She dies in six hours from overheating. *Sputnik 2* goes on to orbit earth 2,570 times before disintegrating.

Cloned: 2005–8: Korean scientists implant cells from the ear of an Afghan hound into thousands of embryos transferred to surrogate mothers. Of the three successful pregnancies, only one, Snuppy, survives, and is named *Time* magazine's Most Amazing Invention of the Year.

Ownership: Americans own 75 million dogs, at an average an-nual cost of over $700.

Chapter 4

How to Be a Game Show Champion

• •

Ken Jennings

Winningest game show contestant in history, with earnings
of $3.6 million and longest *Jeopardy!* winning streak

Ken Jennings' boyhood dream was to appear on *Jeopardy!* The self-proclaimed "trivia nerd" ran home from school every day to watch the show. He grew up absorbing esoteric facts at a rapid clip and developed a competitive edge, playing college quiz bowl while at Brigham Young University. Still, he never expected his *Jeopardy!* dream to come true. He was content to marry, become a father, and take up an uneventful life as a computer programmer. It wasn't until he was nearly 30 that Jennings journeyed from his hometown in Seattle to Los Angeles for a *Jeopardy!* audition. Knowing how slim the odds were of being selected among the crowd of people who all considered themselves to be the smartest person in the room, Jennings returned to his life. A year later, in 2004, when "the Call" came, inviting him to be on the show, Jennings hurled himself into manic preparation. Three weeks later, he won his first game. Then, his next. Then, one after another, 74 games in all, the longest winning streak on the show, as he correctly answered 2,643 questions and earned $2.5 million. Success at doing something he loved changed Jennings' life. He quit his job to become a full-time writer. "Winning made me a lot more confident," he says, "because I'm that guy from *Jeopardy!*, damn it!"

Takeaway: *"If you let go of the outcome and just enjoy the crazy experience of being on a quiz show, you'll do much better."*

1. Learn all the time. Being a quiz show master is a lifelong pursuit. Once, I got a *Final Jeopardy!* clue—"Phoebe Snetsinger, she of the apropos first name, set a record for this activity, about 8,400 species." I knew the answer was phoebe birds, not because I had memorized it from a flash card, cramming for *Jeopardy!*, but because I had read about phoebe birds when I was six. Phoebe birds were in my brain. We trivia nerds pick up new facts all the time. We see something on a billboard or hear something on the radio and our ears perk up. As a kid, I pored over books like the world atlas, the Baseball Encyclopedia and Leonard Maltin's movie guide. As you accumulate facts, you develop a web of knowledge that makes it easier and easier to learn new things. And you never know when you might end up on a quiz show and that fact you memorized when you were six will come in handy.

2. Be TV ready. Producers of a game show don't want a question-answering automaton, or the "Pick me! Pick me!" guy. It's TV! They're looking for fun, pleasant, telegenic personalities. Think of the audition as a kind of beauty pageant. I remember a guy who made the first cut of *Jeopardy!* by answering the very hard 50-question test. But, when the boisterous production guy asked him about his hobbies, the guy answered, "Reading." Just, *reading*? Tens of thousands of people try out every year for about 400 *Jeopardy!* spots. It's easier to get into an Ivy League school. That guy would have made it on the show had he just been a little more likable and smiled or if he had said he was obsessed with lacrosse or raising ferrets. No matter how much smarter you think you are than everyone else, you have to first make yourself interesting and TV ready.

3. Pretend you're on the show. When I finally got "the Call" from the producers, they told me I'd be on the show in three weeks.

I panicked. Cramming for *Jeopardy!* isn't easy. They can ask you any question on any subject in the history of all human knowledge. My wife incessantly drilled me with flash cards—lots of names of cocktails and dead presidents—and I set up my living room to resemble the show. I created a makeshift buzzer from my toddler's Fisher-Price ring-stack toy and stood behind my recliner chair as if it was a podium. Then I played along with *Jeopardy!* twice a day, slamming my thumb down on the ring-stack, calling out answers to the TV. I felt like an idiot, but followed this regimen obsessively. When I was finally on the show, standing behind the podium, it felt like I was in my living room, except, of course, I realized, "Hey, Alex Trebek's here." I was able to transform panic into preparation.

4. Master the math. You need to know when and what to bet to win, so always keep the score in the back of your mind when you make your wagers. If you're behind, know how much you need to bet to win, and if you're ahead, how much you can risk if you get the answer wrong. I saw a lot of people make bad bets and lose. Brian Weikle, who was the all-time *Jeopardy!* champion before me, once misread his own writing when he was working out the math and mistook a six for an eight. He got the answer right, but hadn't bet enough and lost the game by $199. It cost him almost $200,000.

5. Keep cool under pressure. When you're actually a contestant playing on the show instead of watching from your sofa, it can turn dizzying with the lights, the cameras and the dapper Canadian host firing 61 questions at you at a rapid pace. Some contestants freeze up. You can see their deer-in-the-headlights look. I told myself, "You can freak out here. Or not. Your choice." I found if I kept a cool head, probably somebody else wouldn't. Baseball players say when they're in the zone the ball seems to be the size of a beach ball, and that's how it was for me. It was just me and the board.

6. Know what you know (before you know it). The game goes so fast that if you wait until you're sure you know the answer before you buzz, another contestant will probably beat you to it. You have to buzz based on a degree of confidence that even though you don't have the answer on the tip of your tongue, you'll be able to retrieve it in the few seconds that buzzing buys you. It's almost as if your thumb says, "I think we know this one; I'm going to buzz." Then your mind has to race to extract the answer from the recesses of your skull. Once I got a question about the woman from *My Big Fat Greek Wedding*. I felt confident I could retrieve the answer, so I buzzed. Her face just hung in front of me, but nothing came. I tried to think of different connections, and thankfully, finally, I was able to extract the answer—Nia Vardalos!

7. Know what you don't know. Overconfidence can kill you. It can be worse than not being confident enough, because if you get a question wrong you lose money, which puts you behind in the game. Sometimes when people get frustrated, they jump in and start buzzing. If you really don't know the answer, keep your mouth shut.

8. Play against the question writer. To be a *Jeopardy!* champion, you're playing against the question writer, not the other contestants. You are in a psychological game against the writer, who is trying to trick you with misdirection. Don't concentrate on what the answer is, but on why the question is written the way it is. Once I got a question in the category of Literary Pairs: "The film title *Eternal Sunshine of the Spotless Mind* comes from a poem about these ill-fated medieval lovers." I knew the poem was by Alexander Pope because I remembered a reference to the poet in the film. But which poem? I worked my way through the words to see if the question writer had left any clues—"eternal," "sunshine," "spotless," etc.,— but drew a blank. In my mind I ran through all of the star-crossed lovers of medieval romances. Romeo and Juliet? That seemed too easy. Lancelot and Guinevere? I didn't think anyone in Pope's day was writing about them. Then, I became aware that there was something strange about the way the question was phrased. Could the term "medieval lovers" imply that it was about real people who lived during the middle ages? But if they were real, how could they be a "literary" pair? Maybe if one was an author? Then, it hit me: Heloise and Abelard! It was Pope's poem about the real-life theologian Peter Abelard, who was castrated after impregnating Heloise, the teenaged girl he tutored. That was the trick! Think of question writing as an art and pick the writer's brain for clues.

9. Don't take yourself out of it. When I played *Jeopardy!* against an IBM computer, Watson, I was down by tens of thousands of dollars after the first game. But I didn't give up. I actually made a Hoosiers-like comeback on the second day. I didn't win in the end, but it's important to remember that it's never over, no matter how *over* it seems. During my streak, some people thought I was Superman and psyched themselves out of the game before it even started. So I had a huge psychological edge. The woman who finally beat me, Nancy Zerg, was not going to be counted out. She was going to give it her best shot. And that's great advice. Maybe she was just a natural optimist. Maybe she just thought, "Why not me?"

10. Follow your bliss. When I was an English major in college, the joke was always, "What's the difference between an English major and a pepperoni pizza? At least the pizza can feed a family." I thought no matter how much you loved something, it doesn't matter if it's not going to pay the bills. But just getting the callback to be on *Jeopardy!*, I felt like I'd won the lottery. It was my lifelong dream! Once I was a contestant, playing on the show, I became someone who loved his job. The passion that came from that contributed to my winning, and helped me see for the first time that doing something you love really *can* change your life. I leveraged that to quit my old job and become a writer. And now I love what I do every day.

KEN JENNINGS FACTS

Genetics: Jennings' brainy parents are warned by friends not to procreate lest they spawn a super race.

Ken font: Starting on a whim, Jennings makes up "new *Ken* font" signature for every *Jeopardy!* show.

Stealth: Jennings signs confidentiality agreement before *Jeopardy!* run. He travels back and forth to LA, wins 38 games and $1.32 million before his first show is aired, at which time he can legally tell coworkers and friends why he has been away for so long.

Superstition: In order not to jinx streak, Jennings stays every night at same LA "fleabag" motel.

Losing clue: "Most of this firm's 70,000 seasonal white-collar employees work only four months a year." Jennings' response: "FedEx." Correct response: "H&R Block."

Books: *Brainiac, Trivia Almanac: 8,888 Questions in 365 Days* and *Maphead: Charting the Wide, Weird World of Geography Wonks*.

Politics: 2004: Democratic politicians ask Jennings to run for Utah senate seat, but he refuses.

Stumped: 2006: Jennings doesn't know answer when Stephen Colbert asks how many pages are in his own book, *Brainiac.*

Watson: 2011: When IBM supercomputer Watson beats Jennings at *Jeopardy!*, Jennings responds, "I, for one, welcome our new computer overlords."

Unlikely odds: Chances of winning 74 straight games against two opponents: 1 in 20,300,000,000,000,000,000,000,000,000,000,000.

GAME SHOW FACTS

Legend of the "Quiz": 1791: Dublin theater owner James Daly wagers he can introduce new word overnight, hires street urchins to chalk "quiz" on walls around town; by next day, every Dubliner knows word.

First radio quiz show: 1923, *The Pop Question Game*: To boost readership *Time* magazine airs current events quizzes.

"Vox Pop": 1932, Houston, Texas: Radio hosts string microphone out of studio to quiz people on street with random questions; it becomes national hit, broadcast in almost every state.

First quiz show for cash: 1936, Washington, DC: Professor Quiz, ex-Vaudevillian, asks guests questions like, "Are black and white colors?" Correct answers earn up to $25 in silver dollars. By 1938, 200 similar shows exist.

Double or nothing: 1940: *Take It or Leave It* introduces betting into radio game show. Winning contestants "take" winnings or "leave it" in favor of chance at next question. By 1955 show evolves into scandal-plagued *The $64,000 Question* TV show.

Game show heyday: Many new TV game shows introduced in '60s and '70s, including *Jeopardy!*, *The Match Game*, *Let's Make a Deal*, *Family Feud*, *The $10,000 Pyramid* and *Wheel of Fortune*.

Shortest game show run: Three episodes, January 2002: *The Chamber*, in which players answer questions while strapped into a torture chamber.

Longest game show run: 51 years and counting, 1956 to present (with seven-year hiatus): *The Price Is Right*.

Chapter 5

How to Be a Major Leaguer

• •

Yogi Berra

One of Major League Baseball's most beloved players, former catcher for the New York Yankees and sports icon

Perhaps best known for his creatively mangled Zen-like apho-
risms, Yogi Berra is also considered by many to be the greatest
catcher ever to play the game. Lawrence Peter "Yogi" Berra was born
in 1925 in an Italian-American St. Louis neighborhood. Asked how
he liked school, he replied, "Closed," but he was a fanatic for sports.
Berra organized a neighborhood effort to haul off car wrecks from a
nearby dump to create a baseball field. And there, without uniforms
or adult supervision, the kids taught themselves how to play the
game. At 14, Berra dropped out of school. After he was fired from a
job at a coal yard for sneaking off to play ball, his family reluctantly
gave him permission to play professionally. He played for a local
American Legion ball team, where Berra's unathletic bearing and
awkward style of play led one coach to comment: "He does everything wrong, but it comes out right." Signed at 17 to a New York
Yankee minor league team, Berra played for four years and served
in the Navy during World War II. In 1946, he finally made it to the
big leagues, at Yankee Stadium. In his debut game, he hit the first of
his 358 home runs. As catcher, Berra anchored the greatest of all
baseball dynasties, playing alongside such baseball legends as Joe

DiMaggio and Mickey Mantle. With his devotion to teamwork, his perseverance and all-time record of earning 10 World Series championships as a player, Berra wrote himself into sports history. As manager and coach, he led his teams to five more World Series, winning three. Named to the Hall of Fame in 1972, Berra has never lost his humility or his love of the game.

Takeaway: *"You can observe a lot by watching."*

1. Love what you do. All I ever wanted was to be a ballplayer, mostly because I loved playing sports as a kid more than anything. I loved competing, loved finding ways to improve. If we didn't have enough guys for a game, we made up our own games. Ever try hitting a bottle cap with a broomstick? Great for hand-eye coordination. Sure it's different today—there's almost no pickup or sandlot games like we played. Everything's organized, supervised by adults. But I always tell parents, listen to your kid. Don't sign him up for clinics or private instruction or travel teams unless he or she *really* wants to play. If you don't love playing baseball or don't love whatever you're doing, do something else.

2. Play everything. A lot of people think major leaguers played baseball 12 months a year growing up. Not true. Most played other sports, too. Unfortunately, too many kids today commit to only one sport. They say 75 percent of kids quit sports by the time they're 13 or 14, mostly because it's no longer fun. You can easily get burned out doing only one thing year-round. As kids growing up in St. Louis, we played every sport we could. My advice to my three sons was, "Play 'em all." My son Dale was an excellent baseball, hockey and football player in high school. Scouts told him he was going to be a number one draft pick in baseball and should quit the other sports so he won't get hurt. But I told him forget it—if you want to play other sports, keep playing. If an injury happens, it happens. If you're a good enough baseball player, you'll be good enough.

3. Make your own luck. The odds of becoming a major-league player aren't real good. Nowadays, players come from different countries, especially Latin America, where the game is like religion. There are only 600 roster spots in the major leagues. And there are thousands of players in the minor leagues. You better have a plan B. That said, if you have talent and determination, go for it. That goes for any pursuit. When I was 16, I was told at a baseball tryout that I'd never be a major-league player. The guy who told me this was Branch Rickey, then the general manager of the St. Louis Cardinals. I was discouraged but didn't want to believe him. I felt I was still young enough to improve and hopefully get someone to believe I could play. Luckily my American Legion coach liked me. He tipped off the Yankees farm director, George Weiss, who signed me although he never saw me. A little luck never hurts.

4. Get a good mentor. As a young major leaguer, I was an awful catcher. I was a good hitter, but the Yankees basically told me that unless I improved as a catcher, there was no place for me on the team. Fortunately, in spring 1949 they brought in Bill Dickey, a great catcher who retired from the Yankees a few years earlier, to refine me. I owe everything to Dickey. He learned me all his experience, as I used to say. He drilled me on all the aspects of throwing, blocking pitches, catching pop-ups, calling a game—everything a catcher does. Dickey, who was happily retired living in Arkansas, was willing to work with me because I was a willing learner. If it weren't for his mentoring, I'd probably be back home in St. Louis tending bar or working in a shoe factory.

5. Play to your strength. Everybody's different. You do some good things, some not so good. My advice is to play to your strengths and don't go crazy over your weaknesses. The best players improve what they do well. You always hear Ted Williams had no weakness as a hitter. That's because if he had one, he spent most of his energies making any hitting weakness disappear. What I'm really saying is, be the best you can be. Do something better than anybody. If you can't do something so good, that's probably too bad.

6. Be a good teammate. It's easy to get a little self-consumed in baseball. There's a lot of downtime. A lot of time to think or worry about what you did wrong or feel bad for yourself. Sure, baseball is a team game made of individuals. But no team needs individuals who only care about themselves. Once in a World Series game against Brooklyn, our pitcher Tom Gorman and I got crossed up on a pitch that I called and two runs scored. We lost and the reporters were saying it was Gorman's fault. I told them to blame me. If teammates don't support teammates, your team's in trouble. The big reason for our Yankees teams winning was because we were like family—we all pulled for each other. When people said Mantle didn't like Maris and that we as teammates wanted Mantle to break the home run record, that was pure crock. We couldn't care less who hit the home runs. Mickey and Roger were friends, always supporting each other. Mickey was one of the greatest players ever, but most important to him was always helping the team. That's what he wanted it to say on his monument: "A Great Teammate."

7. Get over your slumps. They say baseball is a game of failure. Even the best hitters fail 7 out of 10 times. Sure, slumps are inevitable. Heck, I once went 0-for-32. But I always tried to stay positive—never really considered myself in a slump, only that I wasn't getting any hits. Like a lot of ballplayers, I was superstitious. I used to shower under the same stall when we were on a winning streak. Some guys don't change their underwear if things are going good. During a slump, superstitions are fine, but don't lose your mind. The main thing is getting back to basics. Think about hitting the ball right up the middle and judge yourself on solid contacts, not necessarily hits. Play as hard as you can, do the little things to help your team win. If you stay sane, any slump will be history before you know it.

8. Don't overanalyze. In my rookie year, my manager, Bucky Harris, told me to think about what I was doing at the plate. I told him: "You can't think and hit at the same time." Always felt that was true. To me, there's too much overanalyzing in baseball. It's a game; play loose and have fun. Don't get so caught up watching video or figuring statistics in the computer. They're distractions. One thing I like about many Latin American players is that they just play. They play aggressively and enthusiastically. They play with passion. They play how baseball is meant to be played. They don't play with computers.

9. Keep your eye on the ball. My philosophy wasn't real complicated. If I could see it, I could hit it. Of course, I could always see pretty good. It helps to have good vision, but it also helps to have real good reaction time, especially hand-eye coordination. Especially when you're facing a 95-mile-an-hour fastball. You also need good focus. Meaning you must drown out any distraction, crowd noise or whatever. I always hit good in the late innings because I seemed better focused. I always felt the pressure was more on the pitcher— he had to beat *me*. Truth is, I made some assumptions where the ball was going to be pitched, and how fast, so I was ready. And if you're attentive, you could pick up cues like the pitcher's arm speed. I didn't do a lot of thinking at the plate, but always believed you could observe a lot by watching.

10. It ain't over till it's . . . No success comes overnight. Being a successful ballplayer means you better be committed as can be. Better be prepared to deal with rejection. And you better be willing to make adjustments. Like I mentioned, I was told I'd never be a major leaguer, but I was strongly motivated from within, and willing to do whatever it took. I have a lot of admiration for the thousands of minor-league players who won't yet give up a shot at the majors. They're willing to do things others aren't willing to do. Long bus rides, crummy pay, lousy living conditions. I lived those days myself.

At some point you have to figure out it may never happen. But, if you don't give up, work as hard as anyone, you never know.

YOGI BERRA FACTS

Nickname: Dubbed "Yogi" by a childhood friend because he resembles an Indian snake charmer in a film.

World War II: 1944–46: Berra's baseball career interrupted when he joins Navy and participates in D-day invasion.

Joe DiMaggio's first words to rookie Berra: 1947: "How ya doin', kid?"

Insults: Opposing players call Berra "Neanderthal Man" and make ape sounds. Writers describe him as a "gorilla in flannels." Berra uses insults as motivation.

All-time World Series player records: Most series (14), series wins (10), games (75), at-bats (259), hits (71), singles (49) and doubles (10).

Biggest thrill: 1956: Catching Don Larsen's perfect World Series game (the only one in over 100 years of World Series history). Berra recalls: "I didn't know I'd jump on Don until I jumped on him!"

Museum: 1998, Montclair, NJ: Yogi Berra Museum and Learning Center opens to teach students values of "good character, humility, integrity, fair play, respect and decency."

Yogi-isms: "Ninety percent of the game is half mental." "Nobody goes there anymore. It's too crowded." "It's déjà vu all over again." "I really didn't say everything I said."

BASEBALL FACTS

Baseball goes pro: 1869: Cincinnati Red Stockings is first team to openly pay players.

Reserve Clause: 1878: Team owners collude to prevent players from jumping teams for better pay. (In 1974, free agency allows players to negotiate deals with any team after playing for six years.)

Oddball trades: 1915: Bruce Hopper to Chicago Cubs for a hunting dog. 1931: Shortstop Johnny Jones to Charlotte Hornets for a 25-pound turkey.

Banned pitch: 1920: The spitball, a "freak" delivery caused by applying spit, Vaseline or tobacco juice, is banned; 17 existing spitball pitchers are exempt.

Youngest MLB player: 1944: Joe Nuxhall, 15 years old, Cincinnati Reds.

Oldest player: 1965: Satchel Paige, 59 years old, Kansas City Athletics. (Paige started MLB career at 42 after starring in Negro Leagues.)

MLB players' average salary: 1950s: $14,864. 2011: $3.4 million.

Highest single-season salary: 2009–10: $33 million, Alex Rodriguez, New York Yankees.

MLB total revenue: 2011: $7.2 billion (est.).

Chapter 6

How to Be a Tennis Champion

•••••••••••••••••••••••••••••

Martina Navratilova

Tennis legend with a record-breaking career that spanned
four decades

As a child growing up in Czechoslovakia, Martina Navratilova had the chance to watch the great Australian player Rod Laver—often considered one of the sport's greatest players. Witnessing her fellow left-hander in action, Navratilova recognized a stylistic role model, dreaming that one day she might match his grand accomplishments. By her late teens, Navratilova had become one of the best players in the world. At 21, she had a major breakthrough, besting her rival Chris Evert in the 1978 Wimbledon final. But by the spring of 1981, Navratilova stood at a crossroads. Still among the sport's very best, she remained mercurial, playing with uncertain commitment and prone to puzzling losses. And then, as Navratilova says, "I got religion." Working with basketball star Nancy Lieberman, Navratilova invented a revolutionary approach to training—devoting hours not just to tennis but to the gym, the track, even the basketball court. In the process, Navratilova created the cross-training discipline that is now de rigueur. Next came technical and tactical upgrades to her tennis, drawing on the wisdom of one of the sport's great strategists, Renée Richards. And with a new diet, by the end of 1981, Navratilova had transformed herself. Hours of process led to spectacular outcomes. Over the next six years, Navratilova dominated women's tennis. She was ranked number one in the world. She won a record ninth consecutive Wimbledon singles title in 1990 and an amazing 59 Grand Slam combined titles in singles and same-sex and mixed doubles, including, a month short of turning 50, playing her last match, with victory, in the 2006 US Open mixed doubles final. Over the course of a career that had spanned four decades, Navratilova lived by an important rule: "In the pursuit of excellence, leave no stone unturned."

Takeaway: *"There is a saying that 'You are only as good as your opponent allows you to be,' but I like to think my opponent is only as good as I allow her to be."*

1. Don't specialize. Growing up, I played many sports; I bicycled, I swam, I skied, I climbed trees. I played soccer and hockey. And all that contributed to my longevity in tennis and made me a better athlete both mentally and physically. For instance, if I fell on the court, I didn't hurt myself because I had already learned from my other sports how to tuck and roll. But nowadays, parents specialize their kids too soon. They are so terrified that if their tennis kid rides a bicycle he or she might have an accident and be out of commission for a couple weeks. But tennis players who don't know how to fall the right way will brace themselves with their arms and maybe break their wrists. A kid needs a well-rounded life.

2. Build the body. You are born with athleticism. Even without training, the kid with the fast-twitch fibers in his or her DNA will probably be faster than the next kid. I had that. But when I first went pro there wasn't the focus on physical training there is in the game today. I'd practice maybe an hour a day. In 1981, I was 24, well past the middle of my prime. I had been number one, but I'd become very inconsistent. Then I met Nancy Lieberman [a pro basketball player, now an NBA coach], and I learned from her that trying to play on natural talent and instinct was not enough. I began to practice tennis four hours a day every day. Eventually I could stay on the court forever. I took up weight training to achieve peak conditioning, running and basketball to improve reach and footwork. All that training improved my reaction time and speed. I could hit the ball harder. I could run just as hard at the end of a match as I did at the beginning. I began to win consistently. I was the first to condition myself like that. Even before the men.

3. Dream big. The outcome isn't just decided by endurance. Confidence is just as important. But confidence is hard to get and easy to lose. And, it's difficult to win if you're *not* confident. And until you start winning, you don't have it. In practice I learned to get as close as possible to the whole feeling of a match, the feeling and emotion of the racket in my hand, the physical stroke of hitting the ball, so when I played a match I didn't have to create a physical and mental edge. I just had to recall it. I had the confidence to know exactly what to do. Ultimately, I even anticipated the feeling of lifting up the trophy, how it felt in my hands and muscles and, of course, the emotional elation. I think all the champions do this. The Williams sisters are the epitome of this. They pretended they had the confidence to win Wimbledon before they ever set foot there.

4. Have a game plan. When I started working with my coach, Renée Richards, I learned to ask, "What are my strengths? What are the opponent's weaknesses? What are my best percentages?" We developed a match strategy versus opponents as well as a strategy within a point. I'd have a set play of four or five shots. It would work out exactly as planned, like a football play. But Renée also helped me learn how to mix things up. For example, my rival Tracy Austin had often been able to read my patterns. So rather than always hit the ball to where she'd come to expect it, at certain times in the match I'd change directions just to keep Tracy off balance. Variety is particularly important if things aren't going well. It's tricky out there.

You've got to both make a plan and be nimble enough to subtly alter it throughout the match.

5. Have absolute match conviction. Early in my career, I'd sometimes let up during a match because I'd get a little tired or I'd lose concentration. I might start thinking about the dinner I was going to have or a conversation from a couple of days ago. There were even times when I'd be winning 6-love, 4-love, and I'd debate whether I should try to lose a game. But after I started practicing so hard, my attitude changed. I became very aggressive and intimidating. I couldn't let myself waste all that work by letting up in a match. During a game, I'd tell myself, "I'm not going to take the foot off the gas." I'd put my opponents on their heels. I didn't make it personal. I'd just play every ball to win. When you've got someone down, you need that killer instinct to beat them and get off the court. To be a champion you have to play as if every point is a matter of life and death.

6. Never drop your guns. Sometimes to endear myself with fans, I'd try to finish off my points with a hero shot, even though a sharp rush to the net would have been fine. I had to learn the hard way that when the scoreboard said it was tied at six games, it was not the time to get creative. Your ordinary but effective shots are your weapons. In my case they were my sound serve and volley. If your forehand wins you matches, use it. Don't be a hot dog. Never drop your guns.

7. Evolve. I'm not brilliant, but I'm pretty smart. And my game evolved because I've always been eager to learn new things. Even now, I'm still learning about the game. One of my most satisfying moments was my finals match against Zina Garrison at Wimbledon. I was 33, past my prime. I wasn't going to get any better physically. I needed to figure out how to win. I worked very hard on my footwork so I was able to get to the ball much quicker. And that really improved my game. It was my ninth Wimbledon win. The game evolves. And as a player, you have to evolve, too. For example, the Williams sisters, as great as they are, haven't evolved at all. They've always played the same way, with the same strengths and weaknesses. Other players figured out how to play them. And if those other players could execute their strategy, they could beat them.

8. Take responsibility. It's good to have emotions during a match. It means you care. I always did. But I often lost my temper and got really mad at officials. Finally, I had a trainer tell me, "Martina, your moods are affecting your game. Don't get mad at the officials. Get mad at yourself." After that I did a lot of soul-searching. I threw myself into radically improving my attitude to stay clearheaded to figure out what I needed to do—whether it's tactical or technical—to win each point and eventually the match.

9. Be a good sport. When I was first playing, tennis was still a gentleman's sport. The umpires were amateurs, but if a call was missed, the players would make the call on themselves. I certainly did. That's the way my father taught me. But this happens less now. There's so much more money involved and an attitude of "win at all costs." Recently at a tournament a player returned a drop shot on the second bounce. The umpire didn't call it. And the player didn't call it on herself. It left a really bad taste in everyone's mouth. The player claimed she didn't know. But you *do* know. That's her legacy now. She's going to have to live with it. A player's character really comes through on a tennis court. Part of being a champion is being a good sport, win or lose.

10. Make it fun. I grew up listening to my parents and coach shouting, "Go for it." They just wanted me to enjoy the game. I played for the thrill of hitting the ball where I wanted, and I loved putting all that work and practice into action. I played to win, but I still had fun. Now, particularly on the women's side, a lot of players have lost sight of the fact that it's a game. They've lost the joy of playing. They're so afraid to fail, and with all that pressure, they're miserable and that affects their play. This is a very passionate sport.

To be a champion, you need to love it and treat it like a game. If you're just trying to get rich or famous, do something else.

MARTINA NAVRATILOVA FACTS

Rivalry: 1973: Starting one of the sport's great rivalries, Navratilova and Chris Evert play for first time in Akron, Ohio, and Evert wins. Over their careers, the pair play one another in 80 singles matches—Navratilova wins 43, Evert 37—and exchange number-one ranking 17 times.

Too American: 1975: When Czechoslovak authorities try to limit Navratilova's travel, claiming she's too "Americanized," she defects during US Open. She receives expedited green card and becomes a U.S. citizen six years later.

Ready to rumble: 1981: On first day of basketball pro Nancy Lieberman's relentless 12-step training program, Navratilova falls on track after wind sprints and cries. In 1983, after having transformed herself through conditioning, Navratilova has 86 wins and 1 loss.

Records (for men and women): Most singles title wins (167), most singles match wins (1,442), longest match winning streak (74) and only player to win Grand Slam titles in four different decades.

TENNIS FACTS

Origins: Twelfth century, France: Two players hit ball back and forth by striking it with the palms of their hands.

Take that: Sixteenth century: Rackets are first used and game is called "tennis," from server's announcement to opponent, "Tenez!" which can mean "hold," "receive" or "take."

Wimbledon: Circa 1870, England: Major Walter Clopton Wingfield devises game he calls "Sphairistike," Greek for "skill at playing at ball," that is modern forerunner of tennis. It is played on hourglass-shaped court. Idea spreads to a croquet club in Wimbledon, renamed All England Croquet and Lawn Tennis Club in 1877, when 200 spectators pay one shilling to see Spencer Gore win first Gentlemen's Singles.

First American court: 1874, Staten Island, NY: Young socialite Mary Ewing Outerbridge lays out tennis court at Staten Island Cricket Club on site of what is now Staten Island Ferry terminal.

Love: The term "love," used when score is zero—or "goose egg"—is from the French word for egg, *l'oeuf.*

Extra inches: Ranked number one seven times from 1962 to 1973, Australian Margaret Court's arms are three inches longer than the average woman's of her size.

Meow: 2002: Serena Williams makes headlines wearing a black PVC cat suit during US Open.

Speed balls: Fastest serves: men's, Ivo Karlović (156 mph); women's, Venus Williams (129 mph).

Chapter 7

How to Be Funny (on TV)

∙∙∙∙∙∙∙∙∙∙∙∙∙∙∙∙∙∙∙∙∙∙∙∙∙∙∙∙∙∙∙∙∙∙∙∙

Alec Baldwin and Robert Carlock

Award-winning star (Baldwin) and show runner (Carlock)
of the critically acclaimed *30 Rock* TV show, with 57 Emmy
nominations

"They've ruined me," says Alec Baldwin of Robert Carlock and the writing staff of acclaimed TV show *30 Rock*. "When someone who wants me to host a show pitches me with, 'Soooo . . . you're a Cub Scout master, and you get stuck in . . . ,' I want to tell them, 'I work with the funniest people in the business, and you guys don't know what funny is!'" Baldwin, who plays the charmingly roguish network TV executive Jack Donaghy on *30 Rock*, and Robert Carlock belong to a mutual admiration society. "It is a singer-songwriter thing," says Baldwin of the actor-writer dynamic. "I'm just getting up there saying the lines they write and giving them everything I got." "Comedy is musical," Carlock replies, "the timing and the pitch. And when you've got people like Alec Baldwin doing the acting, you can only blame yourself when it doesn't work." Named the best comedy of the past decade by *Newsweek*, *30 Rock* is a TV show about the behind-the-scenes milieu of a fictional TV show, *TGS with Tracy Jordan*, inspired by the *real* TV show *Saturday Night Live*, where Baldwin, Carlock and *30 Rock*'s creator, Tina Fey, first met. Fey and Carlock were both *SNL* writers, and Baldwin was a regular guest, hosting *SNL* a record 16 times. After Carlock left *SNL* to write for the successful *Friends* and then the ill-fated *Joey*, he was beckoned back to New York by Fey to help her create the characters inspired by their experience at SNL. When Baldwin accepted the role of Jack the three were reunited. *30 Rock*'s writing staff of a dozen or so writers aim so high and work such brutal hours they "look like mental patients around mid-season," Baldwin says. Carlock adds, "We try to tell emotionally grounded stories in as odd of a way as we can."

Takeaway: *"Good ideas come from anywhere, even from bad ideas."*

1. Keep the ship moving forward. ALEC: The writers work ungodly hours. Especially as we get into the second half of the year, they're tired and stressed out. But they don't sit there and say, "We got six episodes in the can. Fuck it, let's just coast." They push themselves. They are the smartest people I've ever met, and what they write is very black-diamond ski course. **ROBERT:** As the season grinds on and we're working 80-, 90-hour weeks, our brains begin to atrophy. We'll be in the writer's room until early morning trying to keep the ball in the air. We need a joke! We need an idea! You pitch your idea to the room. And you know when it doesn't work. There's no more visceral reaction than people not laughing. But when you say something that totally bombs you hope someone else says, "Oh, what I thought you were going to say was X," or "What if it went there?" When you're writing it's as if you're turning something over in your hands and making sure you're looking at every side of it. Is it a piece of coal? Or a lump of shit? But it could be a diamond! What's amazing about the creative process is how at each step you see so much that you hadn't before. It's always a little scary when you're pitching it to Tina or Alec, but a good kind of scary. It's important to create the environment where everyone wants to contribute so that moment of inspiration can happen, because sometimes you're just one step away. And there's nothing more thrilling than when it works.

2. It takes all kinds. ROBERT: There are different kinds of funny, so you want writers who share a comic language—they get your dumb bits and you get theirs. But you also want writers with a diverse range of experiences, so you get that sudden surprise of "Oh! That's something I wouldn't have thought of." Currently our mix includes a former stand-up from Ohio who started writing later in life when he came out of the closet; an Illinois girl by way of Vegas and Amsterdam; the usual, unavoidable contingent of Harvard wangs (you have to hire them—they're really good—but you need to surround them with people who don't care at all that they went to Harvard and make them feel stupid all the time or else they become a monolith); a woman whose father is a Green Beret; a first-generation Indian who is supposed to be a doctor; a singer-songwriter who had a musical produced in LA and Korea; two white Protestants; a first-generation Persian woman; a comic-book nerd writing team who couldn't make eye contact in their first meeting with me and Tina; an Oxford M. Phil [master of philosophy]; and a genius San Fernando Valley dirtbag burnout made good who used to work drunk on a missile-making assembly line. Put all these people in the same room and they not only speak the exact same kind of comedy language but they can laugh at things that the other guy says even though it has no relation to their own frame of reference.

3. Every joke has to count. ROBERT: TV is a medium of limitations. We tell a lot of jokes, but we don't have a lot of time to mess around. Every joke has to accomplish something, whether it's smoothing over a transition, telling us something new about a character we've known for six years, or progressing the story. **ALEC:** We have a lot of great writers. And in only 21 minutes the scripts are very, very nougat-y. I don't want to just call them jokes—they're full of cultural references. The names we drop! And how we drop them. Do you know how good it feels to say, "I can't wait to see you tonight. What are you wearing? Really? You're kidding. Condi! Condi! You're breaking up!'"? We have a basic understanding that unless there's something so glaringly wrong that you think, "I wouldn't say that," we do everything as written.

4. Write it real. ALEC: In the world of sketch comedy, say on *SNL*, you can say the most horrible and offensive things and get a laugh, because when the three-minute sketch is over, that world no longer exists and the characters will never see each other again. Whereas, with *30 Rock*, we can say things to each other on the edge of being offensive, but you can't cross that line, because those characters have to continue to live with each other for years. ROBERT: We have what we call a unified field theory. We try to create a consistent universe in which we ask people to believe. In one of our first episodes, when we were still finding what the show wanted to be, we had written a joke where Jack said, "Did you see the factory explosion on the news? Don't worry about it." The suggestion was that Jack had caused it. Our producer, Lorne Michaels, said he felt that crossed the line. I thought, "We need a joke there. We're just trying to keep this thing moving forward." But Lorne was right. Jack does a lot of things that go right up to the line, but even in our *30 Rock* world, he doesn't blow up factories.

5. Swing big. ALEC: When the writers have written something crazy—either acting-wise, where I play Tracy and his whole family, or some complicated technical production, like split-screen or me talking to me—I'll say to Robert, "Are you sure about that? How are we going to shoot it?" And he'll say, "It's a big swing." ROBERT: I'll always have to ask myself, "Is it worth wasting the crew and the actor's time?" Because if it's not worth it, everybody will be wondering, "Why are we here at 11 o'clock?" ALEC: But it usually works out.

6. Every character has to have their own voice. ALEC: On a lot of TV shows there's no distinction between characters' voices.

They all talk in exactly the same meter. It's beat . . . beat . . . beat . . . joke. Beat . . . beat . . . beat . . . joke. Some of those shows are so successful and we wouldn't mind having a bit of the crumbs from their ratings—but on *30 Rock* every character speaks in their own voice. Tracy has his malapropisms. With Jenna it's a hall of mirrors of self-absorption. Jack's voice is his unerring, hopeless corporate drive. Kenneth's is his suffocating decency, and Liz's is her self-defeating level of awareness.

7. Someone has to give. ALEC: On *30 Rock* every character is not only completely out for themselves, but they're trying to sell everybody else on why they are right. But one person usually has to back down and say, "Okay. I'm not going to think only of myself. I'll sublimate my feelings." **ROBERT:** If everyone is the voice of reason saying, "No, you can't do that," the narrative comes to a screeching halt. In the first season when we were working out all the dynamics, Kenneth [the NBC page] was one of the most helpful characters. He greased the wheels of the story because he was this lovable person who just for his pure love of television and famous people would always embrace the other person's point of view. If Tracy wanted something crazy, like a fighting fish from Chinatown, Kenneth was the guy who would go out and get it. If Jack wanted something, a human mannequin, Kenneth would get it. And that allowed us to break through on a lot of story lines.

8. Mark your words. ALEC: The writing is so smart and well crafted that articulation is critical. We have to really nail it. By the fourth episode, I realized that since the show is only 21 minutes long, the quicker we read the lines the better. And then you have to find all the rhythms to get the juice out of it. I might choose a word to pop for emphasis. And then decide where to take a pause and why. Bada-boom bada-boom bada-boom. Stop. Emphasis. Feeling. Today I had a line, "Do you know the history of this building, Stewart? During World War II, the Bazooka Joe Corporation took a softer version of their gum and made armor-plated bullets . . . [deep breath] . . . *right here.*" Where the line said "right here," I took a pause—as if to savor the line and say, "Can you feel it . . . *right here?* The ground we're standing on?" **ROBERT:** A lot of actors feel like they need to let you know that they know what they're saying is funny. If you do that it breaks the story. The great thing about writing for the actors on our show is that they play it real. The testament to Alec's skills is that he can do an outrageous character like Jack's doppelgänger, the gay Spanish soap opera star Generalissimo. And he plays it so real that you're right there in that reality.

9. Question the script. ROBERT: As we develop a story line, I always ask, what new information have we learned in this scene? How is the story moving forward? How are the stories talking to each other? How is this building? How is the end better than the beginning? Is the end even *in* the beginning? And, most important, am I feeling bored reading this right now? If those questions don't have satisfactory answers, then, however good the jokes are or acting is, you are failing in your duty to create something funny. It might be because of self-indulgence, incompetence, disregard for your characters, audience, or story structure or any number of other possible problems. But the most important question is not "Is this funny?" but "Are we failing at being funny in a larger sense?" And if we are failing, the solutions have to come from the same place the problems started—the writers' room.

10. Be so good they can't cancel you. ALEC: Are there shows that outperform us earnings-wise in a 30-minute half hour? Of course. But does NBC make money off of us? Of course they do. A programming person might come in and say, "I want to take this show that's making $50 million a year off the air because I can come up with an idea for a show that will make $70 or $80 million." That's what network programming is all about. But there is an intangible that I think helps us. There are monumentally successful shows that *nobody* in the business *ever* watches. Never. But we're one of those shows that's a little more interesting, funny and weird, like *The Sopranos* or *Breaking Bad*, that people in the business actually watch. When Lorne Michaels goes to the Grill in Beverly Hills or to Michael's in Manhattan, people turn to him and say, "My son broke his leg skiing. He was in bed and we watched all of season 3 together." Maybe it's my fantasy, but I believe that one of the things that has kept us on the air for six years and maybe beyond is that when these network execs walk into a room, everybody there—and their kids—watches our show.

30 ROCK FACTS

Balls! 1998: Carlock writes infamous double entendre "Schweddy Balls" skit starring guest host Alec Baldwin for *Saturday Night Live*. 2011: Ben & Jerry's introduces Schweddy Balls ice cream with vanilla, fudge and milk chocolate malt balls.

Intended: Tina Fey creates role of Jack Donaghy with Alec Baldwin in mind but is too nervous to ask him to play it. When producer Lorne Michaels takes it upon himself to ask, Baldwin says yes.

Emmy records: 2008: *30 Rock* is only third show in Emmy history (after *The Dick Van Dyke Show* and *All in the Family*) to win the male lead (Baldwin), female lead (Tina Fey) and top show Emmy Awards in same year. 2009: *30 Rock*'s 22 Emmy nominations are the most ever for a comedy show in a single year, breaking *30 Rock*'s 2008 record of 17.

Path not taken: If not a TV writer, Carlock believes he would be in "something respectable and sad, like advertising or law."

Baldwin's only *30 Rock* regret: That actress Jane Krakowski has never won an Emmy for her portrayal of *30 Rock* character Jenna Maroney.

30 Rock **cameos:** Alan Alda, Jennifer Aniston, James Carville, Matt Damon, Edie Falco, Al Gore, Salma Hayek, Jon Bon Jovi, Larry King, Calvin Klein, Queen Latifah, Cyndi Lauper, Chris Matthews, Moby, Conan O'Brien, Jerry Seinfeld, Elaine Stritch, Brian Williams, Oprah Winfrey.

TV on TV: *The Jack Benny Show* on *The Jack Benny Program*; *The Alan Brady Show* on *The Dick Van Dyke Show*; *Six O'Clock News* on *Mary Tyler Moore*; *Itchy and Scratchy* on *The Simpsons*.

TV SITCOM FACTS

First sitcom: 1926, Chicago: *Sam 'n' Henry*, in which two Caucasian actors play African Americans newly arrived from Alabama, first airs on radio. After 586 episodes, the creators rename the hugely popular show *Amos 'n' Andy*, which airs in one form or another on either radio or TV (with an all-black cast) until 1960.

Laugh track: 1950s: Charley Douglass, a sound engineer who notices "God-awful" responses of live studio audiences, develops the "laff box," a two-foot-high device operated like an organ, to play varieties of prerecorded laughter. 2010: Original "laff box" is appraised for $10,000 on *Antiques Roadshow*.

My favorite husband: 1951: When CBS asks Lucille Ball to take her successful radio show *My Favorite Husband* to TV, she insists that her character's husband be played by her real husband, Desi Arnaz. Network is reluctant because Arnaz is Cuban, but show, renamed *I Love Lucy*, goes on to be one of the most celebrated sitcoms in history, still watched by 40 million Americans each year.

Longest running: 1973–2010, England: *Last of the Summer Wine* runs for 37 years until canceled.

Most watched: 1983: *M*A*S*H* series finale seen by 50 million people with a 77 percent audience share.

Seinfeld: 1989–98: Since mantra of the show's producers is, "No learning, no hugging," unlike most sitcoms, there are no happy endings, no moral resolutions and no closure.

Chapter 8

How to Be the Most Fabulous You

• •

Simon Doonan

Creative ambassador at large for Barneys New York,
author, bon vivant, window dresser, fashion and style
commentator

On a spring day, in 1974, 22-year-old freelance window dresser Simon Doonan decided to go for it. He transformed the display window of a men's suit maker on London's staid Savile Row into an outrageous punk-inspired urban alleyway—taxidermied rats with rhinestone bracelets on their necks scampering over tuxedos and garbage cans. Then, he went to lunch. Doonan was born in the grimy factory town of Reading, England, and perhaps it was growing up in a rooming house filled with eccentrics—a lobotomized Narg (Gran spelled backward), a paranoid schizophrenic uncle, and an eternally optimistic mother who teetered through life on four-inch stilettos—that gave him his taste for the outré. At a summer job in a department store in Reading, Doonan was transfixed by two foppish window dressers wearing large wrist pincushions, arguing, laughing and calling each other women's names. Soon after, he left for London to follow in their footsteps and don a wrist pincushion of his own. Returning from lunch that spring day to the Savile Row shop, Doonan saw that all hell had broken loose. The sidewalk in front of his display window was packed with people "screeching in horror and complaining or hooting with laughter." A window dressing star was born. A decade later, as creative director of Barneys New York, the luxury department store, Doonan had become the most famous window dresser on the planet. With his avant-garde attention-grabbing windows, Doonan first transformed Barneys, then himself. He adopted a new role as fashion and style maven, and now Doonan's reach extends beyond his windows as he dispenses cheeky advice on fashion, glamour and attitude through books, columns, radio and TV. He instructs the masses how to attain what he calls that "mysterious, shimmering, you-know-it-when-you-see-it quality that surrounds those that stand out from the crowd," believing that everyone is born with the right—even moral duty—to become their most fabulous selves.

> **Takeaway:** *"Why the hell wouldn't you want to be one of the fabulous people, the life enhancers, who look interesting and smell luscious and who dare to be gorgeously more fascinating than their neighbors?"*

1. Invent yourself. Do you have what it takes to become the most fabulous you? The answer is a resounding *Mais oui!* Evolving your own brand of unique glamour is a process of self-discovery. Reimagine your personal style by uncovering and exaggerating all that is unique about you. Flaunting the idiosyncratic nonconformist that lurks inside of you will leave you feeling gorgeously empowered. Rule number one: Discover your unique style constants that you will become famous for. Whether it's your jet-black ponytail, your green tango shoes or your penchant for white fox fur, think of them as your glamorous foundations, unaffected by the fleeting trends of fashion. Now, punctuate these personal trademarks with a shock of the unexpected—giant rose-tinted spectacles, a pair of gold lamé toreador pants, a vintage Pucci poncho. *Et voilà!* The most insanely fabulous you!

2. Dressing down is a crime against humanity. In 1978, I accepted a window dressing job in the U.S. As I packed, I divided my clothes into two piles: WORK and FABULOUS. The dull work clothes I associated with drudgery; the fabulous, with euphoria. But there was something forlorn about the fabulous pile with its blue and white satin jockey jacket, sharkskin suits and other party clothes. In an overly zealous effort to preserve those fantastic clothes, I had hardly ever worn them. *Quel dommage!* There was only one thing to do. I arrived at LAX with only the fabulous clothes in my suitcase. Moral of the story: Go home and retire your work attire. If you always leave home in the unforgettable ensemble you'd wear to a Lady Gaga concert, your life will *always* be more fun.

3. Go forth and shop. Shopping is a huge opportunity for creativity. Shopping should be like a Hollywood production. You are the costume designer *and* the talent, Edith Head *and* Gloria Swanson. Your mission is to style a very important star: yourself!

4. Be a contrarian. You won't find the fabulously glamorous toeing the line. You'll find them walking on the wild side. Breaking taboos can be a revelation. If indigo becomes the new periwinkle, then start wearing cerulean.

5. Every day is a new photo op. The perfect picture pose is terribly easy to pull off. Run to nearest doorway. Place left foot forward. Place left hand on hip. Place right hand on doorframe. Imagine how much more thrilling life would be if every poseur paused in the doorway and assumed the picture pose before entering the room. Everyday activities such as taking out your recyclables or arriving at the nail salon would take on profoundly glamorous meaning. Each and every picture poser would be doing their bit to change the world, thereby averting wars and other man-made disasters.

6. *Vive la vulgarité.* A dash of bad taste should be an indispensable element of your personal style. As the great oracle and iconic fashion editor Diana Vreeland once said, "Vulgarity is a very important ingredient in life. A little bad taste is like a splash of paprika. We all need a splash of bad taste. *No* taste is what I'm against."

7. Go niche. Want to make a name for yourself professionally? Instead of opting for a showbiz career as a pop star or an A-list actress, you'll be better off choosing a more offbeat profession. Why not become the most famous dog manicurist? Or the meter maid with the biggest hairdo in the world? Just look at me. By filling the windows of high-end luxe boutiques with edgy objects like caskets and snarling stuffed coyotes, I made my mark as the world's most notorious window dresser.

8. Say yes to everything! Real celebrities say no. And they hire cadres of PR flacks to say no for them. My advice is to do the complete and utter opposite. Say YES! Say YES to everyone! I have made myself available to fly-by-night Chilean fashion quarterlies, Polish podcasts and obscure Scandinavian radio stations. Never, ever turn down press. Think of any request from the media as the opportunity of a lifetime. Overexposure, schmoverexposure.

9. Grow old ungracefully. Once you reconcile yourself to the inevitable—that you will wrinkle, wither and die—you can get on with enjoying life. Why blow your money on antiaging creams, Botox injections and boob lifts designed to make everyone look exactly the same, when you can slap on some extra lipstick and mascara and revel in the glamour of every waking moment? And no matter your age, a dab of Arpège can make you feel like the most fabulous movie star.

10. Confidence is the ultimate aphrodisiac. Once you've become the most glamorously fabulous you—with an unshakable belief in your own eccentric beauty—men are going to slip you their business cards and complete strangers are going to offer to pay for your chai lattes. Power up the confidence and get ready for some serious fan worship.

SIMON DOONAN FACTS

Doonan's window dressing tips: Collaborate with artists; draw inspiration from overdressed icons; debunk, lampoon and satirize; don't incorporate sex; don't avoid death; don't tidy up.

Controversy: 1994: Doonan creates Barneys' window Christmas scene with Hello Kitty doll in place of baby Jesus.

The writer's life: 1998: After claiming not to have read a newspaper or book for years, Doonan is asked to write intro for *Confessions of a Window Dresser*, a photo book of his displays. Publisher proclaims the intro "hilarious" and demands he write more.

Columnist: 1999–2008: Doonan writes column for *New York Observer* on such subjects as men who look like lesbians, manscaping and decorator bullies.

Happily ever after: 2008, San Francisco: Doonan marries longtime boyfriend, ceramist and designer Jonathan Adler.

Politically incorrect: 2009: Doonan's White House holiday decorations spark controversy among conservative groups for an ornament of drag star Hedda Lettuce and replica of Warhol's Chairman Mao in drag.

Bull's-eye: 2010: Doonan designs Halloween costumes inspired by reality TV for Target.

Telly: Doonan is a judge on *America's Next Top Model*, appears on *Gossip Girl* and his memoir, *Beautiful People*, has inspired a TV show in the UK.

Other books: *Wacky Chicks*, *Eccentric Glamour*, *Gay Men Don't Get Fat*.

FABULOUS FASHION FACTS

Ancient product: 1800 BC, Babylon: The wealthy powder their hair with gold dust.

Crowned: 800 AD: For his coronation as emperor of the Romans, Charlemagne wears silk tunic embroidered with image of Christ and apostles trimmed with golden scrollwork and crosses, brocaded silk cloak decorated with elephants, red leather shoes studded with gold and emeralds, and jeweled crown.

Vainglorious: Late sixteenth century, England: Elizabeth I, Virgin Queen, covers her breast with white plaster, outlines her veins in blue, has wardrobe of 3,000 dresses and passes laws forbidding others to imitate styles that favor her.

Up with her hair: 1770s, France: Women's hair is stiffened and whitened with flour, piled high and molded into complex constructions. Marie Antoinette's towering hairdos include the "Belle Poule," a model of a French naval vessel.

Original dandy: 1778–1840, England: Fashion arbiter Beau Brummell pioneers style of tailored suits, full-length trousers and knotted cravat. He takes five hours to dress, polishes his boots with champagne and spends inheritance of £20,000 on wardrobe, gambling and the high life. He dies in a lunatic asylum.

Flapper fab: 1920s: Scandalous Jazz Age women style hair in gender-challenging bobs, lose corsets for "step-in" panties and wear sleeveless dresses that fall just above the knee.

Fab forward: 2011: Total U.S. spending on apparel and footwear, $237.2 billion; on prestige beauty, $9.5 billion.

Chapter 9

How to Build a Beautiful Baseball Park

• •

Joseph Spear

Award-winning baseball park designer, director of design
and founding senior principal of Populous
architecture firm

In 1983, when Joseph Spear was offered a job at an architectural firm that designed sports facilities, he remembers thinking, "There might not be much of a market in this." But he joined anyway. And now, 30 years later, Spear and members of his firm, Populous (formerly HOK Sport), have designed or renovated an astounding 19 out of 21 newly constructed or recently renovated Major League Baseball parks (of a possible 30 MLB parks), in addition to a thousand other sports facilities in 34 countries for a construction value of $20 billion. In 1992, when the prevailing architectural style of MLB was the cookie-cutter concrete multipurpose stadium, Spear designed the Baltimore Orioles' Camden Yards—the first of the so-called neo-retro ballparks. Camden Yards was an eclectic, intimate, fan-friendly park, harkening back to a bygone era in its use of brick, steel and stone materials and quirky dimensions. Camden Yards revolutionized the design of future ballparks, which Spear strives to make as iconic as a city's skyscrapers, bridges and churches. "We are framing people's memories," says Spear. "As a kid, I loved baseball. I played on a peewee team, and my dad took me to local games. So I appreciate it's a pretty rare thing to get an opportunity to spend my career designing ballparks. I take a lot of pride in it."

Takeaway: *"What's the most important perspective in the ballpark? We've got 40,000 perspectives to worry about here."*

1. The stupid question is the one you didn't ask. Some architects consider their buildings works of art, and you can't question their work. But I don't reject ideas because they didn't come from between my ears. You'd be amazed at who has a good idea. We sit with the people from the ball clubs and ask, "If you could do anything, what would it be?" And we'll do public forums to learn about what the locals want. Even within our own firm, instead of having people just sitting there and picking colors for the building, we tell them to ask questions and think about what we could do better. You have to keep an open mind.

2. Choose a site that's symbolic. In Baltimore, saving the B&O warehouse was the stroke of genius. We incorporated that eight-story brick railroad warehouse into the design of Camden Yards. It was a local landmark known to everyone, uniquely Baltimore, and it really created a sense of place. After we built Camden Yards, other teams recognized the power of a ballpark's setting. In San Francisco, it was the park right on the bay. In Cincinnati, it was the view of the Ohio River. In Denver, it was the beautiful setting of the Rockies.

3. Design for hometown pride. In the '70s, there was a baseball player who said, "By the time I get to the fourth city on a road trip, I don't know whether I'm in Cincinnati, St. Louis, New York or Philadelphia, because when I walk out of the dugout all these parks look like concrete ash cans." We design ballparks in a way that makes the local fan proud. In Cleveland, for example, the three things most symbolic of the city were the bridges across the Cuyahoga River, the Cleveland Arcade and the Terminal Tower Complex, so we incorporated architectural elements of all three into the design of the ballpark. That connection to local design makes a fan feel, "This one's mine, this one's unique, it's in my hometown and I'm proud of it."

4. It's all about the fans. We design for the entire fan experience, even including aspects like a fan's arrival. Approaching a park should be more exciting than just getting to your seats. Most fans who go to see a Nationals game in DC, for example, ride the Metro. They're crowded in there with 10,000 other people. But we've designed it so that when they come up out of the station, walk down the block and turn the corner, they can see right into the park. There's anticipation, excitement. They feel, "Okay. I've already arrived. I can see the game from here. I can relax, maybe grab a beer." We call that area the *decompression zone*. It can put a fan in the right frame of mind for the next four or five hours they're on site.

5. Create visual variety. There are a lot of different strategies that we've learned, but among the most important was something that a 10-year-old kid once said to me at Coors Field in Colorado: "What I love about this park is everywhere you look, there's something different to see." Whether it's the visual variety inside the park, or the views to the outside, like the spectacular vistas of the Capitol lit up at night in DC, or the view of the Allegheny River and the downtown skyline in Pittsburgh, the beautiful thing about a baseball game is you have enough downtime during the three hours to notice all of the things around you, and we design with that in mind.

6. Welcome fans to the neighborhood. Probably the most famous neighborhood in baseball is the bleachers at Wrigley Field. Baseball is a community and its fans want to be part of the whole.

A neighborhood within a park makes the game richer and more memorable. So we start out by breaking up the forty-or-so-thousand-seat ballpark into smaller, more unique and discernible areas like the Rock Pile at Denver's Coors Field or the park within a park at San Diego's Petco. One of the more interesting neighborhoods we've created is at AT&T Park in San Francisco, where we put arches in the right-field wall so that people outside can look in and watch the game for free. They're so close they can talk to the right fielder. It's a place that's now in the guidebooks, and the fans who watch from there are sometimes called the Knothole Gang, harkening back to the days when kids would watch a game through a knothole in the old wooden fences.

7. Déjà vu all over again. Over time, the classic ballparks had been added to, changed, expanded under different managements and designed by different designers. Very often one seating section didn't precisely match the one adjacent to it. The old ballparks had sort of an ad hoc feel. You don't want to create a caricature, something so convoluted it becomes a joke, like saying, "Well, we'll just re-create the Green Monster at Fenway and put ivy on it." But we do emulate that ad hoc feel by incorporating varied design elements within each park that are unique and arise organically out of the location.

8. Never lose sight of the game. In baseball you have inning breaks, pitcher changes and "human rain delays" like player Mike Hargrove, who had all these little rituals and batting paraphernalia he'd adjust between each pitch. Unlike, say, hockey, where if you go to the restroom you could miss the only play of the game, baseball's pace is such that you can get up from your seat and walk around. We always design our concourses like Ashburn Alley in the Citizens Bank Park or Utah Street at Camden Yards so fans can go for a stroll, get a beer and a hot dog, hang out, talk to their friends, and still keep an eye on the game.

9. When baseball isn't enough, keep them entertained. Back when most of the fans who came to a game were baseball purists, it was enough if your ballpark had correct sight lines, plenty of restrooms and concessions. As MLB has expanded its market to families and people who may not be as baseball-obsessed, we've had to incorporate more amenities and entertainment into our design. It's not just hot dogs and beer; there's sushi, bratwurst, fish tacos, venues for the well-known regional restaurants, as well as full-service bars. We've also integrated spectacle into the design. Teams have their unique ways of celebrating their home runs, like the massive neon Liberty Bell in Citizens Bank Park that lights up and rings, or the foghorn in San Francisco, or the train that blows a steam whistle and comes out of a station in the Houston Astros' outfield. People also love the nostalgic elements we've designed, like the Bob Feller statue in Cleveland or the Hall of Fame walk in Detroit where you'll see a grandfather in front of a plaque telling his grandchild, "I was here for the game when he hit his five hundredth home run." We try to keep everyone happy.

10. Do it right and you'll only do it once. If we're successful at creating a park the fans fall in love with, the franchise will maintain and care for the building and make it last indefinitely. If we do our job right, a ballpark will last forever.

JOSEPH SPEAR FACTS

On building a ballpark: "It's like giving birth to an elephant."

Best professional moment: 1988: Opening day at the first ballpark Spear designed, Pilot Field, home of the Buffalo Bisons, an AAA minor-league baseball team. "The payoff was the newspaper headlines saying, 'They Did It!' and the people of Buffalo, who had suffered all of Johnny Carson's three feet of snow jokes, starting to take pride in their city."

Green ballpark: Washington, DC: With its green design elements—such as installation of water-conserving plumbing fixtures that save 3.6 million gallons of water per year, reducing overall water consumption by 30 percent, and recycled materials used in 20 percent of the ballpark's construction—Nationals Park is first ever U.S. professional stadium to get LEED (Leadership in Energy and Environmental Design) Silver certification.

Point of pride: 2000–2007, Pacific Bell Park (now AT&T Park), San Francisco: When slugger Barry Bonds is at bat, fans await home run balls while bobbing in a flotilla of small boats in San Francisco Bay just outside of right field.

From start to finish: Due to ownership changes and multiple referendums, AT&T Park in San Francisco takes 15 years from conception to completion; Washington, DC's Nationals Park is quickest, taking only three and a half years.

Populous' popularity: Number of seats in Populous-designed sports facilities worldwide: 18 million. Spectator attendance in these facilities since 2000: 520 million.

BALLPARK FACTS

Ballpark history: 1845, Hoboken, NJ: Elysian Fields is site of the first organized baseball game. 1862, Brooklyn, NY: Union Grounds becomes first enclosed park, home to Brooklyn Eckfords. 1923, New York, NY: Record crowd of 74,217 attends inaugural game at Yankee Stadium.

Oldest ballpark still in operation: Fenway Park, Boston, opened 1912.

Disco demo: 1979, Comiskey Park, Chicago: On "Disco Demolition Night," 90,000 fans overfill stadium, chanting "Disco sucks" and throwing projectiles onto the field. As giant pile of disco records is blown up in the outfield, fans storm the field, light fires and tear bases out of the infield until field is cleared by riot police.

Annual attendance at all MLB parks during regular season: 1940, 9.8 million; 1975, 29.8 million; 2011, 73.4 million.

Official ticket prices: 2011: Cheapest seats: Milwaukee Brewers, Uecker seats, and Atlanta Braves, Skyline seats, $1. Most expensive seats: New York Yankees, Legends Suite, $1,500/game.

Chapter 10

How to Create a Great Company Culture

• •

Tony Hsieh

CEO of Zappos, a leading online shoe company, and author
of the bestseller *Delivering Happiness*

When Tony Hsieh was nine years old, he read that when you cut a worm in half, both halves would grow into new worms. With an investment of $33.45 from his native Taiwanese parents, Hsieh [pronounced Shay] began his first business, a hundred-head earthworm farm in the backyard of his Marin County home. Within a month, his entire stock had either escaped or been eaten by birds. But Hsieh wasn't discouraged. He went on to other precocious entrepreneurial pursuits, including Christmas card and custom photo button businesses. "The first company I actually sold worked out pretty well," Hsieh said, a characteristic understatement. In fact, LinkExchange, a company he cofounded when he was just 22, sold to Microsoft for $265 million. It was 1998, Hsieh had over $80 million, and he was only 24. Unsure of what to do next, he started a venture capitalist firm, Venture Frogs. But he found investment boring. "I missed building something," he said. And since he didn't *have* to work, he wondered, why go into an office with people he didn't want to be around? Enter Zappos, a fledgling company that came to Hsieh for investment. Within a year, Hsieh was CEO and soon he was doubling revenue of the online shoe company every year, hitting the $1 billion mark in gross sales in 2008. As Zappos' workforce grew, Hsieh's preoccupation became how to create a company culture that employees would not only embrace but embody, and that would contribute overall to the company's long-term success. With a bestselling book and a seminar-based company, Zappos Insights, that helps other companies discover their best company culture, Hsieh is pioneering ways to develop a culture at Zappos that joins employees in unified purpose, not just to sell shoes, but, as Hsieh puts it, "to make the world a better place."

> **Takeaway:** *"Great companies have a strong culture of values. It doesn't matter what those values are; what matters is that you have them. If you want your company to be great, you have to figure out what your values are."*

1. Discover your personal values. Before you can determine your company values, you have to discover your own personal values. First map out a timeline of your life. Examine the peak moments. You will see that one or more of the values you prize was present. Some moments may have different meanings for different people. Winning the high school football championship for one person may represent the value of a sustained individual effort and for someone else teamwork. Then look at your low moments. These will reveal the absence of certain values you prize. Also, make a list of your friends. You will usually have one or more values in common. Then list the people you don't like, and you'll find there is a values disconnect. Even making a list of exes is helpful. You liked them once! And figuring out why you broke up can reveal some subtle (and sometimes not so subtle) value differences. Defining your own personal values is the first step to creating the core values of your company.

2. Align your company's values with your employees' values. If there are just a few of you starting out, the value exercises are ideal, but what if you're already bigger than that? At Zappos we didn't realize we'd need a set of core values until we already had over a hundred employees. Values resonate more with employees if they participate in establishing them, even better if the values are in the employees' own words. We sent out an email asking all our employees: "What should Zappos' values be?" We got a whole range of responses. After a year of back and forth, we had a list of 35 potential core values that we then condensed, combined and edited to come up with a list of ten that we could not only remember but actually commit to. It took a lot longer than I expected, but doing it this way increased the sense of participation and feeling of ownership of the culture among all the employees.

3. Hire and fire for values. It's much harder to find someone who is a great culture fit than someone with technical expertise. When we hire, we interview for the standard stuff—relevant experience and technical skills—but we also have questions for every one of our core values. Because when we find a person whose personal values match ours, they automatically fit in. On the other hand, when you first establish your core values there may be people in the company who don't connect with them. Some of those people could be your superstars. Most businesses will say, "Well, he's our top performer; we can't let him go." But if you keep making those compromises, by the time your company reaches a certain size, your culture will be gone and your losses will be greater. The process of firing based on values took us half a year. It was really tough. But taking that step was the turning point. The employees saw that everyone, no matter how important a position they held, was committed to the company's core values.

4. Get out of the way. My goal as CEO is to make as few decisions as possible. The best decisions are made from the bottom up. A manager's job is to remove obstacles.

5. Promote connection. Being surrounded by a lot of people in a large company can actually leave you feeling isolated. At Zappos we try to knit our employees together. We configured our building so we all enter and exit through a single reception area. People bump into each other and all sorts of serendipitous encounters occur. And in the digital world, there's our "Face Game." Everyday, when we log into our computers, someone's photo pops up—a randomly selected Zappos employee. We take a multiple-choice test to guess the colleague's name. After that, the person's profile and bio come on the screen. We do whatever we can to promote connection.

6. Keep the culture alive. Our company culture is driven by our employees. They decide how they want the culture to evolve based on what would make them happy to come to work every day. They come up with the most amazing and random ideas. About seven years ago someone had the crazy idea of doing a parade through their department. The idea caught on and now it's become a tradition at Zappos. You never know when or where a parade will occur. Every week or two, one goes by in honor of superheroes, underwear, Oktoberfest or anything else. They make a lot of noise, there's music playing, they might even hand out food. A customer may call up with an order and hear music playing and a ruckus in the background, and our person on the phone will say, "Oh, that's just a parade going by." That customer won't forget us. We try to create an environment where employees feel energized, where work doesn't feel like work. You're just living life the way you want to live it, and it happens to make money as well.

7. Instill the "WOW." Our first company core value is "To deliver WOW through service." We use "WOW" as a verb. Everyone has his or her own definition. For me it's about doing something that's so above-and-beyond that people literally say, "WOW." Ten years ago when we offered free shipping both ways, that was a huge WOW. A customer could buy ten pairs of shoes, try them on with different outfits and send the ones they didn't want back free of charge. Now that's become an expectation, so we keep

raising the bar. We trust our reps. They decide when to add surprise upgrades. Sometimes they'll send customers flowers or hand-
drawn thank-you cards. And we don't stop there. We WOW our
coworkers, our vendors, and, in the long run, our investors. It's as
important a part of developing our company culture as anything
else we do.

8. Build your brand one interaction at a time. When you
think about a brand, you don't mentally pull up a list of bullet
points; you either think "I love this company" or "I don't." Ultimately a brand is a shortcut to a set of emotions. Coke and Pepsi's
strategy to create emotional connection is to spend millions on TV
commercials. But that's a very expensive way to build a brand, and
it was more relevant 30 years ago. The Zappos brand emanates from
every employee. We make an emotional connection person to person, one interaction at a time. One of the best branding opportunities is the telephone. We don't script our customer reps. If we give
them enough freedom and they feel strongly about our brand, they'll
build a unique personal connection with each customer. They have
the customer's undivided attention for five to ten minutes. And, if
he or she gets that interaction right, something so unusual in today's
world, the customer is going to remember it for a very long time and
tell their friends and family all about us.

9. Prepare your employees for the future. Zappos is growing all the time. Who knows what we'll be doing in the future? The
top technologies or jobs ten years from now haven't even been invented yet. We'll always have to take up new challenges and solve
new problems. A workforce needs to grow and learn on an ongoing
basis. We believe our employees have more potential than even they
realize, so we invest in training, mentorship and offer all sorts of
classes. Employees can take classes on happiness, wellness, life
skills, personal money management. The range of topics is always
evolving. Our goal is that our employees will still be Zappos employees a decade from now. The only way that will happen is if

everyone continues to grow with the company both personally and professionally.

10. Have a higher purpose. As an employee, it's not just about the work you do or making another dollar for your company but the meaning behind your work. Think of the bricklayer who isn't just laying bricks but is inspired by his job because he's building a cathedral. All great companies have a vision that encompasses a higher purpose beyond profits or being number one in the market. And the irony is that the higher purpose enables these companies to generate more profits than their peers. Our higher purpose, at Zappos, for example, is to make people happy. If you inspire your employees by having not just stated values—framed and hung in the corporate lobby—but actual, practiced values that match their personal values, you can accomplish so much more.

TONY HSIEH FACTS

Job history: Age 9: worm farmer, profit $0. Age 10: greeting card salesman, profit $0. Age 12: mail-order button maker, profit $200/mo. Age 14: video game tester for Lucasfilm, $6/hr. Age 16: computer programmer, $15/hr. Age 16: mail-order magic trick salesman, loss $790. As college student: pizza shop proprietor in Harvard dorm, profit $2/hr. Age 22–24: founder, software start-up company LinkExchange, profit $80 million.

Favorite shoes: Running shoes (preferably ASICS), unless he needs to dress up.

Influences: *Good to Great* by Jim Collins, the TV show *Mac-Gyver*, and Rave culture with its emphasis on PLUR (Peace, Love, Unity and Respect).

Hsieh's bet: On an out-of-town business trip, a Skechers rep bets Hsieh that if he anonymously calls the Zappos hotline, the customer rep will refuse to locate the nearest late-night pizza delivery. Hsieh wins.

Hsieh's desk decorations: Jungle vines and an inflatable monkey.

Next mission: Building a Zappos campus in the old Las Vegas City Hall to connect to and help revitalize the downtown area.

The future: "Thirty years from now I wouldn't rule out a Zappos airline that was just about the ultimate customer experience."

ZAPPOS FACTS

Zappos core values: (1) Deliver WOW Through Service, (2) Embrace and Drive Change, (3) Create Fun and a Little Weirdness, (4) Be Adventurous, Creative and Open-Minded, (5) Pursue Growth and Learning, (6) Build Open and Honest Relationships with Communication, (7) Build a Positive Team and Family Spirit, (8) Do More with Less, (9) Be Passionate and Determined, (10) Be Humble.

Shoe varieties sold by Zappos: 50,000.

Cash to quit: After intake training, all Zappos employees are offered $2,000 to quit "to weed out those that are just there for a paycheck." Ninety-seven percent turn down offer.

Employee fringe benefits: Free lunches, 25-cent vending machines (profits go to Nevada Childhood Cancer Fund), company library, nap room, free health care and freedom of choice in workspace decor.

Longest customer service call: Over eight hours.

Managers' mandate: Spend 10–20 percent of working hours "building culture" with employees outside of the office.

Fortune's **Top 100 Companies to Work For, 2011:** Zappos, number six.

Customer service survey: Among 300 online shoes, clothing and accessory retailers, Zappos is number one.

Amazon purchase, 2009: Concerned with maintaining Zappos company culture when many of the company's board of directors want to maximize profits, Hsieh engineers Zappos' sale to Amazon for $1.2 billion.

––––––––––

Chapter 11

How to Create a Mind-Bending Crossword Puzzle

∙ ∙

Will Shortz

Crossword puzzle editor for the *New York Times*, puzzle
master on NPR's *Weekend Edition Sunday* and founder and
director of the American Crossword Puzzle Tournament

Thinking of clues can keep Will Shortz up at night. "Just as I'm about to drift off to sleep I may think of a terrific clue," says Shortz, who comes up with an astounding 16,000 clues a year. "It's the eternal writer's dilemma. I have to either wake up and write it down, or think really really really hard and hope the idea will still be there in the morning. Usually, I choose the latter." Shortz began constructing puzzles at eight. He sold his first one at 14. In 1974, he completed the first ever—and world's only known—degree in enigmatology, the study of puzzles, at the University of Indiana. Ever since, he has been on an enigmatological pursuit, as editor at *Games* magazine, as founder and director of the American Crossword Puzzle Tournament, and at the *Times*, where he has elevated the crossword to a minor art form with his "twisty" wordplay sensibility where Gauguin can coexist with Gaga in the same grid. His loyal fan base numbers in the millions, and, in fact, in addition to his evangelizing for crosswords and puzzles in books, on radio and in the tournaments and contests he hosts around the world, Shortz spends a good amount of time each week listening to solvers' feedback. "We're faced with problems every day in life, and most of them don't have clear-cut solutions, so we just muddle through the best we can and move on to the next thing," says Shortz. "But with a crossword, we're challenging ourselves to create order out of chaos. Although you might think, 'Boy, this is hard and I don't really have time for it,' it gives you a rush to fill in those last letters, and immediately . . . you want to do it *again*."

Takeaway: *"Put yourself in the solvers' shoes."*

1. Get the right tools. When I was eight or nine my mom had a bridge club over for the afternoon. To keep me quiet, she had ruled a sheet of paper into squares and showed me how the words interlocked to make a puzzle. I constructed my first crossword, if you want to call it that. I didn't know "the rules." There were no books on how to make crosswords then. I learned from looking at published crosswords and I winged it. For someone starting out I recommend getting some graph paper, a pencil, and an eraser to get an idea of the constraints. It's useful to have print editions of a dictionary, thesaurus and almanac and *The Million Word Crossword Answer Book*, which lists possible crossword answers up to seven letters by every combination of two letters in every possible position. Nowadays, though, most of the tools you need can be found online for free.

2. Appeal to as many people as you can. When I first started at the *New York Times*, I edited crosswords just as I had for *Games* magazine, which has a younger, hipper audience. A lot of *Times* solvers complained that I was dumbing the puzzles down, making them too easy. So I said, "You want puzzles hard? I'll show you hard!" I went to the other extreme, and you can imagine the letters in response. "You think we're all geniuses?! This is impossible!" I modified my style again to find a happy medium. Of course, at the *Times* we have easier puzzles in the beginning of the week, harder ones later on. It's like a circus. I try to get as many people into the tent as possible by having different "acts" and appealing to everyone at least some of the time. A crossword has a natural level of difficulty. One of the biggest mistakes a constructor can make is to create a puzzle with a simple theme and easy vocabulary . . . and then have tricky clues. That's out of sync. An even bigger problem, because it causes me more work: a puzzle with a tricky theme and hard vocabulary and then easy clues.

3. Create a theme. Thematic crosswords took root in the 1950s and '60s, and then became common in the '70s. The Monday to Thursday puzzles at the *Times* always have themes, which makes a crossword more than a collection of words. It's almost a narrative. A themed puzzle provides a few smiles, wordplay discovery, and when you as a solver are done you feel you've accomplished something. Themes can be puns, wordplay or something straightforward, but they should be as narrowly focused as possible. A theme for a recent *Times* puzzle involved film titles containing exclamation marks— *Viva Zapata!, Mamma Mia!, Oliver!, Avanti!, Airplane!,* and *Hello, Dolly!* The constructor also managed to plant the 15-letter answer, "EXCLAMATIONMARK," running smack across the middle of the grid. That was ambitious, but nice. My colleague, Merl Reagle, likes to "cook" a theme by using all the best examples of it in his puzzle. If any other constructor ever repeats a theme of Merl's, whether accidentally or not, they'll have to repeat some of his examples.

4. Construct the puzzle. In everyday life we use words linearly. They run across the page in one direction. But with crosswords, they have to run in two directions. To design the physical puzzle you have to be able to recognize patterns and see how words interlock. It's a math-type skill, and a lot of crossword constructors are computer programmers, math professors or musicians. Most crossword grids are symmetrical. If you rotate the grid 180 degrees, the pattern of black squares will look the same as it did right side up. When constructing the puzzle it's best to place the theme entries first. Next, place the black squares to break up the grid into workable chunks. Then, fill the grid with words, starting with the parts that are the most constrained—for example, answers crossing two theme entries, or areas with several adjacent long answers, or, say, a spot where you need a four-letter word ending in *q*. Save the easiest sections for last.

5. Write clues. Every answer must be a legitimate word, name or phrase. For definitional clues, the clue and answer must be in the same part of speech and be interchangeable in a sentence with the same meaning. A good clue writer should be tuned in to pretty much everything in the world, from popular culture to the classics. Also, for the *Times*, a little humor and personality are nice. Our culture has become so fragmented that nowadays 18-year-olds know different things from 40-year-olds who in turn know different things from 80-year-olds. Try to represent everyone's culture in the clues. Clues about movies from the '40s and '50s can coexist with a rap hit from 2008. But emphasize vocabulary and knowledge from our common culture that everyone knows.

6. Be relevant. Somebody sent me a crossword back in the late '90s with the title of the Britney Spears hit "Oops! . . . I Did It Again." The song had just come out a month or two earlier, and I didn't think it had sunk in enough in the popular consciousness to be worthy of a spot in a *Times* crossword. I rejected it, but I told the constructor if the song did turn out to have staying power, send the puzzle again. Well, the song did, so I accepted the puzzle the second time around and was happy to run it. New words or names are always entering the popular consciousness. Puzzle makers are always looking for new, short, vowel-heavy answers, which are very useful in construction. We were delighted when the singer Adele made it big. There's so many ways to clue her! When Elena Kagan was nominated for the Supreme Court, constructors cried "Hallelujah!" Whether you like Justice Alito or not, you have to love his name. If the vocabulary can be kept up to date, solvers will see part of their culture in the crosswords, which will keep puzzles relevant and fun.

7. Make it "twisty." With difficult puzzles I try to write some twisty clues that will stump the solver. The most satisfying clues for the solver are the hardest ones for the constructor to write. These are the clues that by using trickery and deception and not being dependent on a straightforward definition can lead the solver down the wrong path. Crosswords are a game, so you could say that I'm the solver's opponent. But it's no fun for the solver if they're completely stumped. You want them to get the answer eventually. I try to write clues that will stymie the solver for a while, so when they finally have that head-slapping moment and go, "Aha!," they get the ultimate solving satisfaction.

8. Avoid obscurity. I hate clues that even after you've solved them, make you go, "Huh?" You figure out the answer from the crossings, but you don't understand why. Even with the crosswords I edit, that's going to happen once in a while, but I don't want it to happen often. I really hate clues that a majority of solvers are not going to understand. Never let two obscure words cross. And avoid tired obscurities like "ESNE," which is an "Anglo-Saxon slave." This used to be a frequent answer in crosswords, because it has four very common letters and it starts and ends in a vowel. But you could read every story in the *New York Times* for 10 years and never come across "ESNE," so why should you have to know it? A word like that is a black mark on a puzzle and a sign of desperation.

9. Listen to feedback. It used to be that the only feedback constructors got was from me, the editor, and maybe a friend or family member. Nowadays, though, there are at least four daily blogs on the *Times* crossword alone. Constructors go there to find out what solvers like and don't like. The bloggers and people posting comments are very demanding. In the old days, you could throw in the name of a South Pacific island that no one's heard of in order to make your corner work, and solvers really had nowhere to complain. Now, you *know* you're going to be raked over the coals if you do something like that. Everyone is more accountable.

10. Think outside the box. At the American Crossword Puzzle Tournament in 2012, we had a puzzle titled "Boustrophedon," which is a style of ancient writing. In boustrophedon writing, the first line reads from left to right, the second line reads from right to left, the third from left to right again, and so on. Maybe that was the easiest way to write if you were chiseling a stone. At the tournament the puzzle's theme was: *Things that move from left to right and back*—like "PLOWING A FIELD," "DOT MATRIX PRINTERS," "MOWING THE LAWN," etc. And the crossword answers actually worked that way. The first row went from left to right, the second one from right to left, and back and forth. Most of the solvers loved it. But a computer program, Dr. Fill, which entered in the contest unofficially, had not been programmed to solve a puzzle this way, and it just got killed. Puzzles that go against expectations are a real pleasure because they twist the solver's brain in a whole new way.

WILL SHORTZ FACTS

Collection: Shortz has world's largest private library of puzzle books and magazines—25,000, dating back to 1533.

Shortz on *The Simpsons*: 2008: After Homer bets against Lisa in a crossword champion tournament he enlists Will Shortz (played by himself) to win back her love.

Quality control: At the *Times*, Shortz sends edited puzzles to four test-solvers for "solvability" and comments (one of the testers fact-checks every clue and answer again), then on to a fifth solver for further comments and finally to a sixth solver for a final look. On average only five mistakes appear in the *Times* crossword each year, out of more than 32,000 clues.

Favorite crossword clue: "It may turn into a different story." Answer: "SPIRAL STAIRCASE."

Favorite puzzle: Election day, 1996: One clue: "Lead story in tomorrow's newspaper." Two answers (either one correct, each interlocking with crossing words): "CLINTON ELECTED" or "BOB DOLE ELECTED." All day long, Shortz's phone rings. Some irate readers say, "How dare you presume that Clinton will win?!" Others, who filled in "BOB DOLE," think *Times* has made "a whopper of a mistake!"

CROSSWORD PUZZLE FACTS

First crossword: 1913: By Arthur Wynne in the Sunday "Fun" section of the *New York World*.

Crossword crowd: 1921: New York Public Library reports, "Latest craze to strike libraries is the crossword. . . . Puzzle 'fans' swarm to the dictionaries so as to drive away readers and students who need these books in their daily work . . . can there be any doubt of the Library's duty to protect its legitimate readers?"

New York Times on crosswords: 1924: "A sinful waste in the utterly futile finding of words, the letters of which will fit into a prearranged pattern. . . . Not a game at all, and it hardly can be called a sport. . . ." 1942: The *Times* starts to publish its own crossword.

Code breaking: 1944, London: Crosswords in the *Daily Telegraph* include secret code names for D-day invasion, including landing sites "Utah" and "Omaha." Investigations conclude it is not an attempt to pass messages but constructor's use of overheard soldiers' conversations.

England vs. America: American puzzle makers are called "constructors" because American crosswords emphasize grid construction and interlocking words, while in Britain they are called "composers" because there is a much looser, easier-to-fill grid interlock and more emphasis on the clues.

Prolific puzzler: UK: Roger Squires has had over 70,000 crosswords published.

Chapter 12

How to Create One of the World's Most Popular Blogs

• •

Mark Frauenfelder

Founder and coeditor of *Boing Boing*, one of the most
popular blogs of the last 12 years

Mark Frauenfelder inherited his love of all things technical from his father, an electrical engineer. Together they built radios, electric eyes and assorted gadgetry, and in time, young Frauenfelder even assembled smoke bombs in the family kitchen. Mechanical engineering seemed like a sensible career. But, after eight years, Frauenfelder felt something was missing. He had no creative outlet for his many passions that ran from cyberpunk to underground comics to Timothy Leary. That is, until he discovered the world of zines, amateur-made publications devoted to personal obsessions. In zines, Frauenfelder saw that anyone could connect with others with similar interests. In 1988, Frauenfelder and his wife, Carla Sinclair, began to publish a zine of their own, *Boing Boing*, to explore "the coolest, wackiest stuff" they could find. At the dawn of blogging in 1995, Frauenfelder moved *Boing Boing* online, where it became and remains one of the Internet's most popular blogs. Defying the corporatization of the blogosphere, *Boing Boing* has remained a curio of oddities, tech news, gadget tips and real-life marvels with 2.5 million unique visitors a month. Now, Frauenfelder shares daily blogging duties with five of other passionate editors, including Cory Doctorow, David Pescovitz and Xeni Jardin. After 12 years, his enthusiasm hasn't waned. "The recipe for an excellent blog is to be so deeply obsessed with something that you need to communicate it to others," says Frauenfelder. "If *Boing Boing* stopped making money tomorrow, I'd still need to do it."

Takeaway: *"Make the blog that doesn't exist yet, but that* you'd *want to read."*

1. Tap into the zeitgeist. If you can tap into the right cultural moment you'll have a lot of fans. Jann Wenner, founder of *Rolling Stone*, was the ultimate groupie. He didn't do focus groups to see if there was an audience for a magazine about rock 'n' roll, he just went ahead and created it. It turned out there were enough fans out there that shared his viewpoint to make it a success. Same thing with Hugh Hefner—he had a vision of where people were headed in postwar America. Riding on the crest of the Pill and new attitudes toward sexuality, *Playboy* magazine appealed to enough people to make it a cultural phenomenon. The same sort of lucky thing happened with *Boing Boing*. I started it when computers were just becoming cheap enough for people to buy. I was fascinated by what would happen when computers got into the hands of creative people, how our future would be reimagined through this consciousness-altering technology. It just so happened there were enough people out there interested, too. You can't really plan it, but sometimes you have the good luck of being the messenger for a larger cultural movement. Once we were out there, we had the advantage of being first.

2. Be original. If you try to emulate a successful blog, you'll just be a second-rate version of something already out there, and who needs that? Make the blog that doesn't exist yet, but that *you'd* want to read. Some people may collect vintage guitar string envelopes. They look really cool, and if you started a blog on that with really beautiful pictures, I guarantee, within a short amount of time, every vintage guitar-string envelope collector would be visiting your blog. Depending on your idea, starting a blog might not be the way to make a lot of money, but it is a way to live a fulfilling and engaged life.

3. Make the connection. One fax machine was worth nothing, but once you had two or three fax machines, they started to gather value because they connected with each other. It's called the "Network Effect," and it's the same with computers or the Internet. Those tools become more valuable with every new user who brings in their new connections. We're living in an amazing age. What's killer about the Internet is that anybody can create a worldwide community that connects to other people with the same interests. If you spend too much time obsessing on the minutiae of digital marketing techniques, you'll lose sight of the mission of a blog, which is to share information with like-minded people.

4. Get an attitude. Without a point of view, your blog is unfiltered mush. Whether you love or hate a blog, you still want it to have a unique perspective. As a kid, I was influenced by the *Mad* magazine attitude of poking fun at institutions and conventional wisdom. At *Boing Boing*, we share that subversive attitude. We tweak institutional powers—banks, the government and large corporations—to expose them for being foolish, to get back at them for sometimes making us feel like helpless victims of their rules and red tape. Our readers appreciate it. They come to us to get in on the joke. We're not afraid to post items that are a little bit mischievous and may get people upset, because that's a good way to stimulate discussion and promote counterarguments. We've had people wishing for us to die fiery deaths for some of our more controversial posts, and we're okay with that.

5. Don't waste people's time. We're all professional journalists at *Boing Boing*, and we always keep in mind that people are busy. They resent it when you waste their time. When the reader comes to our site, they're not going to land on a post that says, "This is amazing," and forces you to click on the link. Our posts explain what's important about what you're reading and why. Often that explanation is enough for the reader. Unless they're especially interested, they don't necessarily have to read the entire article to take something valuable away. It may be tempting to write cute headlines, but the most important function of a headline is to sum up what the post is about. If you've developed a trust with your readers that they'll get good value for the time they invest in visiting your site, they'll be back.

6. Mix it up. We try to make an art of combining fun, poppy stuff with heavy news content on the site. Posts that are easy to grasp in a couple of seconds—a bit of shopping news, helpful tips or gossip—get lots of hits and move fast. But, if that's all you focus on, it dumbs down the site. You'll have lost any type of gravitas. You have to have an editor's gut feeling to get the mix right. All of our editors go for that kind of a balance every day. We're as likely to have a post about a chilling political development as something on the frothiest bit of pop culture.

7. Appeal to the novelty gene. It's good to blog frequently, but the stuff you blog about has to be unexpected or people will lose interest. They say that there is a novelty-seeking gene. It causes people (like me!) to crave excitement, and to want constant hits of surprising things that don't fit the conventional model of the way the world works. I have subscriptions to hundreds of blogs and RSS feeds to search for items that surprise me. Ninety-nine percent of what's out there is crap. Our job is to put in the hard work to find that 1 percent that's fascinating, because a lot of our community has the novelty-seeking gene, too.

8. Let feedback change you. I think of myself as being pretty sensitive to other points of view, but once upon a time I was less so.

For example, once I posted a video of a guy who had squirrels eating food out of his bird feeders. He had a contraption that flung the squirrels out of the bird feeders, and I got a lot of emails saying, "That's no way to treat an animal." And they were correct. I thought, "Wow, that was really dumb." Another post was a beauty contest of women who were in jail—a *Hot or Not* of incarcerated women. Readers complained and explained that the majority of women in prison are dealing with tough circumstances, bad domestic situations, mental illness and drug addiction. It would be unthinkable for me to post something like that now. The community feedback has made me more aware of my insensitivities, and the blog has evolved because of it.

9. Think of a friend. Blogging can be paralyzing if you worry about trying to please a million people. If you start thinking, "Well, this person might object to that," or "Some people won't understand this point," it's really going to take the life out of your writing. So to get over blog stage fright, when I post something, I'll often have a friend in mind who has the same sense of humor as me. Someone I know who will get a kick out of it. And often that person will email me saying, "That was great!"

10. Keep it real. Although I search a lot online, I try to limit the echo chamber of the blogosphere. The best material for the blog is usually found in the real world from real-life experiences. All of our editors travel a lot. We take our cameras and come across interesting people, strange finds, all kinds of surprising things in the world of nature and humanity. Readers also send us their real-life stories and pictures, and we may post them. I can even find good material in my own backyard. Recently, I saw a few big fat weird bugs called Jerusalem crickets, and I took a picture of them next to a quarter. That post got a great response. People love to hear about real life, as if they're sitting there with you, experiencing it. Once in a while I'll get sick of the Web and being on the computer, and that's when I'll pull out my paints and do some artwork or go out and do something with my kids like fly a kite.

MARK FRAUENFELDER FACTS

Romance: 1983: Frauenfelder meets his wife and collaborator, Carla Sinclair, when her band, Rap Race, opens for his, the Elephant Boys. They now have two daughters.

How *Boing Boing* got its name: Frauenfelder's wife's grandfather stayed out drinking at a Jewish mafia club in LA. Whenever he came home drunk, his wife pelted him with rolled-up socks, yelling "Boing!" every time one hit him on the head.

***Boing Boing* motto:** "Brain candy for happy mutants."

South Pacific adventure: 2003: Frauenfelder and family set up house on remote island, using coconuts, twigs, shells and various items to make clothes and food. They last only five months but produce a popular blog, *The Island Chronicles*.

Books: *The Mad Professor*, a kids' book on science experiments; *Rule the Web: How to Do Anything and Everything on the Internet—Better, Faster, Easier*; and *Made by Hand, Searching for Meaning in a Throwaway World*.

Do It Yourself: Frauenfelder is editor of DIY *MAKE* magazine and cofounder of spin-off *Maker Faire*, where creatives show off their DIY projects.

BLOG FACTS

Proto-blogs: 1994: Swarthmore College student Justin Hall begins *Links.net*, a compilation of links considered by many to be the first blog.

JenniCam: 1996: 19-year-old Dickinson College student Jennifer Kaye Ringley posts one of the first live webcam blogs allowing users to view another human's daily activity.

Term "blog" coined: 1999: "Weblog," a compound of "web" and "log," is jokingly broken into the phrase "we blog."

First Weblog Awards ("Bloggies"): 2001: Weblog of the Year is Zannah's *#!/Usr/Bin/Girl*, a "collection of interesting links to distract you."

You're fired! People fired for blogging: 2002: Heather Armstrong of *Dooce* fired from a dot-com start-up. 2004: Ellen Simonetti of *Queen of Sky: Diary of a Dysfunctional Flight Attendant* fired from Delta Airlines. 2004: Jessica Cutler of *The Washingtonienne* fired from job as a congressional assistant.

Viral: 2006: Teenager Bree's Lonelygirl15 "confessional videos" on YouTube cause a sensation but are later revealed to be film promos done by 19-year-old actress Jessica Rose.

Jailed: 2007, Myanmar: Nay Phone Latt sentenced to 20 years for posting a cartoon of Head of State Than Shwe.

Payout: 2005: Arianna Huffington's blog *The Huffington Post* launches. 2010: Sells to AOL for $315 million.

Number of blogs worldwide: 1999: 23. 2011: Over 150 million.

Chapter 13

How to Cultivate an Exceptional Wine

· ·

Randall Grahm

Award-winning vintner and founder of Bonny Doon
Vineyard in California, and bestselling author of *Been Doon
So Long: A Randall Grahm Vinthology*

R andall Grahm is a serial dreamer. After having been exposed to "an ungodly number of great French wines" as a floor sweeper at a wine shop in Beverly Hills, Grahm began to fantasize about a life as a winemaker. He studied plant science and purchased a vineyard in the hills above Santa Cruz, California. His lofty goal was to grow the Great American Pinot Noir. But it didn't work out. Pinot Noir varietals were not suited to the soil or climate at his Bonny Doon Vineyard. Grahm did go on, however, to make a success of the winery with Rhône wines and Italian varietals, ultimately selling as many as 450,000 cases a year. His zeal for winemaking and love of tinkering led him to grow obscure varietals and experiment with oddball techniques. Through his writing and lectures—a mélange of rollicking parodies and cosmic musings—he became a bestselling author and an entertainingly contrarian voice in the stuffy world of wine. But the wines Grahm was most passionate about were not his own. His true love was the great wines of Europe, *vins de terroir*. These wines so embody the essence of the soil and microclimate from whence they come that when tasted the wines express a profound sense of place. "Am I capable of such a transcendental feat?"

Grahm wondered about these wines that require the vintner to cast aside manipulation and let nature take its course. "It took generations in the Old World—how do I make it happen here in a single lifetime?" Full of doubt and hope, Grahm is now off on his next quixotic quest to create the wine of his dreams, a *terroir* wine in the New World.

Takeaway: *"Let nature do the heavy lifting."*

1. Make wines that matter. For a long time I tried to make wines that other people would buy, drink and enjoy. But whenever I said, "I've got to make this fruitier," "I've got to make this softer," "I've got to make this *this* way, or *that*," it never worked. Instead, I've had to ask myself: "What wine does the world truly need?" It is *terroir* wine, because a *terroir* wine carries within it a deep, almost elemental psychic force and resonance that has the capacity to enrich the world. Ultimately, if I'm going to be a vintner, that's the wine I want to make.

2. Put up or shut up. The riskiest thing is to stay the course and pretend that things are normal. Nothing is normal; the whole world is upside down. You have to be fairly extreme to have any shot at succeeding. I actually dreamt of a place where I could start my experiment to grow *vins de terroir*. When I saw the property in San Juan Bautista, the one I had envisioned in my dreams, it was my moment of truth. I was scared shitless. I had to tell myself, "Okay, Grahm, you've been raving on about the transcendental value of *terroir* for a decade. Life is short and if this is really what you love about wine, well, for Chrissake, just go for it." And so I did.

3. Honor the place. A 22-year-old from Burgundy who inherits the Pinot Noir vineyard from his grandfather would never say, "Jeez, I wish I weren't here. I wish I were in Bordeaux or the Rhône." He doesn't have to think about what he *should* be growing. Pinot Noir! Those are his grapes. They're in his blood. His grapes are perfectly adapted to the terrain and climate of his vineyard. They've been grown by his family for fourteen generations. But, in the New World, we've only been growing wine for a generation. Here, we're free to choose whether to grow Pinot Noir or Riesling or Bordelais grapes or really just about anything. But that doesn't mean we should. In order to respect the land on which you grow, then, the question to ask is not the narcissistic, "What variety do *I* want to grow?" but "What grape varieties will honor *this* place?"

4. Listen to the land. Once you've accepted your duty to honor the place, how do you divine which varieties or mix of varieties are actually best suited to accentuate its unique soil types? The information exists on some level, but there's no one to ask except the place itself. And, when you do ask the place, "Should I plant Grenache or not," it's like a game of Twenty Questions. This might sound strange and more than a little New Age-y, but you can access this information by communing with nature spirits. I've taken my cue from a very peculiar book called *Perelandra: The Garden Workbook* by Machaelle Wright. Her theory is that if we can bring ourselves to the right level of relaxation/attention, we can participate in the intelligence of nature itself. You use your own muscular system as a feedback loop and then act on that information, asking yourself a series of yes/no questions and observing the differential reaction of your own body to these questions. Accessing the information has required me to sink my own roots into this new place in a very new and different way; it has required me to become a lot more present. If I'm unwilling to learn what this place has to teach me, than I am nothing but a fool.

5. Let nature do the heavy lifting. There must be human intelligence in vineyard design, but the goal for a *terroir* wine is to allow nature to do her thing. There are a few holistic principles such as sowing seeds or harvesting to the position of the planets and the phases of the moon. You can design a polycultural vineyard with a genetically diverse grouping of grape varieties planted alongside varied flora and fauna. Plant peach trees in the middle of the vineyard, or olive trees, rosebushes, a row of lavender; carefully select your cover crops—grasses and legumes—between the rows. This promotes the emergence of multiple species of beneficial insects, butterflies and honeybees. With each passing year there will be a deeper biological diversity that will lead to a more pestilence-free vineyard, negating the need for man-made, chemical solutions. Growing under these conditions amplifies the sense of place and often leads to the most interesting wines.

6. Water like a god. Plants learn the way animals do. They think, "If some guy turns on the water every two weeks, why do I need to grow roots?" But, to make a wine that will transmit the quality of the soil to the grapes, your roots will absorb more minerals by snaking out and exploring every square inch of soil. In some drier circumstances you may have to irrigate. But there are more benign ways of doing it. To get your roots to become explorers, you have to trick 'em. Do it more like rain—scattered, unpredictable, a sprinkle here, a shower there, a heavy downpour every now and then—just the way God would do it.

7. Stay true to your grape. After cultivation, we vintners control things in the fermentation and cellaring. We use whatever trickery we can muster to make wines more delicious by using oak chips, designer enzymes and yeasts on wine made from grapes grown in climates too warm to allow for proper acid balance—we'll even take the wine for a spin in the spinning cone! Because of all of this manipulation, these wines are easy to like but hard to love; they reflect the intelligence of the winemaker (which is quite limited) rather than the intelligence of nature. To make a wine that is truly exceptional, just like cooking a dish that truly reflects the origins of the ingredients, you have to minimize manipulation and let the grape speak for itself.

8. Subsidize the dream. The wine industry is in a rather perilous state. Almost every country now makes wine. It seems like every human being with disposable income has decided, "It's been great being a rock star, a race car driver, a film director, an orthodontist, a plastic surgeon; now I need to be a winemaker, too." It's a rather grim zero-sum game as we each vie for a diminishing slice of the pie. To make a great wine requires such risk that one must throw away the idea of making a profit. First, you need a business model that makes money, by selling, for example, some lines of decent and salable wines. Then you'll have the financial security to experiment and goof around to hopefully create something new and strange and possibly, if you're lucky, even great.

9. Challenge the taster. Taste is a complex proposition. It's not just the wine, it's not just the taster; it's a collaboration. Today, many wine growers are risk averse. They are economically dependent on the killer wine scores of very influential wine tasters who shall remain nameless. (Such as Robert Parker, for example!) Tragically, many wines are beginning to taste more or less the same, following a certain stylistic prescription that pleases the Parkerian or *Wine Spectator* palate. Wines that express *terroir* have a strong personality with their minerality and surprising flavors. Some tasters find them extreme, even offensive. But great wine challenges. Of course, it's up to the taster to engage or not, but the hope is, over time, most wine consumers will develop a deeper appreciation of the wines that reflect nature's vast intelligence and complexity.

10. Set the wine free. The more life force or *qi* in a great *terroir* wine, the weirder and more unpredictable it is from experience to experience. What it tastes like in the morning is different in the afternoon and different still from day to day. Wine is sensitive to environmental phenomena, to barometric pressure, to phases of the moon, temperature, and, undoubtedly, your own physiology and affect—are you angry, happy, sad, comfortable? I believe exceptional wine has something of a consciousness where it is sensitive to the belief system or the state of mind of the people who experience it. It is freaking perverse, but a *terroir* wine just does what it wants. And, if I as its creator think, "I want you to taste *this* way," it says, "Sorry. Not going to do it. I'm just not going to taste that way today." Expectations go straight out the window. *Que syrah syrah.*

RANDALL GRAHM FACTS

Inaugural vintage: 1984: Le Cigare Volant, created in homage to wines of France's Rhône region, where 1954 ordinance outlaws flying saucers (or "flying cigars," as the French call them) from landing.

Asteroid: 1992, Arizona: Ted Bowell of Lowell Observatory names "Rhôneranger asteroid" in Grahm's honor.

Bonny Doomed: 1995: Bonny Doon's main vineyard wiped out by bacterial killer, Pierce's disease, transmitted by an insect: the glassy-winged sharpshooter.

Corked/Screwed: 2002: Grahm adopts screw caps, holds mock funeral for the cork.

Doonsized: 2006: Grahm shrinks Bonny Doon production from 35 wines to 12 wines to focus on attempting *terroir* wines.

Labeled: 2008: Not legally required, Grahm includes comprehensive ingredient lists on Bonny Doon labels because, "If you have to put it on the label, you think twice before adding anything, and it makes a better wine."

Bestselling wines: Big House Red and White, Cardinal Zin (a Zinfandel) (these brands were sold in 2006); Muscat Vin de Glacière (dessert wine "of the icebox") (discontinued); Pacific Rim Riesling (brand sold in 2010); Le Cigare Volant (a Rhône blend).

Awards: 1989: Grahm is inducted into Who's Who of Cooking in America. 1994: Receives James Beard Foundation's Wine and Spirits Professional of the Year. 2009: Beard Foundation's Book Award for *Been Doon So Long: A Randall Grahm Vinthology*. 2010: Inducted into the Culinary Institute of America's Vintner's Hall of Fame.

WINE FACTS

First known wine: 7000 BC, China: Rice wine made with honey and fruit.

First biblical bender: Noah: "And he drank of the wine, and was drunken; and he was uncovered within his tent."

Oldest known bottle of wine: Fourth century AD: Ancient Roman glass amphora buried in stone sarcophagus found in Germany.

Patriot after-party: 1787: Following drafting of the U.S. Constitution, its 55 signers consume 54 bottles of Madeira, 60 of claret, 8 of whiskey, 22 of port, 8 of hard cider, 12 beers and 7 bowls of spiked punch large enough that "ducks could swim in them."

Grapes in average bottle of wine: 500–600.

Old wine: 1961: Wine critic Hugh Johnson opens a bottle of 1540 German Steinwein and declares it "still lively," but after two mouthfuls, the wine turns to vinegar.

Biggest drinkers: 2010: United States surpasses France as world's largest wine-consuming nation.

Most expensive bottle of wine: 2011: $117,000 for an 1811 Château d'Yquem sweet Sauternes from Bordeaux.

Chapter 14

How to Fight for Justice

• •

Constance Rice

Prominent civil rights lawyer and activist, author of
Power Concedes Nothing

From the moment she saw Barbara Jordan, the booming-voiced black congresswoman from Texas on TV during the 1974 Watergate hearings, Constance Rice was inspired to devote herself to fighting for justice. As a Harvard- and New York University–educated civil rights lawyer in Los Angeles, Rice waged a legal war against entrenched power centers with innovatively crafted lawsuits. The suits, aimed at improving the quality of the lives of Rice's clients—LA's ignored underclass—succeeded in winning $2 billion to improve LA's public transportation system, $1 billion to build 147 new schools and significant cases to curb police abuse. But in the wake of the 1992 LA riots sparked by the Rodney King verdict, Rice had an epiphany—even though she was winning lawsuit after lawsuit, her clients were losing their lives. Rice's urgency, focus on solutions and fearlessness led her to use unorthodox and unlawyerly tactics. She stepped outside of her comfort zone and into the violent communities of south LA, where she began a decades-long relationship with the population she calls "the invisible people." Confronting and engaging one of the forces most responsible for the ills she was trying to cure—the gangs—she helped to broker a truce between Crips and Bloods that stands to this day. And once an archenemy of the LAPD, through media pressure, legal force and political infighting, Rice became a powerful influence, helping to change their mind-set from paramilitary policing to community-based policing. Although crime is down and the LAPD's most barbaric excesses have been curtailed, Rice believes her work is not yet done. Her sense of urgency is as strong as ever. "People are afraid of me," she said. "I don't have any money. I don't have a gun. I only have a big mouth and an iron will."

Takeaway: *"Be willing to step back and say, 'Okay, this is how life is. Now, how should it be?' And go out and make that happen."*

1. Know yourself. I've understood from a very young age that I'm hardwired for fighting for justice. I get up every day and I can't wait to get back to work. A lot of people want to help one human being at a time—drug abuse counseling or taking in foster kids. That's important work. But I knew that I didn't want to do that. I wanted to work the systems' end. I wanted to take on the big challenge of the second phase of the civil rights movement that Martin Luther King talked about—realizing equality by radically restructuring our economic and political systems. That informed the choices I made. I joined my high school debate team to sharpen my verbal skills. I enrolled at Harvard to learn rigorous thinking and earned a law degree to get the tools to fight power.

2. Be better than everyone else. I did some of my best work before I became a lawyer. This was in the summer of 1982, when the Supreme Court effectively ended what had been a national moratorium on the death penalty. I was just a law school intern at the NAACP partnered with another intern. Without much supervision we defended inmates on death row who had been victims of miscarriages of justice. We pored over records and trial transcripts, devised creative legal arguments and became investigators when there were gaps in the facts. We ignored hierarchy and didn't ask permission. The stakes couldn't have been any higher and our dedication couldn't have been any greater. We saved many lives. If you're like us—Robin Hood lawyers with no money—you have to do it with a lot less. And you have to be better than the corporate lawyers and entrenched bureaucracies.

3. Be ready to go to war. Sometimes the best approach to a situation is persuasion. But when the only way to accomplish a goal is to fight—my opponents know I'll come at them like Xena the Warrior. I don't have the fear gene. I'll walk into Klan meetings. I'll walk into gang meetings with Crips and Bloods. I went after LAPD when that was a dangerous thing to do. It's only afterward I'll wonder, "What was I thinking?" But soon enough I'll say to myself, "That went well. I'm going back down there again."

4. Get creative with the law. In the 1980s we were winning police abuse lawsuits against the LAPD—which at the time was a fearsome paramilitary force that often terrorized the black community. Those cases were the only thing that held LAPD accountable, but the verdicts weren't leading to systemic change. The judge would look at our clients, regular people or budding gang members, and say, "I'm not going to meddle with police culture based on your client." And the politicians wouldn't rein in the police because LAPD operated like J. Edgar Hoover—they had secret files on every politician in LA. Then one day a retired deputy chief of LAPD came into my office and told me, "You've got to represent cops." He explained that there was only one way to persuade a judge to order LAPD to reform—we'd have to find police officers who would tell the judge that LAPD had to change. The potential reformers and change agents were the black, Latino and female officers who had suffered mistreatment and thwarted promotions. They were hiding inside the department, but some of them were so fed up that they were ready to take a stand. With them, we fought LAPD for 15 years with class-action suits over blatant racial discrimination and mistreatment of female cops that was sometimes violent. LAPD retaliated against these officers with threats, investigations on trumped-up charges, and even endangerment on the job. Many officers lost their careers or quit, but it was the first step in changing LAPD's culture.

5. Listen. Sometimes you have to put your ego in a box. In 1992 I went for the first time to the Jordan Downs housing project in Watts—which was so violent and lawless it was like an American favela. This was right after the LA riots. Smoke was still rising from burning buildings as I waltzed into the housing project looking like a black Republican, wearing a St. John suit and more pearls than Barbara Bush. Another lawyer and I were there to persuade the African-American residents to try and make peace with their out-numbered Latino neighbors. But it backfired. A woman got up in my face and exploded, "Where were you when they gunned down both of my sons in a gutter? Where were you when the bullets were flying through the walls so bad that we had to put our babies to bed in the damn bathtub?" Her anger yanked me out of my middle-class lawyer's world. I realized that these women were living in a kill zone. And if they had no safety, nothing else mattered. I said to the woman, "Yes, ma'am, you have a right to be angry, because we *haven't* done anything for you. But I'm here now." I asked them what *they* needed. When they calmed down they said, "Help our men. Stop the bullets. Stop the killing." And that's what I vowed to help them with.

6. Get out from behind your desk. Nothing I had learned at Harvard or as a lawyer would help me to figure out how to stop the violence. To learn that, I'd have to learn about the community first-hand. The women at Jordan Downs directed me to a trailer where their men were having a meeting. I knocked on the door and told the man who answered, "I'm Connie Rice from the NAACP Legal Defense Fund, and I'm here to help you." Inside I could see hard-core gang members—the ones with red bandannas on one side of a

table and the ones with blue bandannas on the other. Bloods and
Crips. They slammed the door in my face. Three minutes later the
door opened, and a guy said, "You're a lawyer? We're trying to set
up a cease-fire. Can you get us a copy of that agreement that the Jews
and the Arabs have? If they can work their shit out, we can too."
When I went back to my office my boss read me the riot act for driving down to Watts and meeting with gang members. But I didn't
stop. Sitting at my desk waiting for clients wouldn't reduce violence.
Even though they were the ones running drugs, terrorizing the community and creating the epidemic of violence, I felt I had to work
with these men. I went back the next day with the Camp David Ac-
cords to help them work out their gang truce. It's held to this day.

    7. Speak the truth. Many problems don't get solved because
people are afraid to speak up and say, "Even though you're my best
friend, you're in the way of the solution." And then, not only are
you *not* going to be invited to the Christmas party, but you could
easily become a pariah. That's what I went through in 2001 working
against the reappointment of LA's first African-American police
chief, Bernard Parks. He was a brilliant and charismatic man, but
he ruled through absolute fear and had even told me once that when
it came to LAPD, "I am the law." Police officers were terrified of
him. LAPD was falling apart. And, just as important, Parks made it
clear that he was never going to change the warrior culture of
LAPD. The head of the policemen's union, a white woman who
wouldn't publicly come out against the chief, asked me to come forward because, as head of the NAACP Legal Defense Fund and one
of the top black civil rights lawyers, I could be a racial shield. I went
on a campaign, writing editorials and doing radio and TV shows.
There were bomb threats at our office. Other black leaders who remained silent out of fear of being ostracized offered me private en-
couragement. At a debate in a black church where some of the 1,000
people in the audience chanted, "Save our chief," a lady demanded,
"Miss Rice, how can you go against a black chief when you are a

civil rights lawyer?" I explained that I didn't back police chiefs because they were black. I backed them because they do the right thing. It was one of the hardest things I ever did. And it left scars. But it was one of the best things I ever did because it paved the way for the appointment of William Bratton as chief, who was the beginning of the turnaround for LAPD.

8. Change the system from within. If you see a need for change you have to ask yourself, "Who has the power to get it done?" Sometimes it's the voters. When it comes to gangs, it can be gang members and their communities. When it comes to police reform, it's the police. I wouldn't get the opportunity to create change from within LAPD until the new police chief, William Bratton, heard what he called my "provocative remarks" on the corrupt LAPD Rampart's CRASH unit. Even though I was LAPD's archenemy, Chief Bratton asked me to head a panel on what lessons had been learned from the Rampart case—the biggest police corruption scandal in American history. While conducting the investigation with hundreds of hours of interviews of LAPD officers, my own mind-set changed. I learned that the cops felt that not only did no one care about the people in the poor communities; they also didn't care about the cops who risked their lives to police them. "We're not paid to protect people in South LA; we're paid to contain them," was their very clear message to me. By working within their system, I was able to make a case to Chief Bratton for changing LAPD's style of policing from a paramilitary style of policing to community-oriented policing.

9. Keep up the pressure. Most politicians don't focus on poor people unless forced to. So you have to create pressure. When I was hired to write a report on gangs in 2007, the city expected me to do what others had—write what they wanted, get paid and then go away. The report, named "A Call to Action," was a thousand pages and created headlines for nearly a month. The politicians felt like they'd been hit in the head with this 12-pound report filled with radical ideas about restructuring the way LA dealt with gangs, including the appointment of a Gang Czar that the politicians wouldn't be able to control. The politicians wanted me to quietly submit the report so they could kill it. But I made sure we had a public hearing. We packed City Hall with a thousand people, black and Latino gang intervention guys sitting together, Chief Bratton, the sheriff, the city attorney, the DA, law enforcement officers, prosecutors, mothers of murdered children and religious leaders. We showed them our political power. Even though the police were solidly behind it, City Hall still wasn't. I had to make my final push with the mayor. We really had it out. He was angry and said, "I'm supposed to be the Education Mayor, and you're going to turn me into the Gang Mayor?" And I made the case that kids in gangs don't learn. And to his credit, a month later, during his State of the City address, he backed it. His entire speech was about gangs.

10. Outlast everyone. There are a lot of folks who are a lot smarter than me. But I am more persistent. I'm more determined and I've got more passion. So I outlast everybody. The LAPD basically said, "She's never leaving, so we may as well marry her."

CONSTANCE RICE FACTS

Heritage: One part Native American (Cherokee, Seminole and Cree), one part African, one part Scotch, Irish, Welsh and Anglo-Saxon.

Home base: Rice is raised as Air Force brat; family moves 17 times to Air Force bases in the United States, Europe and Japan.

Martial arts: In her junior year at Harvard, Rice is physically assaulted by fellow undergrad; enrolls in tae kwon do and earns black belt. She credits practice for her fearlessness.

Witness: 1993, Watts neighborhood of LA: Among worst of gang crime's effects on children that Rice encounters is a nine-year-old assassin, Pygmy. This and other horrors push Rice to redouble efforts in community.

Honoree: 2000, LA: Rice is invited to meeting of gang prevention group; arrives in ballroom of airport hotel and finds white roses, pink tables and banner reading, "To the women in our lives, thank you for loving us when we did not deserve to be loved." During ceremony, reformed gang members stand, confess sins and ask for forgiveness from wives, girlfriends, mothers and daughters. "Without y'all we'd all be dead," organizer tells Rice. She leaves with rose, sits in car and weeps.

Parallels: 2008: After Rice's report on gangs, "A Call to Action," is published, Department of Defense official, drawing parallels between insurgencies in Iraq and LA gangs, calls to ask Rice for her strategic help.

On family differences: Rice says of cousin Condoleezza: "She has a Chevron oil tanker named after her. I'm working on getting a Greenpeace trawler."

Alt universe: Rice says if she weren't a civil rights lawyer, she'd prefer to be a queen, abbess or lady pirate in the nineteenth century.

Favorite quote: "Power concedes nothing without a demand. It never has and it never will." —Frederick Douglass

CIVIL RIGHTS FACTS

Roman law: 439 BC, Rome: 12 bronze tablets listing laws that define private rights are posted in Roman Forum. A Roman historian writes, "Every citizen should quietly consider each point, then talk it over with his friends, and, finally, bring them forward for public discussion."

Rights of man: 1774, United States:Thomas Jefferson writes that "a free people [claim] their rights as derived from the laws of nature, and not as the gift of their chief magistrate."

Feminism: 1848, Seneca Falls, NY: Founding document of American women's movement is signed by 68 women and 32 men. Local paper describes document as "the most shocking and unnatural event ever recorded in the history of womanity."

March: 1930, India: Protesting British Raj's salt tax, Gandhi marches 241 miles to the sea to make salt himself and is joined by thousands of Indians along the way. Sixty thousand people are imprisoned.

Arrested: 1963, Birmingham, AL: Martin Luther King is arrested and jailed during antisegregation protests and writes "Letter from Birmingham Jail," arguing that individuals have moral duty to disobey unjust laws.

Opening doors: 1989, Prague, Velvet Revolution:Tens of thousands gather nightly in peaceful protests. Jingling keys to symbolize unlocking of doors, they sweep Communists from power. Dissident Václav Havel becomes president.

Arab Spring: 2010–present: Strikes, demonstrations and social media raise awareness of human and political rights abuses, forcing leaders in Tunisia, Egypt, Libya, and Yemen from power. Protests follow in over a dozen Arab countries.

Chapter 15

How to Find Extraterrestrial Life

. . . .

Jill Tarter

TED Prize–winning leader at the Search for Extraterrestrial Intelligence (SETI) Institute

Imagine going to work every day for nearly 40 years, searching for answers believed to exist in a vast expanse. Then imagine that this expanse is so large that if it were the equivalent of all the world's oceans, in half a century you would only have examined the contents of a single glass of water. But that's not all. Imagine you must do so in the face of having no certainty about what you are searching for or how long the search will take—decades, even centuries—with no guarantee of success. Jill Tarter doesn't have to imagine this. She has devoted her life to it—raising tens of millions of dollars to assemble an elite team of experts, then develop, build and operate multidisciplinary technological systems in the world's most ambitious search to find extraterrestrial intelligence. "As a kid, I remember taking walks at night along the beaches in southern Florida with my dad," said Tarter. "I'd look up at the stars and think there must be other children walking along *their* beaches up there with *their* dads looking up at *their* stars. It was obvious to me that we were not alone in the universe." At the time, of course, Tarter had no idea that she would become a leader of SETI. But by the age of eight Tarter *did* know that she wanted to be an engineer. She was the only woman in her engineering class of 300 at Cornell University. Shortly after she earned a PhD in astronomy from the University of California, Berkeley, her knowledge of an obscure computer programming language led to a job offer at one of the world's first SETI experiments. "How wonderful that I was alive at just the right time to be a part of this great scientific experiment!" said Tarter. "I was hooked."

Takeaway: *"My biggest wish is to enable earthlings everywhere to join in the search for cosmic company."*

1. Think big. Ultimately we actually all belong to only one tribe—earthlings. I hope that if SETI does nothing else, it will change the perspective of humans on this planet. That would be one of the most profound endeavors in history.

2. Define the search. If a distant civilization were searching for signs of life on Earth, the easiest way to find us would be from the radio waves we've been leaking into space for the past 80 years. If an extraterrestrial culture were similar to ours it might be emitting radio waves as well. And that's what we're looking for. SETI uses the tools of astronomy to search for radio waves, which might be evidence of a distant life-form's technology. But we have no idea what form these signals might take, so we have to search by process of elimination. We detect and clarify over 3,000 signals each hour. And then we have to screen out all of the noise that occurs in nature as well as the man-made noises of satellite, microwave, aircraft and cell phone transmissions. If and when we do find an interstellar signal that cannot be explained as a natural or man-made signal, it could mean we've found alien intelligence.

3. Show me the money. Searching for extraterrestrial life is not cheap. The equipment and computing power carry a steep price tag. NASA used to fund our SETI search, but in 1993 Congress cut off all funds. We had to either close down or get creative and turn to private sources. I used to primarily be a researcher, but now fundraising and making people aware of our project is 100 percent of my job. I'll do whatever it takes, and in fact, SETI is now experiencing one of its funding roller coasters. Paul Allen, a founder of Microsoft, funded the construction of the first phase of the Allen Telescope Array ($25 million), an incredibly powerful tool that will eventually include 350 small satellite dishes. When these dishes are wired through computers they act as a single virtual dish and are one of the largest and most sensitive radio telescopes in existence, not to mention the fastest tool ever built to hunt for extraterrestrial signals.

4. No noise is good noise. A single transmission signal from a cell phone is enough to overwhelm the ultrasensitive receivers of the antenna conducting our search. Once a cameraman shooting a documentary shut down the whole telescope array just by arriving with a cell phone in his pocket he hadn't turned off. The ideal setting to base a search for alien life is probably just what you'd imagine from the movies—a peaceful deserted valley far from human population or industry, like our observation site in a valley in Northern California, 290 miles northeast of San Francisco.

5. Expand the search. We are searching through an enormous cosmic haystack for signs of intelligent life. In our galaxy there are 400 billion stars, and beyond that there are 100 billion other galaxies. In the past decade, we've searched through a thousand star systems—the equivalent to scooping a single glass of water from all of the oceans. In the next decade we will have searched through a million star systems. But it's still a fraction of what's out there. The exponential increase in our technical capabilities is breathtaking, and a big part of my job is making sure we harness the new technologies to expand our search, because the coming years will bring opportunities we can't predict. The more of the universe we can cover, the better our chances of success.

6. Get smarter. As in any scientific experiment, it may turn out our methodology is misdirected, which is why one of our rules at the institute is to reserve the right to get smarter. To try and predict what is going to exist 50 years from now is impossible. We may discover we should be searching for extraterrestrial life in entirely different ways. We have to be open to new ideas constantly.

7. Crowd-source. There's a joke that you could fit all the SETI experts in the world into a single phone booth. For years we existed in splendid isolation. But now we are so swamped with SETI data that we can only process a little more than 10 percent of what we gather. To get help in processing the other 90 percent, we published our code as open source and put our data online. Now for the first time we have a global brain trust of non-SETI specialists that helps us improve our searches. Soon we will launch a global citizen science project based on an application now in beta test. One of these new participants from anywhere in the world could come up with valuable research that could *move the telescope*, astronomy-speak for the honor of directing where to focus the telescope next.

8. Eureka! We have a plan. When a signal of intelligent life is found, here's what we'll do: (a) Open the champagne (currently a bottle of $10 Freixenet sitting in the observatory fridge); (b) verify our findings; (c) get independent confirmation from a qualified facility to make sure it's not a hoax; (d) call the directors of all SETI-related observatories; (e) send out an official notice of discovery that goes to all the astronomical observatories of the world; (f) inform our major donors; (g) complete and immediately send to be published the scientific paper we've already prepared a template for; (h) alert our *interpreters*, astronomers designated to explain our findings to regional and local news media; and (i) hold a press conference to announce the discovery to the world, because the signal isn't being sent to our observatory in California; it's being sent to planet Earth and planet Earth deserves to know about it. Carl Sagan envisioned such a moment as a circus springing up and surrounding the discovery site. A SETI facility director once said, "Honestly, I wouldn't know whether to call for protection or porta-potties."

9. Take the world view. How are we going to respond to an extraterrestrial civilization if we receive one of its signals? As much as some of us would love to establish contact, there will be a lot of difficult questions to answer first. Some, like Stephen Hawking, believe that firing back something immediately could get the whole neighborhood destroyed, and others believe that kind of attitude is rooted in paranoia. Our mandate is to wait for a calm and reasoned global consensus on what to say and how to say it. Then again, once a signal has been detected, anyone with a transmitter can get on the horn and shout back out whatever they want.

10. Take the long view. I don't get out of bed every morning thinking, "Will I find extraterrestrial intelligence today?" But I do think every day, "How can I improve the search?" Fifty years of silence doesn't mean SETI is a failure; it means we're just getting started. We may not succeed tomorrow or next year or next decade or even next century, but a critical part of our job is passing on what we've learned to the future generations of cosmic scientists.

JILL TARTER FACTS

Youth: Growing up, Tarter takes apart and reassembles radios under her father's watchful eye. When pieces are left over and she asks for help, her father directs her to take it apart and try again.

Early influences: Arthur C. Clarke books and *Flash Gordon* serials.

Coined: 1975: Tarter coins the term "brown dwarfs," a classification for dark substellar objects floating freely in space.

"Aha" moment: 1975: Tarter reads 300-page "Project Cyclops Report," an early study on using radio telescopes to search for extraterrestrial intelligence, cover to cover. She has worked in the SETI field ever since.

Contact: 1997: Jodie Foster's character in the movie *Contact*, alien hunter Ellie Arroway, is inspired by Tarter's life. 2011: When SETI is forced to shut down operations due to lack of funds, Foster and many other private donors raise hundreds of thousands of dollars to keep it going.

Favorite quote: "Chance favors the prepared mind." —Louis Pasteur

EXTRATERRESTRIAL FACTS

Earliest recorded UFO sighting: Circa 1500 BC, Egypt: "A circle of fire coming in the sky . . . became more numerous . . . shone more than the brightness of the sun . . . extended to the limits of the four supports of the heavens. . . ."

National Radio Silence Day: August 22, 1924: All U.S. military radio stations are commanded to be shut down for eight hours to listen for radio signals from Mars.

The "wow" signal: 1977, Ohio: SETI scientist discovers possible signal from extraterrestrial source and writes "wow" on the computer printout. This signal is never detected again.

Notable pop-culture aliens: *War of the Worlds* (Martians), *The Day the Earth Stood Still* (Klaatu), *Invasion of the Body Snatchers*, *My Favorite Martian*, *Star Trek* (Klingons, Vulcans), *Star Wars* (Wookies, Ewoks), *The Man Who Fell to Earth*, *Close Encounters of the Third Kind*, *Space Invaders* video game, *Alien*, *E.T.*, *Alf*, *X-Files* (various), *Avatar* (Na'vis).

Theories on why we haven't found alien life: (1) Alien life doesn't exist; (2) alien civilizations die out because they destroy themselves, are destroyed by others or are destroyed by natural events; (3) alien life exists, but we haven't found it because they are too far away, we haven't searched long enough, we don't know what to search for or they purposely hide their existence; and (4) alien life exists, but the evidence is suppressed.

———————

Chapter 16

How to Find Love Online

· ·

Sam Yagan, Chris Coyne, Max Krohn, Christian Rudder

Founders of OkCupid, the fastest-growing (and possibly
hippest) online dating site, with over 7 million users

Ask a prospective date if she likes the taste of beer. If the answer is yes, she is 30 percent more likely than women who say they don't like the taste of beer to sleep with you on the first date. This is just one of a blizzard of fascinating facts about human social behavior divined from the statistical data of the users of the online dating site OkCupid. The site's genius? Its founders' commitment to applying high-level number crunching to the oldest equation in human history: sorting people into pairs. The four Harvard math whizzes behind OkCupid sold their first online venture, SparkNotes, a digital CliffNotes, to Delia's for $30 million in 2000. After their payday, the foursome turned their attention to a compatibility algorithm they had developed that ingeniously measured the match worthiness of people based on their answers to questions. In 2002, OkCupid was born. Although the founders (who are all happily married) claim no lothario-like superpowers, based on their teeming mass of statistical data and observational evidence they can provide a commonsense approach to finding someone online.

Takeaway: *"Getting 99 percent of the people to kind of like you is a waste of time. Accentuate your eccentricities and find the people who will love you as you really are."*

1. Quit bitchin'. The single people we feel sorriest for are the ones who say, "Do you know anyone?" And we say, "Yeah, thousands of people! On OkCupid!" And they say, "Oh . . . I don't know." For some people there is still this negative mythos that online dating is sketchy; that it's for losers. But it's no sketchier or more desperate than off-line dating. If you're not meeting anyone in "real" life, quit bitching and get online.

2. Start a conversation with your picture. The old saying that a picture's worth a thousand words has never been truer than with online dating. If a profile picture is a close-up of someone's beautiful face, the viewer knows that person is attractive and then can say something like, "Nice glasses . . . I wear glasses, too!" But, really, your profile photo needs to start a conversation. If you're playing a guitar up on stage, then we know something about you. You're in a band. Now, we have a conversation: "Oh, you play guitar? I do, too." If you're standing in front of the pyramids of Egypt, someone can say, "Oh, I've been there." Now you've got something started. Our statistics show that profile pictures of people actually doing something interesting lead to a much higher quality of contacts.

3. Give them the hook with your profile. The whole point of your written profile is to start a dialogue. Anything insanely long or too personal is not going to accomplish that. Same with selling yourself too hard. Think about it: A guy goes up to a girl at a bar. What does he try to do in the first thirty seconds? Get her to laugh. Once you get a girl at a bar to laugh, you're in. Maybe you're even taking her home. But, if you're sixty seconds in and she's straight-faced and saying, "Uh huh. Uh huh," your night is over. The best tone for profile writing is conversational banter. Be witty. If you can add a little self-deprecation, someone may think, "That's kind of funny, that's kind of smart. I want to get to know that person." It's also a good idea to include questions in your profile. List the places you like to travel and then ask, "What are your favorite places?" Give readers a hook—favorite bands, books, bars, whatever. There's a chance something you have in common will start a conversation.

4. Accentuate your eccentricities. Getting people to *kind of* like you is a waste of time. You're looking for the two or three people who will love you as you really are. If Dungeons and Dragons is your thing, you want that person who will say, "Oh my god! *You* love D and D? *I* do too!" And the same goes for your photo. We see so many images that are designed to minimize some supposedly unattractive trait, like the close-cropped picture of a person who's overweight. Women with tattoos and piercings have an intuitive understanding that when they show off what makes them different some people won't like it, but they'll get lots of attention from the men who do. We have mathematical evidence that men will message women that they believe appeal only to them before messaging women they believe will appeal to everyone. So, if you have something that makes you unique, even if some might consider it a flaw, flaunt it. Flaunt your big nose, curvy full figure or weird snaggletooth, and you'll attract the kind of person who finds it exciting.

5. To lie or not to lie? The goal of your profile is to meet people *in person*, so it's really never a good idea to lie. Especially about physical things like your height. Eventually you have to show up, so lying is going to lead you to go on a lot of dates that will suck because the person is expecting someone else. If you could have one lie, age might be the one to go with. It can help you avoid being filtered out. This applies especially to those who are older but look younger. If you see a woman at a bar, her age isn't plastered to her head. You might think she's really cute. You might go talk to her. When you find out, "Holy crap, you're fifty-five?!" you may end up realizing no matter how old she is, you want to see her again.

6. Cast a wide net. You may have a picture in your mind of who you're going to marry, someone of *this* religion, race or age. But people are always marrying people they didn't expect to. Most people just want somebody that they'll really love. A question that we ask on the site, like, "Would you prefer wealth or power?" is going to tell you a lot more about who you are compatible with than, "Would you date someone who's black or Caucasian?"

7. Get thee to Starbucks. The point of sending someone a message is to determine if that person is worth meeting for twenty minutes, not if he or she is "the one." Even though it's online dating, the basic rules of courtship haven't changed. Reply quickly. If you make someone wait while their message sits in your inbox, when you do eventually reply those people will have probably moved on, thinking, "Screw you, I'm not going to write back." So be timely. But not instantaneous! It's best to put some thought into your messages. Mentioning something from someone's profile shows interest. And, of course, you want reciprocity. We also recommend that you keep your messaging casual. You don't need to get into debates about religion to determine whether to go grab a coffee. And when you do meet for the first time, don't plan to go to the opera and then have a four-course dinner. That's insane. It should be more like, "Let's grab a beer," or "Let's go to Starbucks." If you like the way things are going, you can take that next step and say, "Let's get some dinner."

8. Take the pressure off. If you take online dating too seriously, if you think, "I can't believe this person didn't reply to me. I'm too good for this!" you're going to have a bad experience. Dating is emotional. It's messy. Bad things happen. People will send you lame messages. You're going to go on bad dates. You're going to date someone who's not who they claim. But, if you have the attitude that, okay, the whole process of dating and mating kind of sucks but it's necessary, you just might be able to roll with it, take the pressure off, and have some fun. Otherwise, with the pace of online dating and the sheer number of potential dates, you'll burn out fast.

9. Have game. If you're an older woman in the singles' scene the odds are not in your favor. But here's the good news: according to our research, attractiveness trumps age. So, if you're attractive, you're still fine. You might think that once you reach a certain age you should look more sophisticated, but we've found that older women who wear provocative clothing in their photos get more messages. So look sexy. Even if you're 40, you're in competition with a 25-year-old because chances are she'll sleep with that 35-year-old guy you're interested in. Show that you have game. Be more aggressive. Send more messages than your younger counterparts. You're signaling to potential partners, "I know you're searching for someone of a certain age, but I think I could roll with 28-year-old girls. Let me prove it." Guys may not go out of their way to write you first, because men's age preferences tend to skew so much younger, but any guy likes attention from a woman and may be happy to respond.

10. Follow the stats. We constantly crunch the numbers of Ok-Cupid's online interactions so that our members can enhance their "brand." Plus, we're just curious. We've found with photos, using flash skews your attractiveness to that of someone seven years older, so go for natural light. The most successful pose for women is the MySpace angle, holding your camera above your head and being coy. Women flirting into the camera get the most messages; women flirting to someone off camera, the least. The cleavage shot garners women 49 percent more contacts, and the ratio goes up with age to 79 percent for 32-year-old women. Best pose for men is mysteriously aloof, unsmiling, looking off camera. A 19-year-old showing his abs gets twice as many contacts, but the rate falls off sharply for older men. When it comes to messaging, reply rates plummet for misspellings, bad grammar and Netspeak. And, general compliments like "awesome" and "fascinating" have much higher reply rates than physical compliments like "sexy" and "beautiful." There are a few common lies to look out for. The more highly a picture is rated *attractive*, the more likely it is out of date. Eighty percent of self-identified bisexuals are only interested in one gender. Both men and women inflate their income by 20 percent. And lastly, we've found that the three questions tested above all others in determining if you and someone else have long-term potential are: "Do you like horror movies?" "Have you ever traveled around another country alone?" and "Wouldn't it be fun to chuck it all and go live on a sailboat?" If you find someone that answers all three the same way you do, the two of you might just belong together.

OKCUPID FACTS

Origin: 2002: Cofounder Coyne calls fellow cofounder Yagan from bar to say, "We should make a dating site!" Yagan's reply: "Call me when you're not drunk." A few months later, OkCupid is launched.

Love stats: OkCupid's blog, OkTrends, is a popular source of stats such as, "iPhone users have more sex."

Match request: Each OkCupid match involves millions of computations and takes 30 milliseconds.

WikiLove: WikiLeaks founder Julian Assange's (alleged) OkCupid profile: "Passionate and often pigheaded activist intellectual seeks siren for love affair, children and occasional criminal conspiracy."

Kink: The OkCupid Salt Lake City user base is kinkiest in country.

Founder status: All four founders are married. All met wives off-line.

Payoff: 2011: Match.com buys OkCupid for $90 million. Founders stay on.

Mission accomplished: On first time an OkCupid member sent in baby pictures, site cofounder Yagan says, "We thought,

'We affected the creation of a life!' Now, we've done that tens of thousands of times over."

ONLINE DATING FACTS

First computer dates: 1964: Clients pay $5 to answer 100-question survey that is put onto punch cards and fed into IBM computer named TACT (Technical Automated Compatibility Testing). Five matches for each client are spit out of computer.

Internet ready: Average length of time for online daters before tying the knot: 18.5 months. Real-world daters: 42 months.

Score: One in six new marriages are result of online dating site meetings.

For cheaters: Dating site Ashley Madison specializes in connecting cheating spouses.

Lies online: 81 percent of people misrepresent height, weight or age in profiles; women on average describe themselves as 8.5 pounds thinner, and men, 2 pounds; and men lie more about height than women, adding an average of 2 inches.

Outsourcing: Busy execs can pay Atlanta-based Virtual Dating Assistants $1,200 to maintain online dating profiles and secure five dates a month.

Gov't sponsored: LoveByte (Singapore, 2009) and Fukui Marriage-Hunting Café (Japan, 2010) are launched in hopes of reversing declining national birthrates.

Meet market: 2010: U.S. online dating site revenues exceed $1 billion.

Chapter 17

How to Get the Funk

· ·

George Clinton

Front man of the legendary, influential and oft-sampled
Parliament-Funkadelic and P-Funk All Stars

In 1976 George Clinton emerged from the hatch of a spaceship
wearing a four-foot-long blond wig, full-length white ermine fur
coat, matching hat and nine-inch platform boots and sauntered
down the spaceship's stairway to the stage as 20,000 people roared.
The Mothership had landed. Clinton's funk dynasty, Parliament-
Funkadelic, made up of over three dozen musicians, singers and
hand-clappers, toured throughout the country with their version of
controlled musical chaos that Clinton described as "James Brown on
acid." Called by a journalist a "showman, shaman, satirist, satyr . . .
and bona fide genius," Clinton was born in an outhouse in North
Carolina, in 1941. At 14, having moved with his family to a small
town in New Jersey, he persuaded four friends to form a doo-wop
band, the Parliaments. When the band's soul-inflected "(I Wanna)
Testify" became a hit in 1967, Clinton moved the band to Detroit to
try to get signed by Motown. But it was too late. The '60s, with their
cacophonous rock 'n' roll, race riots and psychedelic drugs, had
changed Clinton. "One day I put on a sheet and cut my hair in a
Mohawk and walked around town," he said. "I thought if nobody
kicks my ass or arrests me, we're gonna take this craziness to the
stage." Within a couple of years, Clinton had become a grand funk

provocateur. Under his management style, a sort of anarchistic humanitarianism, the musicians of his sprawling funk collective have flowed in and out of the bands that Clinton formed, splintered and merged, putting on outrageous shows and recording music that reflected America's counterculture and black consciousness. Now in his 70s and still touring with the P-Funk All Stars, Clinton owns a musical legacy that began in the era of doo-wop and remains a staple of the era of hip-hop. Rappers have sampled his songs so voraciously that one *New York Times* critic wrote, "Mr. Clinton's music virtually replaced Motown as the blueprint from which young black musicians worked." Or as Prince once said, "They should give that man a government grant for being so funky."

> **Takeaway:** *"Funk is an attitude. Funk is something that saves your life. Funk is anything you need it to be at any given time."*

1. You might as well be the ringleader. I was 13 when I organized a baseball team even though I couldn't play baseball. I started our little doo-wop group, the Parliaments. We were all in love with Motown, waiting to be discovered, teenagers trying to get a hit. I'd go into New York City, knocking on doors to try and make the deals. After we got our hit "(I Wanna) Testify," I moved the band out to Detroit because I wanted us to be the Temptations. I was always pushing something, until years later we had so many people coming and going on different labels with different acts, I got us our own studio, even our own record label. Sure, it felt like *responsibility*, but the guys always left it for me to do all the business stuff, so I took it upon myself. Someone's got to be in control, and if you know what you want, it might as well be you.

2. Grab what you like and bring your own thing. Keep your eye on what's happening. By the late '60s, Motown was going pop and that wasn't right for us. The white boys—Eric Clapton and the

Rolling Stones—were playing the hell out of the blues, so they were able to *own* it. We missed out on that. I made sure we weren't going to miss out on the funk. Funk was the future, it was dance music, party music, and it was coming up big. We saw Cream and Vanilla Fudge take soul, flip it upside down and make it loud. We saw Jimi Hendrix bring psychedelics to the rock 'n' roll sound. You see what you like and grab it. Then, you got to bring your own thing. We took the discipline of Motown. We took the blues and speeded it up. We added the psychedelic sounds and just made it *chewy*. We took the hard stuff of MC5 and the Stooges, the churchy stuff, the R&B stuff, Jimi Hendrix, James Brown, Eric Clapton, the Beatles—and we were all of them at once. We mixed it all up and called it funk.

3. Free your mind. In the '60s, acid and the hippies busted things wide open. Where I came from it was, "Watch your back and do it to them before they do it to you." So, when I saw the hippies trying to do it another way, raising consciousness, it really meant something. I saw we could do it, too. But we were going to deliver *our* message *our* way, to the black community. No boundaries. On the records we'd just talk about the shit that was going on—inequality, greed, corporatism, the war taking our babies and drugs turning people's minds into maggot brains. We wanted people to get their own consciousnesses going, get some black pride; *free your mind and your ass will follow*. It's not that we were into preaching. We were just into having people think. And if the people didn't want to listen, the music was good enough that they could just bump.

4. Mix it up. At Motown there was so much talent that whenever an artist got cold, they'd shift him to the next set of producers and get a fresh sound and maybe another hit record. I started doing that—mixing up the artists I was working with. I took the Parliaments and we just flipped it, put the musicians up front—guys like Eddie Hazel, who played guitar like Hendrix, and Bernie Worrell, a keyboard genius, who can just take any groove and make it

Beethoven—and put the Parliaments singing behind them. We changed the name to Funkadelic and we just started making crazy, tripped-out rock funk. When we got Bootsy Collins on bass from James Brown's band, we made a new group—not the Parliaments but Parliament. It was mostly all the same guys—just as funky, but with a more commercial sound. Then we added the horns, Maceo Parker and Fred Wesley—they brought that slick James Brown sound. I could put all the artists together with all their different styles—not just Parliament-Funkadelic but Parlet, Brides of Funkenstein, Bootsy's Rubber Band and the Horny Horns—and they'd come up with nothing anybody had ever heard, some of the funkiest stuff out there.

5. Take it to the stage. Around the mid-'70s, I saw that bands were coming up with theater concepts like Pink Floyd's *Dark Side of the Moon*, the Who's *Tommy* and even *Hair* on Broadway. So when we started looking at some real money I told Neil Bogart at our record company Casablanca, "Get me a spaceship." I wanted to make a funk opera with Afronauts coming from outer space—our version of *Sergeant Pepper*. I knew it would really blow some minds. The other guys in the band wanted houses and cars with the money we were making, but I told them, "As soon as we stop making hit records they'll repossess our cars, but they can't repossess the Mothership!" We had a designer from Broadway make us a spaceship for $275,000. We landed it in Times Square at five o'clock in the morning. The next morning, we landed out in front of the United Nations. We went out on a monster tour, playing the big, sold-out arenas. Onstage, we had so many musicians all in crazy costumes and our massive skeleton head smoking a six-foot joint lit by a five-foot Bic. A guitar player, Garry Shider, wore a diaper with a rig under it so he could fly out over the audience shooting everybody with this strobe light bop gun. Glenn Goins sang in his churchy way, "I think I hear the Mothership coming, I think I see the Mothership coming," as the spaceship landed. Then I'd come out the door as Dr.

Funkenstein with my outfit and cane, and the crowd would just go crazy. It was ridiculous how good it felt.

6. Create characters. The thing about characters is they live longer than people. Bugs Bunny, Porky Pig, Mickey Mouse—they're ageless. I started creating strange characters in about '75—Dr. Funkenstein, Sir Nose d'Voidoffunk, Mr. Wiggles, Starchild—as part of an ongoing black cosmic funk opera. These characters had their own mythology that went back to the creation of the earth. That's when the funk flowed freely before it was hidden away from man in the pyramids. The characters were battling to bring the funk back into the world—the battle of Funkentelechy versus the Placebo Syndrome. They were heroes and villains, like in the comics; we wrote them into our songs and into the stage shows. They were different incarnations of us, and you can keep being them 'cause the other thing about characters is, you don't have to be young and sexy to play one.

7. Transfer the funk. At our shows the audience *and* the band were acting the fool like they never thought they could, waving their hands, shaking their ass, doing the idiot jerk. We had *every* kind of person in the audience: blind, crippled, crazy, black, white, tall, short, aliens. Through the music and the energy and how much fun we're having on stage, we'd transfer the funk to the fans until they got the message. I never wanted them to feel like they were just an audience. I wanted them to feel like they were in the band, too. We had the call-and-responses and chants. Some people thought it was spiritual, but I didn't want them putting a God thing on me, so I'd just tell them, "Ain't nothing but a party y'all." One night in St. Louis before we came out we heard them chanting, "We want the funk. We want the funk." I turned to someone and said, "Damn, we gotta put that on a record." We put it in "Give Up the Funk (Tear the Roof off the Sucker)," and it became our first certified platinum single. We let our fans know, "You hear us. We hear you back."

8. Stick together. Being a bandleader is about getting everybody together 'cause they *want* to be there. James Brown ran his band like the Army. I ran ours like a collective. I'd suggest, but I didn't *tell* the guys what to play or where they could play or couldn't. If you're going to put your players through all that, you better be paying them all the money in the world, which I couldn't. By the mid-'70s we already had so many artists playing in so many bands and record deals on different labels, I had to maintain that friendship thing with all of them. The minute they have to make appointments to see you, it's all over. A band is a family. You fight, fuss, kiss, love, and make up and start all over again. And if anybody gets in trouble, we're all going to stick with that person no matter what. They're all our little brothers and sisters, all the people who grew up together. If you've ever been in the Funk, you're in it forever.

9. Don't go crazy (offstage). The advice I'd tell a young musician is play crazy, act crazy, but don't ever go crazy for real. You can spend so much energy worrying about what people can do to you that you don't have the energy to do your thing. Your feelings are the one thing you can take control of. I survived 'cause when things would get crazy, I'd think, "Okay, *I'm* not going to go crazy. I'll do another thing." And it's worked so far.

10. Keep chasing the dream. It's easy to get tired at 70 years old, but I'm not successful yet. There's always more ground to cover. If you get to the top and catch up with happy, you got a real problem because you'll get bored. I'm not trying to catch up with being happy—because it's the *pursuit* of happiness I'm after. I want to be so close behind it I can almost touch it. That's what keeps me looking forward to moving ahead.

P-FUNK FACTS

First gig: 1957, New Jersey: As teenagers, Clinton's band, the Parliaments (named for the cigarettes), sing for barbershop customers at the Uptown Tonsorial Parlor in Newark and later at the Silk Palace in nearby Plainfield.

Amped: 1967, Fairfield, CT: When their equipment doesn't arrive on time for a show, the Parliaments borrow a double stack of Marshall amps, a triple stack of SVTs and an oversize fiberglass drum set from support band Vanilla Fudge. Inspired by the booming sound, the Parliaments order same equipment delivered three weeks later.

Most embarrassing stage moment: '70s: Clinton, notorious for getting naked onstage, fears a moment when the music will stop and the houselights go on. One night, when it actually happens, Clinton hits the floor and crawls through musicians' legs.

Going to the chapel: 1971, Detroit: Funkadelic plays frequently with Motor City's Ted Nugent, Iggy Pop and the Stooges and MC5. Pop's manager suggests that Pop and Clinton stage a wedding as stunt, but they never make it to altar.

Ahh . . . the name is Bootsy, Baby! 1972, Toledo, OH: Former bassist from James Brown's band, Bootsy Collins, is "discovered" (by Clinton's girlfriend's sister) playing in his own band, wearing a body stocking and hot pants, with a tambourine taped to one foot. Clinton immediately hires Collins to join band.

Flash light: 1978: Clinton sets out to make a Michael Jackson–style song. He includes a Bar Mitzvah chant ("da da da dee da da da da da da da") sung by a chorus of over 50 people. "Flash Light" hits number one on the R&B charts.

Bow wow wow: 1982: Months after Parliament-Funkadelic disbands, Clinton gets a hit with funk-electronic "Atomic Dog," one of the most sampled songs in hip-hop history.

Hall of famers: 1997: Clinton and fifteen members of Parliament-Funkadelic are inducted into the Rock 'n' Roll Hall of Fame.

FUNK FACTS

Early funk: Circa 1900: "Funky Butt" was one of New Orleans jazz innovator Buddy Bolden's most famous songs, with the lyrics, *I thought I heard Buddy Bolden say | Funky butt funky butt, take it away.* A fellow musician claimed it was about the smell of an auditorium packed full of sweaty people "dancing close together and belly rubbing."

Inspiration: After James Brown's idol Little Richard writes "Please, Please, Please" on a napkin, Brown carries it around and vows to write a song based on the words. In 1956, Brown's band, the Flames, has their first R&B hit, "Please, Please, Please," selling over a million copies.

First mention: 1966, Phoenix, AZ: Dyke & the Blazers write riff-based song "Funky Broadway," the first soul song to use the word "funky." It is about Broadway Street in Phoenix, not New York's Broadway. Band breaks up shortly afterward. 1967: When Wilson Pickett records song, it jumps to number one on the Billboard chart.

Rise and Fall: 1968: Sylvester Stewart of the Family Stone, who had recorded his first song at the age of eight, becomes so big that even James Brown records a cover of one of his band's songs, "Sex Machine." Threats from black militants, drug problems and band acrimony eventually lead to dissolution of the band.

Known in the future as Prince: 1975, age 7: Prince Rogers Nelson writes first song, "Funk Machine."

Call and response: 1975: AWB (the Average White Band) releases James Brown–style "Pick Up the Pieces," which climbs charts to number one. In response, Brown releases song called "Pick Up the Pieces One by One," under the name of AABB (the Above Average Black Band).

Chapter 18

How to Get the Inside Scoop

....

Barry Levine

News director of the *National Enquirer*

When Barry Levine started his journalism career at the Associated Press in 1981 intending to become a sports reporter, he never imagined he'd end up at ground zero of the tabloid universe—the *National Enquirer*. But when Levine was offered his first tabloid job at Rupert Murdoch–run *Star* magazine, he was amazed at the size and professionalism of the reporting staff. At *Star*, he flew around the country on private planes and helicopters, following celebrities into top hotels, chasing down one story after another. "I was exhilarated and fascinated," says Levine. "It was like a romantic throwback to the wearing-a-press-card-in-your-fedora, Chicago *Front Page* days." Now news director at the *Enquirer*, Levine is proud and unapologetic about the paper's mission to doggedly investigate and report stories on celebrities and newsmakers of the day. Often maligned as "supermarket sleaze" or "tabloid trash," the *Enquirer* is gaining a newfound respect by scooping the mainstream press on high-profile stories like John Edwards' adultery and love child, Tiger Woods' mistresses, Michael Jackson's death, Rush Limbaugh's drug addiction and Bristol Palin's pregnancy. In 2010, the tabloid was even considered for the Pulitzer Prize for its reporting on John Edwards.

Takeaway: *"We'll do anything to get the story."*

1. Know your audience. America has a fascination with celebrities and newsmakers, their secrets and romances, their health
issues, addictions, alcohol, drugs, sex. The names have changed
from Liz and Dick to Lohan and the Kardashians, but the formula's
the same. Showing that Hollywood actors and TV stars don't have
perfect lives helps people accept their own problems. As an old *Enquirer* editor once said, the big news organizations tell people what
they *think* they should be interested in, whereas we try to give them
stories they *are* interested in.

2. Preparation is the key to success. That was something an
experienced news editor at AP told me when I was just out of college working my first job there as an office assistant. It starts in the
office. We answer phones on the first ring and we never take any
story lightly. If we're going to interview a celebrity we go through
every news clipping. At big events we encounter the unexpected, so
if it's a celebrity's wedding, we get the names of all the relatives and
try to contact them ahead of time to pick up details. Sometimes before a wedding, we'll rent helicopters to fly over the site to figure out
how to photograph on the actual day. We prepare maps and dossiers
on the couple. We do everything possible to pick up details to provide the inside story to the readership down to the type of cologne
the groom is wearing. They can't be at the wedding, so we need to
give them everything we can. When Liz Taylor got married to Larry
Fortensky on Michael Jackson's ranch it was like the tabloid Super
Bowl. It literally took months of preparation. We even found out
who was going to be catering the wedding and who was going to be
delivering flowers to get jobs in those venues.

3. Feed the beast. Back when I was at *A Current Affair*, a former Fox-TV tabloid-style TV show, the O.J. trial had totally captured the public's imagination. You couldn't rest because you had to

go out the next morning with a new story. I came up with 300 straight stories over the course of months and months. To keep the narrative going in a huge national story like that you have to go behind the scenes of every side character and tell their life stories. Like Kato, O.J.'s houseboy. We did a hugely popular story on him that even included his baby pictures. These characters can become as interesting to the public as the main subjects.

4. Information is king. We'll do anything to get it. My reporters have to be journalists but also like secret agents in the ways they gather intel. They develop long-standing relationships with sources, stepping in to be a sympathetic ear as a big brother or sister, if need be, to convince them to help us get information. Sometimes info gathering is more about the research. During the O.J. trial, for example, there was the bloody shoe print of an Italian Bruno Magli loafer that O.J. denied owning. It was before my time, but the *Enquirer* went through thousands upon thousands of images in search of an image of O.J. wearing those shoes. And, in those days, you had to go through old negatives. Finally, they came across a picture in which a photographer testing his new telephoto lens at a stadium had a shot of O.J., head to toe, wearing the "ugly ass shoes," as O.J. had called them. The *Enquirer* published the image, and the attorneys at O.J.'s civil trial used it to show that O.J. owned the shoes, which contributed to the civil court judgment that he was responsible for the murders.

5. Get the shot. Photography is a huge part of what we do. Our bestselling issue featured a photo of Elvis in his coffin and sold 6 million copies. When Tiger Woods was in sex rehab, our photographer stood in the exact same place for days outside an open gate of the rehab center. When he finally caught Tiger leaving his dormitory to walk to another building on the compound, the photographer had a split second to get the shot through a narrow opening. The result was a searing picture of Tiger Woods with a few days' growth of beard. After we published the photo, it was reproduced all over television. The *Washington Post* published a long essay on the photo itself, about how it was the kind of image of Tiger Woods you'd never seen before.

6. Know where you're headed. My hero, Ernest Hemingway, would always leave off writing at the end of the day at a point in his story where he'd know just where he'd pick up the following morning. Our stories can involve very complicated investigations and reporting, but when I hit a brick wall at the end of the day, I always think up my next chess move. That way, I can come in the next day and start fresh. In the John Edwards story, for instance, we believed John Edwards' mistress, Rielle Hunter, was pregnant and hiding out in North Carolina in a gated community, but we couldn't find her. I thought about it one night and determined that the next morning we'd identify all of the gynecologists in the area she'd likely be going to. And then we'd stake them out. That was the breakthrough idea. We finally found her and got a picture of her—clearly pregnant.

7. Prove it. Why do individuals come forward with information? Sometimes they're looking for money, sometimes revenge. In the case of John Edwards, a lot of sources came forward with info because they felt that Edwards' betrayal of his sick wife was wrong. They felt that presenting a false picture of himself while running for president was wrong. Whatever the reason, we go through a great deal to make sure that the information we're printing about someone is true. Our standard operating practice is to put sources under extensive lie detector tests administered by law enforcement professionals. We'll videotape sources' testimonials and have them sign legal documents, so if we were ever called into court they would have to testify on our behalf. Sometimes we even do background checks on sources to make sure they're who they say they are. If information comes from a paid source we'll try to corroborate it with other individuals who aren't paid from different aspects of that celebrity's life. Oftentimes I may have a half dozen reporters working on the same story and they don't know who the other reporters are talking to, so we'll get redundancy in terms of the information. And then I have to face a trial by our own in-house attorneys, who will question me over the sources' identities and how they know what they know. I treat every story that comes across my desk as if it's false and I have to prove it to be true. And it has paid off. Because of our newfound credibility, I'm getting a much higher quality of information now. In the past, sources very high up the food chain might have called the *New York Times* or *Washington Post*, but now they'll consider us.

8. Pace yourself. No matter how big a story is, you can't let it overwhelm you, because you have to be back at your desk at eight o'clock the next morning to work on other stories. Years ago, I was afraid to leave my desk. But these days, no matter how busy I am, every day I'll leave my office, walk around the block, get lunch or go to the gym. It's a marathon, not a sprint.

9. Never get too high or too low. There have been days when I've been featured on the front page of the *New York Times* business section or interviewed on *Nightline* and other days when I come into the office and there's a legal letter from a Hollywood attorney or somebody on the phone screaming his head off at me, threatening to sue. In my line of work, you can never get too high or too low. For the most part, you live your life in the balance. You have to embrace your success and think hard about the failures that come your way, but you can't obsess on either. When it gets into people yelling "How do live with yourself?" or "How do you face your children or your wife?" you have to keep a sense of humor about yourself or you're not going to last very long in this business.

10. Accusation is motivation. We're not vindictive, but when a story subject tells the media we're reporting a bunch of lies and we're in the same category as papers reporting on space aliens, it propels our reporters, photographers and editors to do the long stakeouts and spend the extra hours finding that one source that's going to put the story over the top. I don't have anything against John Edwards as an individual, but when he came after us and said, "You're tabloid trash," we were absolutely determined to get pictures of him with his then-mistress to establish that we were telling the truth. A year later when he was at the Beverly Hilton on a secret meeting with Hunter and their baby, we finally caught him. As the saying goes, "Never pick a fight with people who like to fight!"

BARRY LEVINE FACTS

Quote: "If I were in Russia, I'd be taken out by a hail of bullets, because that's what happens to investigative journalists over there."

Scariest moments: 1988: Mike Tyson threatens to kill him for asking if he's gay. 1989: Levine's helicopter shot at over Don Johnson and Melanie Griffith's wedding. 1991: Levine's news team is "attacked" by a swarm of tarantulas after sneaking onto Michael Jackson's Neverland Ranch for wedding of Elizabeth Taylor and Larry Fortensky.

Craziest assignment: 1988: Two reporters wearing sheep costumes cross a field trying to get into Michael J. Fox's wedding.

Favorite shoes: Bruno Magli loafers (the type O.J. wore).

On the Pulitzer Prize nomination: 2010: "Mainstream media would rather see the earth explode before they give the *Enquirer* a Pulitzer."

Dream story: An exposé of the Obamas.

NATIONAL ENQUIRER FACTS

Incarnations: 1926: William Griffin, a protégé of William Randolph Hearst, founds the *New York Evening Enquirer*, a Sunday afternoon broadsheet newspaper. 1952: Inspired by watching gawkers at auto accidents, new owner Generoso Pope Jr. revamps *Enquirer* into a sensationalist sex and violence weekly with headlines like "I Cut Out Her Heart and Stomped on It." Late '50s: Paper's focus changes to celebrity and scandal. Late '60s: *Enquirer* adds stories on UFOs and the occult.

1980s slogan: "Enquiring minds want to know."

Scoops: 1987: Photos of presidential candidate Gary Hart with mistress on his knee on the yacht *Monkey Business*. 1997: Based on tip, weapon used to murder Bill Cosby's son is found. 2001: Jesse Jackson's love child. 2003: Rush Limbaugh's addiction to painkillers.

British Invasion: 2005: In response to circulation plunge, 20 British journalists are hired and *Enquirer* offices are moved to New York. 2006: Change fails, British journalists are fired and offices move back to Boca Raton, Florida.

Sued the *Enquirer*: Carol Burnett, Frank Sinatra, Cary Grant, Johnny Carson, Liz Taylor, Raquel Welch, Redd Foxx, Cher, Tammy Wynette, Clint Eastwood, Engelbert Humperdinck, Tom Selleck, Roseanne Barr, Lisa Marie Presley, Brooke Shields, Martha Stewart, Eddie Murphy, Kate Hudson, Cameron Diaz and many more.

Chapter 19

How to Grow Killer Weed

· ·

Ed Rosenthal

Guru of Ganja, cannabis cultivation expert and author of
12 books on how to grow pot

It was the sixties, and Ed Rosenthal, who listed his future career as "plant geneticist" in high school, had discovered pot. After college, living in an oversize apartment in the Bronx, Rosenthal decided to grow his own, and his long love affair with marijuana began. At first, he just plucked and rolled and smoked the leaves like other novice growers. But with a background in botany, Rosenthal soon began to produce higher quality pot than the Mexican weed on the street. Within a year, he was producing grow systems for people. The day he was featured in an alternative New York newspaper, a line of people stretched out his door to observe his growing techniques. "At the time it was just a way to make a living," he says. "I had no idea I'd spend the rest of my life doing it." Proclaimed the Guru of Ganja by *High Times*, Rosenthal has been a godsend to both the home-growing hobbyist and the commercial grower. He has authored a dozen books on marijuana cultivation, and his popular grower's advice column, "Ask Ed," ran in *High Times* for two decades and is syndicated internationally. Although an avid pot smoker, when it comes to cultivation of the plant, Rosenthal goes against type. He is a solid pragmatist with a scientific bent. To enter Rosenthal's world of horticultural advice is to journey to an all-things-pot planet where you can study everything from 24-hour terpene fluctuations to breeding for marijuana's intricate flavor palate. "It just goes to show the thoughtlessness of youth," says Rosenthal. "I write about pot, so I get a lot of free pot. Maybe I should have been writing about diamonds and gold?"

Takeaway: *"Marijuana may not be addictive, but growing it is."*

1. Know the consequences. Face it, pot isn't legal yet. There are almost a million marijuana arrests in America every year, so before you start to grow, think about what'll happen if you get caught. If you get busted in Oklahoma for growing a single plant you can get two years to life. Know your local laws, both state and county. Ask yourself, "Is growing worth it?" and "Can I afford a lawyer?" In some states a medical doctor can lose his license for cultivation. A student can lose rights to scholarships. You can lose your right to adoption or public housing or even your driver's license or right to vote. The police blotter is full of stories of people who didn't think it through.

2. Design your garden. Cannabis growers can be highly opinionated about how to grow the best pot. They'll argue over hydroponics versus soil, seeds versus clones. Get into a discussion on lights and you'll have to sort through a dizzying array of pros and cons over sunlight, fluorescents, sodium, ultraviolet and LED lights. But what's important is to determine the best garden design for *your* particular circumstances and needs. If you're squeezed for space, you can grow in a closet. Need a fast turnaround time? Plants grown hydroponically mature more quickly. Don't want to risk being busted with an indoor garden? Find a small hard-to-detect plot with sufficient water, sun and soil, and grow a guerrilla garden. If you're licensed to grow medical marijuana, you might be legally limited to a certain number of plants, so you'll want to design your garden for maximum yield of each plant.

3. Know your limits. When some people first get started growing, they want to do too much and they get in over their heads. I knew a first-time grower who planted a 400-square-foot indoor garden. He bought sixteen lights and had the idea to do everything by hand. No irrigation system. No help. Halfway through the first grow cycle he realized, "There's not enough time!" He was having a nervous breakdown. I told him, "Shut off half the lights and do what you can." Growing cannabis is not a fly-by-night project. Start small. Get some experience. Then you can expand into a larger system.

4. Choose your variety wisely. When you grew back in the late '60s, you collected seeds from friends or whatever marijuana happened to be left around—Columbian Gold or Panama Red. But those plants were actually more suited to tropical climates. Then the breeders came along, legendary guys like Neville Schoenmaker, who gained access to some of the world's greatest strains of cannabis: Skunk #1, Haze and Pollyanna. They opened mail order seed banks. For the first time you could select strains suited to various climates that grew faster and had much better highs. After 40 years of breeding, the marijuana plant has evolved. Now, you have at least a couple of hundred seed banks. Any novice can buy top-quality genetic seeds—Silver Pearl, Lemon Haze, Big Bud Skunk, etcetera—or find first-rate clones to choose from. You can select for taste, aroma and, of course, the high. Want a couch potato high? Go for Easy Rider. Something more cerebral? Go for Green House Thai. Prefer a party buzz? Try Euforia. Medical marijuana patients can choose from strains to relieve particular ailments. If you are going to go to the trouble of growing, why not select the best plant for you?

5. Remember: Marijuana is NOT a magical plant. Some pot smokers believe that marijuana is their mystical ally, like Don Juan talked about in the Carlos Castañeda books. They get so excited that they think they can plant a seed in the ground and a few months later they'll be smoking killer pot. But marijuana plays by the same rules as everything else in the plant kingdom. Just like an orchid or a head of lettuce, marijuana requires the right amount of light, CO_2, nutrients, water, oxygen and temperature. Your plants may give you great joy, but they won't grow to their full potential unless you educate yourself about the principles of cultivation.

6. Believe your eyes. A plant's reactions to stimuli can be as instantaneous as an animal's, but you have to learn to read the cues. As you tend your garden, step back to watch the plants. They'll indicate their health. Are they getting enough water? The right spectrum of light? There's a telltale sign for almost every nutrient deficiency. No matter what you've learned from books or other growers, you have to trust your eyes. Once, returning home after a week away, I noticed my plants had drought damage. Just by looking I could see they hadn't been watered correctly. I shocked the plant sitter when I asked him, "So, how come you didn't water my plants last Thursday?"

7. Harvest no bud before it's ripe. You wouldn't eat a green peach. Or, a hard pear. So why go to all of the work of growing a marijuana crop only to harvest the buds before they're ripe? A ripe bud gives you the most potent high. Know the cues. Get yourself a photographer's loupe. Up close you'll notice that the buds glisten in the sun as if sprinkled with tiny crystals. That's when the magic moment has arrived. Some growers get lazy and harvest plants all at once, but even buds on the same plant don't mature at the same time. Of course, in outdoor gardens you can't control the weather, so keeping on top of forecasts is crucial since you may need to harvest a few days early to avoid rain. Any kind of moisture can cause mold, turning even the most magnificent buds to mush.

8. Don't get busted. There are a million ways to get busted. Any one of these might work: tell everyone about your garden, act suspicious, throw late-night parties, wave a gun around, don't pay your taxes, be a lousy neighbor, spread a lot of cash around in town, piss off the garbage man, post pictures of your garden on Facebook or grow a garden next to a major airport. Every time you tell someone about your garden, assume you've just told ten people. Anybody—an angry spouse, a disgruntled roommate—can turn you in. Some people go to great lengths to keep their gardens under wraps. I know an Australian grower whose garden grows on a section of unused railroad track. He built a shed without a floor on wheels, so whenever he hears the helicopters coming he slides the shed right over his plants. He can do it in 90 seconds flat, and he's never been found out.

9. Evolve. Thirty years ago your typical grow room was a couple of hanging lights and a fan. Obviously, the science of marijuana cultivation has changed radically over the years, but some growers think they've got it down. They think they know everything. I visited a grower once with a terrible garden, a real throwback to the '70s. I took some of his pot to some people, and no one would even smoke it. The best growers realize they have a lot to learn. From homemade aeroponics systems to decarboxylation, cultivation technology is always changing, which can be overwhelming. But that's the way it is.

10. Legalize it. A lot of potheads don't even vote, but every change in the marijuana laws has been the result of a struggle. A lot of people don't have the time to fight for legalization or they don't want their faces recognized, but anyone can make a contribution to the cause. If the 20 million regular users donated $10, that would be $200 million toward marijuana law reform, and the law changes would be immediate. If marijuana was decriminalized, a hundred thousand people would be released from jail and 10 million would have their criminal records expunged. We could look forward to free-market marijuana that would offer us the choice of how we'd want to benefit from this incredible plant. Are you for legalization? Then act on your beliefs.

ED ROSENTHAL FACTS

Cannabis curator: 1987: Rosenthal opens Marijuana Museum in Amsterdam; police confiscate entire inventory.

Arrested: 2002: Convicted for cultivation and conspiracy for growing medical marijuana in California; faces possible sentence of $4.5 million fine and 100 years in jail. 2003: Federal judge sentences him to a $1,000 fine and a day in jail.

***New York Times* on Rosenthal:** 2003: He's "the pothead's answer to Ann Landers, Judge Judy, Martha Stewart and the Burpee Garden Wizard all in one."

Author: *Marijuana Growers Handbook, Closet Cultivator, The Big Book of Buds.* Editor of *Hemp Today.* Over 2 million books sold.

On marijuana legalization: "This isn't a fight about a drug. It's about civil liberties and people being able to do what they want to do."

Tommy Chong on Rosenthal: "He holds the distinction of turning more people on to pot than Cheech and Chong."

MARIJUANA FACTS

First import: 1492: Christopher Columbus brings cannabis to the New World.

Colonial law: 1619: Jamestown settlers are all required to grow cannabis.

Cannabis Rx: 1850–1941: *U.S. Pharmacopeia*, a medicine and supplements authority, lists marijuana as useful for nausea, rheumatism and labor pains. Marijuana is sold at pharmacies and general stores until 1930s.

Pot and the temperance movement: 1890s: Marijuana is recommended as a substitute for alcohol because it doesn't lead to domestic violence.

Busted: 1937: Samuel Caldwell is first person arrested under Marihuana Tax Act; fined $1,000 and sentenced to four years hard labor.

Not your parents' pot: 1970s: THC (the primary active ingredient of marijuana's high) concentration, 2–6 percent. Today: Up to 20 percent.

"War on Drugs": 1971: Term first used by President Richard Nixon.

iPot: 2010: Mobile app "Cannabis" lets users find nearest (medical) marijuana dealer.

Emerald Triangle: Northern California's Mendocino County, where pot trade generates an estimated $1 billion a year, up to two-thirds of local economy.

Pot slang: Baby Bhang, Bammy, Blunt, Catnip, Cheeba, Chronic, Dagga, Dinkie, Doobie, Gasper, Giggle Smoke, Grass, Herb, Hot Stick, Hydro, Jive Stick, Kush, Locoweed, Mary Jane, Muggle, Reefer, Sensi, Shake, Shwag, Skunk, Tea, Wacky Weed.

Chapter 20

How to Hunt Big Game

Chad Schearer

Master hunter, outdoorsman, guide and host of the TV
show *Shoot Straight*

While he was studying business law in college, Chad Schearer, a fifth-generation hunter, took a part-time job as a hunting guide. When told there would be a cameraman along, Schearer thought, "My first guided hunt is going to be a TV show?!" That morning he called out a five-point elk bull for the cameras. "The host got bull fever, froze up and didn't get a shot off," says Schearer, "but I was hooked for life." Schearer became a master hunter not by virtue of overwhelming firepower but by developing sensitivity to his surroundings, the weather, the moods and habits of the animals he hunts. Experience has not only sharpened his observational powers but taught him patience to wait for the right moment to strike. A world champion elk caller and writer on hunting, Schearer has run more than 700 hunting seminars and spent over 3,000 days hunting over the last 20 years. His TV show, *Shoot Straight*, features his wife, Marsha, their young sons, Wyatt and Walker, and special guests who hunt with a variety of weapons in destinations around the world. "I spent a lot of time hunting in the field with my dad," says Schearer. "The lessons I've learned hunting—patience, persistence, learning from mistakes and not giving up—can be applied just as well to business and life. When you go out in the woods you never know what's going to happen. You could not see anything or you might take the animal of a lifetime."

Takeaway: *"Look at the cards that are dealt to you that day and be ready to change up your tactics."*

1. Make practice a dress rehearsal. You can't just go walk out into the woods with a weapon and hope for something to happen. You have to prepare. When you practice, simulate the conditions you'll be facing in your actual hunt. Become familiar. Practice in the clothes you'll be wearing with the weapon you'll be using. Run forty yards till your heart is pounding and you're out of breath, then pick up your weapon, try to control your breath, settle in and practice your shot. This will re-create the heart-pumping adrenaline you'll have in a hunting situation.

2. Know your terrain. Speak to local wildlife managers, sporting goods store owners, and sportsmen's clubs about the area you'll be hunting. Preseason scouting helps you become familiar with the terrain and identify the animals' habits by game trails, tracks, droppings, damaged trees and other signs of activity. When animals bed they are often in the cover of dark timber. They can smell you coming from behind and see you coming from below, so you want to position yourself in a spot where they'll come out into the open to feed in a meadow or water at a stream. I can look at a map and realize, okay, those animals are going to bed on a north-facing slope in the thicker timber, and they're going to feed on the south-facing slopes where the grass grows. Once you are on your hunt, spend a lot of time with binoculars or a spotting scope, looking over an area to make sure of what's out there so you can position yourself to improve your odds.

3. Do not disturb. When you hunt you have to be careful not to spook animals. I learned this lesson on my very first time out—a spot-and-stalk hunt for mule deer with my dad. We walked right by a rattlesnake den. My dad was within two feet of a snake. I pulled out a pistol to shoot the snake, but my father said, "Wait! Those deer could be right over this ridge." He got clear of the snake, and sure enough, we went 100 yards and I got my first buck. Had I shot that snake, it would have spooked the deer out of there.

4. Read the animal. We call it taking an animal's temperature when we try to figure out what kind of mood it's in and why. Is it rut? Is it pre-rut? Is it post-rut? If you know how fired up he is, you can anticipate his next move. It's like playing the ultimate game of chess. What's he going to do? Where's he going to go? There's no book to tell you how to do this. Sensing it comes from hours of trial and error in the field. Once when I was bow hunting in Montana for elk, I'd been watching a bull that I'd determined was in rut. Toward evening five or six cows from his harem started moving toward a stream to water. I hit a couple cow sounds to fool the bull into thinking one of his cows had gotten away. After that, I hit the bugle, the male call, so he'd think there was a bull out there with his cow. I knew that would be a threat to him; that he'd step out to challenge the bull he thought was there. And he did just that. He came out of the brush 43 yards broadside. I got my shot and the arrow hit its mark.

5. Play the wind. Big game animals have incredible noses—if they catch your scent, they're gone. One of the biggest factors in hunting is playing the wind. If you know which way it will blow, you can be upwind of the animal so they can't smell you. A few years ago I was guiding hunters on a mountain in Montana. It was morning and typically as the sunlight heats up a valley, the wind is drawn uphill, and so we were staying up above the elk. As the sun sets and the temperature cools, it's just the opposite; the wind is drawn downhill. We were working our way toward the elk. There were eight bulls with thirty or forty cows, and I thought, "Man, this is a perfect setup." Then, all of a sudden, the wind changed. It was heading downhill toward the elk. I was stumped. While we sat and waited, I watched the sky and noticed these big cumulus clouds. I realized that when the clouds passed in front of the sun, the valley cooled down and the wind was drawn downhill. I thought, "I've been doing this for fifteen years and I've never noticed that." I knew if we timed the clouds just right, as soon as the sun came out from the cloud, the wind would get going back uphill. And that's what happened. We moved really aggressively toward the elk. I was cow calling, and brought in a bull 35 yards to one of the hunters. Unfortunately, he shot a tree.

6. Be patiently aggressive. Patient aggression is an oxymoron, but in hunting it truly applies. When I was younger, I hunted much more aggressively. If I heard an elk bugle, I'd start calling back right away, trying to bring the bull in even if it was two miles away. But, as I've gotten older, I sit back and look more carefully at the scenario. How can I stack the odds in my favor? Now, if I'm hunting and animals are too far away, I'll take my time, sneak in as close as I can, then hit the call. One call at the right time is more valuable than a hundred calls from a long way away.

7. Don't leave game to find game. Hunting is about constant change. You may go into an area with the mind-set, "This is how I'm going to hunt it," and all of a sudden a quality animal you weren't expecting pops out in front of you. When opportunity knocks be flexible and adjust your plan. Don't pass on that animal. Stay with it, even if you end up covering several miles in a different direction than you thought you'd be going.

8. Don't guide the guide. When I go to a new destination, I'd rather hunt with a local guide who knows the terrain and animals than with the best hunter in the world. Even a rookie guide may make a few mistakes, but he knows the area. Once in Zimbabwe I was hunting with the guide Rory Muil, who is a specialist on Cape buffalo. Many times we were within seventy yards of buffalo, but they were in herds of 40 and 50 with no big trees for us to jump behind. I'd look at Rory and he'd say, "Chad, it's not right. If you shoot, the herd will charge." After five days a buffalo whose tracks we'd been following through the sand got tired of us tracking him. All of a sudden we heard this big horrific bark, "Aoooff!" We looked up and this buffalo had turned to face us. Rory said, "Are you ready?" The buffalo came straight at me. Rory called, "Chad, shoot!" And I shot him straight on. It was an incredible hunt. I ended up taking a tremendous Cape buffalo with a muzzle-loader because I was tuned into the guide's expert skills.

9. Pick your spot. When I first started hunting I placed a sticker right on my bow that read, "Pick your spot." Sometimes when you've got a big animal out there you're looking at the antlers and thinking, "Wow, this thing's incredible." But if you want to take that animal, quit looking at the rack, and aim for the vitals: the heart or the lungs. Focus on where you want to put the bullet and shoot. Sometimes people pull the trigger, lift their head and drop their weapon because they want to see if they dropped the animal. But if they lift their head, they tend to shoot over the animal.

10. The worst mistake in hunting is not hunting. There are times when you're out there and think, "Oh, it's going to be a horrible day, the conditions are all wrong, I'll just stay in camp." There have been days when I thought that, and—*boom!*—we've had success. Once, we had been hunting deer down in Greensburg, Kansas, for a week. The weather wasn't cooperating. It was hot and then turned cold. The deer were in a crazy pattern. Trespassers came in and blew out deer we were hunting right in front of us. Everything was going wrong. It was the last afternoon of the last day of the season and I could have said, "Ah, let's head to the airport and take off," but we knew there were a couple big deer in this wooded draw, so I tried a scent drive, a technique that isn't often used. We set it up and all of a sudden this monster buck, a 174-inch record-book buck, came walking out. I was able to take him because we hung in there and didn't give up and that was the biggest whitetail of my life.

CHAD SCHEARER FACTS

Schearer's wife: Working as a dentist's office manager, Marsha has only one unsuccessful hunt before meeting Chad. Within a month of their marriage she becomes camp cook. A year later she is guiding. "When I met Chad, I was hunting for a husband," she jokes. "And now I'm hunting *with* my husband."

Sixth-generation hunters: At age six, Schearer's son Walker takes his first mule deer; at age five, Wyatt takes his first whitetailed deer.

Meat eaters: Schearer and family eat the meat from the animals they hunt.

Favorite hunting joke: "If an elk could see like a turkey and a turkey could smell like an elk we'd never see either one."

Most memorable hunt: 2010: On hunt in Montana, Schearer teaches sons, Walker, age nine, and Wyatt, age eight, to call elk, promising he will take any elk they can call to him. Walker makes cow elk sounds and Wyatt bugles, bringing in a five-point bull to 40 yards, and Schearer takes him with bow and arrow.

HUNTING FACTS

First known complete hunting weapon: Circa 400,000 BC: Wooden throwing spears are discovered with animal remains in Germany in 1995.

U.S. hunting stats: 2006: 12.5 million people hunted for a total of 220 million days and spent $22.9 billion; 91 percent of hunters are men.

Fair chase: According to century-old American tradition of "fair chase," a hunt involves a sportsman tracking free-ranging wildlife that have every opportunity to evade him. The objective is the hunt, not the kill.

Hunters by state: Most: 19 percent of Montana residents hunt. Least: 1 percent in California, Connecticut, Massachusetts and New Jersey.

Danger: Injury rates for sports per 100 participants: football (5.3), cheerleading (1.2), hunting (0.05). The only two sports that have lower accident rates than hunting are billiards and camping.

Chapter 21

How to Inspire a Student

· ·

Erin Gruwell

Inspirational teacher of at-risk students, bestselling author
and founder of Freedom Writers Foundation

Shortly after the Los Angeles riots, Erin Gruwell, an idealistic young teaching novice, stepped into Room 203 at Wilson High School in Long Beach, California. But her students, whose lives were plagued by poverty and violence, could not have cared less about Gruwell's plans for teaching Homer's *Odyssey* or Shakespeare's sonnets. "It became painfully obvious," said Gruwell, "that every theory I had learned in my graduate courses paled in comparison to the raw lessons I would learn in my urban classroom." Through a process of trial and error, gradually Gruwell began to reach her students. She worked tirelessly to make her classes relevant and break down barriers between herself and the students, and the barriers between the students themselves. When she asked them to journal about their lives, they wrote with reckless abandon and dubbed themselves "the Freedom Writers" in honor of the Freedom Riders who marched to end segregation decades before Gruwell's students were born. Collected stories from their journals went on to become the *New York Times* bestseller *The Freedom Writers Diary*. Her students were transformed into critical thinkers, thoughtful writers and engaged citizens of the world. Four years later, after witnessing the jubilation of their graduation, Gruwell left to teach other teachers. Through the Freedom Writers Foundation that she and her students had started back in the classroom, Gruwell formed the Freedom Writers Teacher Institute to teach educators the innovative techniques that she used to inspire her students.

> **Takeaway:** *"The best part of teaching is when your students take a lesson out of the classroom and back into their own world."*

1. Become a student of your students. On my first day at school, in my pearls and polka dot dress, I thought I was going to change the world. But I didn't have a clue. My students checked their pagers, reapplied their eyeliner and laid down their heads on their desks and took naps. I dodged a paper airplane made out of my syllabus and tried to make myself heard over the "Yo' mama" jokes. As the bell rang, one student said, "I give her five days." I felt like a failure. My first step was to throw out everything I'd been taught. I had to become a student of my students. I had to learn to speak their language instead of expecting them to speak mine.

2. Connect your kids. Teenagers often identify themselves by externals—the color of their skin, the sneakers they wear, the cliques they belong to. In Room 203 the Latinos sat on the left, Asians on the right, African Americans in the back and a couple of Caucasians huddled together in the front. Their hostility toward each other was going to make teaching impossible. One day my students were laughing at a note being passed around. It was a racist caricature of one of my African-American students that reminded me of images from Nazi propaganda depicting Jews as rats. Something inside me snapped. I was angry. "This reminds me of the Holocaust," I told them. But when I realized no one knew what the Holocaust even was, I wondered if this was the kind of opportunity to break down barriers among them I'd been waiting for. I asked them, "How many of you have been shot?" and nearly every hand went up. They started telling stories, pulling up their shirts to show their stitches, scars and bullet wounds, interacting with each other. As I listened my anger turned to empathy.

3. Make your classroom a home. I was going to show my kids that no matter what happened with their parents, parole officers and other teachers, I wouldn't give up on them. I let them know, it matters to me that you come to class, it matters to me that you try, it matters to me when you succeed. There's food in the corner if you're hungry. This room is a place you can come to before or after school. We took photos and covered the walls with snapshots of every single student. The kids loved that. We turned our crazy, messy, dilapidated classroom into a home. The message was clear: "You belong here."

4. Engage your students. I thought my students might relate to teens overcoming hard lives. When we read Anne Frank's *Diary of a Young Girl* one of my students, Maria, said, "Anne Frank is not even Latina. She doesn't speak Spanish. She is not from my 'hood." But when Maria, a hardened third-generation gang member who was on house arrest and came to school wearing an ankle monitor, read that Anne, confined to her attic, felt trapped like a bird in a cage, something in Maria clicked. She began to ask me questions like, "When is Anne going to smoke Hitler?" One day she stormed into class and threw the book across the room. With tears in her eyes, she yelled, "Why didn't you tell me that Anne doesn't make it, and if she doesn't make it what are you saying about my chances?" A couple of weeks later she asked me if there was a way to buy the book in Spanish. When I asked why, she said, "My mama wants to read about the little girl that changes my life."

5. Help your students find their voice. Every kid has a story. Hoping they'd been inspired by the examples of Anne Frank and other teens who had turned negative experiences into something positive by writing about them, I handed out notebooks for my students to journal about their lives. I had no idea of how they would respond. There was some initial resistance. But then the stories poured out of them, full of anger and sadness. They wrote about sexual abuse, gang violence, hurt and hate. Many of them were stories they hadn't told anyone. It wasn't just the writing, but hearing and editing each other's stories was cathartic for my students, really a profound healing process. Once they began to write their own stories, it opened them up to the possibility of being able to rewrite their endings.

6. Find role models. Some of our greatest lessons came through discussions with guest speakers who had made a difference in the world. When we discovered that Miep Gies, the woman who had helped to hide Anne Frank, was still alive, my students wrote to her, imploring her to come. Miraculously, she agreed. She was 87. She told us how the Gestapo held her at gunpoint as they took Anne off, and how she risked her life to try to bribe the Nazi soldiers to set Anne free. She said, "There's not a day that goes by that I don't think about Anne," and told us how she went up to the attic and found Anne's diary pages scattered across the floor. "You must act when injustice happens," Miep told my students. She told them not to wait for leaders to make the world a better place and to "Please make sure that Anne's death was not in vain." One of my students, Darrius, who had lost two dozen friends to gang violence, stood up. He fought back tears. "I've never had a hero before," he told Miep, "but you are my hero."

7. Fight for your students. When I went to get *Catcher in the Rye* for my students from the English department storeroom, the cochair took the book out of my hands and said, "Your students are too stupid to read it." I thought, "I'll show you!" I asked my dad for a cash advance on my Christmas present to buy every student a copy. They were shocked to get brand-new books. Realizing I'd gone out on a limb for them, they worked that much harder. When a field trip to Washington, DC, we had organized to meet the secretary of education was vetoed by my principal, I wouldn't let my kids be denied. I took the risk of going over his head to the superintendent of the entire school system. He not only helped make the trip happen; he came along with us. You need to find advocates—in your school system, in your community, enlist CEOs, appeal to friends and family for extra pairs of hands. You'd be surprised at how much people are willing to help.

8. Find emotional support. Being a teacher can be isolating. You go in your room, you shut the door, you're by yourself. You may battle condescending administrators, disgruntled parents, long hours of afterschool work. You try things that fall flat. You work two, sometimes three jobs to make ends meet. Disillusionment is totally normal. Some teachers feel that if they ask for emotional help, they're a failure. But teaching is a team sport. You have to find allies who understand what you're trying to do and will boost you up when you're down. If they're not at your own school, find them in your community, through organizations or in other schools. You're no good to your students if you let yourself collapse.

9. Make your students citizens of the world. We pushed hard for it and traveled to Auschwitz. We traveled to Sarajevo. We went places where the students could experience the lessons of fighting against intolerance firsthand. Eventually, the kids were so inspired that they became instrumental in organizing community events to field trips themselves. That's the beauty of education: kids taking lessons out of the classroom and back into their own world where they can positively affect their family, their friends and their greater community. I take pride in my students. They didn't think they were going to make it to their eighteenth birthday, but they went to college, they're getting married and having children. They've also become true citizens of the world.

10. Transform education, one classroom at a time. Seeing all 150 of my students graduate, many the first in their families to do so, made me wonder if the teaching techniques I'd been instinctively developing could be replicated in other classrooms. Through the Freedom Writers Foundation, with many of my former students, we developed a program that emulates and universalizes the lessons we learned in Room 203 to inspire the youth of tomorrow, regardless of age, race or socioeconomic background, to make a difference in their communities and the world.

ERIN GRUWELL FACTS

Namesake: Gruwell's father, a baseball scout, names daughter after great slugger Hank Aaron.

Inspiration: 1989: Man who stood in front of tanks in Tiananmen Square inspires collegiate Gruwell. "Maybe I can stand up to adversity and discrimination, too."

Bad advice: Education professor: "Don't smile until Christmas. And never, ever let your students see you cry."

Nickname: "Ms. G." (At first Gruwell is unaware "G" stands for "gangsta.")

Moonlighting: To supplement teaching salary, Gruwell works as concierge at Marriott Hotel, sells lingerie at Nordstrom and teaches education courses at National University.

Gruwell's writing advice: "Just like a miniskirt, make your paper long enough to cover everything but short enough to pique someone's interest."

Books: *The Freedom Writers Diary, Teaching Hope, Teach with Your Heart.*

Rockstar moment: At book event, Taiwan: "It was like Beatlemania. The Taiwanese people revere educators. I wish educators in America got the same kind of reverence we give to athletes and reality pop stars."

Doppelgänger: 2007: Academy Award winner Hilary Swank plays Gruwell in the feature film *Freedom Writers*.

Favorite quote: "Whoever saves one life saves the world entire." —The Talmud

EDUCATION FACTS

The Six Arts: 1045 to 256 BC (Zhou Dynasty), China: School-boys learn Six Arts: ritual, music, archery, chariot driving, calligraphy and math; girls learn ritual, deportment, silk production and weaving.

Warrior class: Fifth, fourth centuries BC, Sparta: Education system trains boys, age seven on, to become warriors with complete obedience, courage and physical perfection. Boys live at barracks, and with harsh discipline are taught sports, endurance and fighting.

Early textbook: 1450: The hornbook is a wooden paddle with the alphabet, Lord's Prayer and Roman numerals hand lettered on parchment that is laminated on with a sheet of transparent sheep or cow horn.

Graduation rate from U.S. high schools: 1919, 16.8 percent; 1930, 32.1 percent; 1970, 75.9 percent (all-time high); 2009, 75.5 percent.

High school graduation rates by state: High: Wisconsin, 89.6 percent. Low: Nevada, 51.3 percent.

Spending per student, U.S. public school: 1961–62, $393; 2008–9, $10,297.

Oldest and youngest grads: 1990: Michael Kearney, 6, graduates from San Marin High School, Novato, California. 2002: Cecil Smith, 94, earns General Educational Development (GED) degree, California.

Teachers who quit their day jobs: Lyndon Johnson, Benito Mussolini, George Orwell, Gene Simmons (of Kiss), Stephen King, Sting.

On education: "He who opens a school door, closes a prison." —Victor Hugo

Chapter 22

How to Live Life on the High Wire

• •

Philippe Petit

High-wire artist and multidisciplinary performer who
perpetrated the artistic crime of the twentieth century

On a summer day in 1974, a 24-year-old Frenchman stepped
onto the world stage with one of the most astonishing performances in modern history—walking back and forth on a wire illegally rigged across the void between New York's World Trade
Center Towers, three quarters of a mile above spellbound onlook-
ers. It all began six years earlier when the young Philippe Petit was
inspired by a rendering of the not-yet-constructed towers he saw in
a magazine. He spent the following years preparing "like a madman." He refined his wire walking skills, made two trips to New
York City and countless visits to the towers to plot how to surrepti-
tiously enter the buildings, and solved the complicated logistics of
rigging his wire between the swaying towers. But, for all of his
meticulous preparation, Petit bristles at any attempt to systematize
his methods. "My life was usually a total mess," says Petit. "I'd
throw all types of cables and equipment in the truck and drive in a
frenzy to the place and arrive exhausted with no money and no
organization. I'd do everything by myself and have sometimes 12
seconds to change from my dirty rigging clothes to my performance
outfit." Asked to explain his artistic process, he says, "It has evolved
from six to sixty years old, but can be boiled down to a few words—

from chaos to total control to perfection." Petit has gone on to perform many other spectacular wire walks. He has also authored over half a dozen books, produced theatrical performances, and single-handedly built a barn using eighteenth-century tools and design. Whether on the high wire or not, Petit's philosophy is epitomized in his response to reporters shouting "Why?" after his dramatic Twin Towers crossing. Petit's answer: "The beauty of it is, there is no 'why.'"

> **Takeaway:** *"Ask a great artist why they do what they do and the answer will be, 'Because I have no choice.'"*

1. Let life be your teacher. How can you achieve greatness if you haven't experienced the hard lessons of life? To become a great theatrical director, a great actor or a Renaissance man, you have to do all the jobs most people don't want to do, like washing dishes and shoveling horseshit. When I was young, I did everything myself. I had so much to prepare before my shows I had no time to sleep. If I had 27 minutes before a performance, I had to fall asleep in a minute flat to have 26 minutes of sleep before this very important moment in my life. I had to learn to sleep in any position on anything—a bumping bus, a concrete floor. You will never learn that by googling "how to" from a comfortable armchair.

2. Court disaster. When I first became a magician, a juggler and a wirewalker, word was out. I was so arrogant that no circus director would hire me. It was as if I made sure that the whole world was against me, which forced me to do things without permission. There is positivity in putting your nose in disaster, in fiasco, in accidents. If you go where trouble is you will find a magnificent transformation. After all, if I had followed the rules, would I have traveled across the ocean to a foreign country and illegally snuck into and then wire-walked across a building a quarter mile above the ground?

3. Make your art a joyful adventure. When I begin a new project, I embark upon an adventure that has many forks in the road. At each one I must decide, "Should I take the left or the right?" This joy of exploration is childlike, though not childish. It carries me along and gives me my energy to fight and succeed. Without this sense of a solitary, joyful journey of a child who is free to go where he or she wants, I would not do good work. If I were to sit at a desk, write a list, make a schedule, and go and meet the building and then make a plan to do a high wire walk in the most safe and intelligent way, I would not have that sense of adventure and exploration. And there would be no point in living. Although today I would add wisdom to my madness!

4. Be a madman of detail. If I go to climb a place that is rocky, I will find out what kind of rock it is. If the rock is rotten, the rope I'm hanging from will dislodge pebbles that will break my head. I would be a fool to *hope* that the rock is healthy. Before I walked the Twin Towers, I gathered information with cunning and precision. This door in this place opens to the left this wide with this many steps of a certain thickness, the 450-pound cable must be brought up this way to avoid detection, and so on. There were at least a thousand other details to solve. When it comes to doing my homework, I'm obsessed. I want to live to be very old. A half a millimeter of mistake, a quarter second's miscalculation, and you lose your life.

5. Improvise. Improvisation is turning away from a well-polished plan within a millisecond because there's no such thing in life as a well-polished plan. One of my favorite activities is to jump from rock to rock in a running torrent in the bed of a river. When I jump, I do not know where I'll land. I'm in the air and there are six rocks around me and in a millionth of a second I see that I'd slip on the one to the right because it's covered with moss, the one to the left is a little too far and I decide to come down on that little flat rock just ahead. But, before landing, I'm planning my next move. Of course, in our twenty-first century full of helmets and knee-pads and "don't-try-this-at-home," people will say, "You should go with three people observing you, just in case you fall, so they can rush you to a hospital." But, if you put all your energy, talent and intelligence into an action such as landing on the right rock, then failure is not an option. You cannot slip. You cannot fall. You cannot land in the water.

6. Banish doubt. To get on the wire, I must be fearless. I must be in total control. I cannot take the first step if I'm not sure that the last step will be a success. When incidents occur on the wire that are very dangerous, let's say a problem with the rigging, or if someone touches something they shouldn't, I can't let myself fall prey to doubt. Fear will invite losing all your strength. You need faith in yourself, faith in the wire and the millions of hours of rehearsing. Sometimes, strangely, fear comes after the walk, when I look back and think, "Oh my god, I did that? In those conditions? I am crazy."

7. Make the gods your accomplices. I am not a religious man in the way the term is normally used, but I believe in mysterious forces. When I walk on a wire I have subliminal, invisible encounters with the god of the void, the god of the balancing pole, the god of the cable. If I drop my balancing pole, I won't be able to balance. I'll be killed. The balancing pole is a god, and I have to hang on to it and negotiate with its mood, so it will never, never leave my hands. If you rise up to be higher than a god and condescend you will fail. I talk to these gods as an accomplice. When I walked the World Trade Center, I spoke to the swaying gods of the Towers, "Let me go, let me pass, let me reach you." Each time I place my feet on the wire, it's not an imposition of my personal strength; it is a communion with mysterious forces that are much stronger than myself.

8. Listen to the song of the wire. A wire is alive. Tie a wire between two points and slap it with your hand; you'll see the three natural moves of the wire. It will sway left and right. It will sway up and down. And it will turn on itself. That is the song of the wire. If you bang your feet across the wire, disregarding the wire's song, you will be a very ugly walker and you will not go very far. To be a true walker you must recognize that the wire is alive. You have to research its breathing. And once you feel you are getting it, you will synchronize your own breathing, your steps and the shifting of your weight to the song of the wire. You're in tune. The wire will not be an enemy. The wire will become your friend.

9. Don't congratulate yourself too soon. You're never victorious until you've walked the entire wire, crossed to the other side and stepped onto the platform. Many wirewalkers have died three feet before arrival because in their heart, they said, "Hey, I did it! I did it!" The audience screams and cheers, you think of your dinner or your paycheck. And then you die.

10. Be effortless. When I first saw circus wirewalkers with their stunts and tricks to prove they were risking their lives by doing dangerous things, I knew my life was going to go in the opposite direction. I knew as a wirewalker, I would be a poet who writes in the sky. Art happens when you work millions of hours not to make it look hard but to make it look effortless. The beauty for an audience is to be inspired and awestruck because you made them forget that the wire was even there.

PHILIPPE PETIT FACTS

Ne'er-do-well: As a teen, Petit is expelled from five schools.

Criminal Mind: 1973, Sydney: Immediately after wire-walking Sydney Harbour Bridge, Petit pickpockets arresting policeman's watch.

Twin Towers obsession: Annie Allix (Petit's girlfriend at the time): "One day he showed me a photo of two buildings in a magazine. There was a real madness in his eyes, a real rage. It was truly, 'I'm going to do this no matter what.'"

Financing: Petit subsidizes Twin Tower "coup" by juggling in the streets of Paris and New York City.

Arresting officer's comment: 1974, World Trade Center: "We asked him to get off the high wire but instead he ran back into the middle. Everyone was spellbound. I figured I was watching something that nobody would ever see again in this world."

High wire walks: Notre Dame Cathedral, Eiffel Tower, Grand Central Terminal, Valley of Hinnom in Jerusalem, Lincoln Center, Paris Opera, Cathedral of Saint John the Divine and many more.

Other skills: Street juggling, magic, horseback riding, fencing, eighteenth-century barn building, rock climbing, rigging and knot tying.

Documentation: Petit's WTC feat is documented in his book *To Reach the Clouds*, which is the basis for the Oscar-winning, critically acclaimed documentary film *Man on Wire*.

HIGH WIRE WALKING FACTS

Early practitioners: 500–700 AD, China: Images of tightrope walkers are drawn in Thousand Buddha Caves in Flaming Mountains.

Crown caper: 1385, Paris: Anonymous tightrope walker slides down rope stretched from Notre Dame to Pont Saint-Michel to place crown on head of future Queen Isabeau, who is part of a royal procession. The walker whisks away, departing up rope, holding two torches seen for miles, causing villagers to believe he is an angel.

First Niagara crossing: 1859: Frenchman "the Great Blondin" crosses the gorge on tightrope. He repeats act several times, always with new twist—blindfolded, draped in a sack, manacled, pushing a wheelbarrow, on stilts, carrying a man on his back, sitting down midway to cook and eat omelet and standing on a chair with one chair leg on rope.

Only woman to cross Niagara: 1867: Maria Spelterini crosses backward with peach baskets attached to her feet and paper bag over her head.

The Flying Wallendas: 1940s: Famous wirewalker family performs their greatest trick—a woman standing on shoulders of a man balanced on a chair on top of a bar between shoulders of two men riding bicycles on wire.

Longest skywalk: 1961: Rudy Omankowski Jr. skywalks three quarters of a mile between mountaintops in France.

Longest time on wire: 2010: Adil Hoshur (fifth-generation Uighur wirewalker) lives 60 days on rope above Beijing's Olympic Stadium.

Chapter 23

How to Live Life on the Road

. . . .

Ray Benson

Founder and front man of the nine-time Grammy-winning
Western swing band Asleep at the Wheel, who have been
on the road for 43 years

Ever since the twelfth century, when troubadours toured Europe, musicians have taken to the road to support themselves. In 1970, at the age of 18, the six-foot-seven-inch Ray Benson gathered the founding members of Asleep at the Wheel in a cabin in Paw Paw, West Virginia. To make the money they needed to keep the band together they had to go on the road. Since then, there have been over 90 band members and Benson has spent two-thirds of his life crisscrossing the country, traveling 3,000,000 miles and playing over 10,000 gigs. Having played in every state in the nation, as well as internationally, the band's pace has slowed, but only slightly, from the 300 gigs a year they used to play. Disgruntled travelers could take some tips from Benson's copacetic embrace of the road, where he can be found holding court in his tour bus, golfing, seeking out-of-the-way places to eat or doing what he loves most—playing music. "My uncle played sax on cruise ships," said Benson. "Everyone said it was a wonderful hobby that wouldn't pay, so he gave it up. But I was stubborn, because I had the dream. This business chews you up, burns you out and spits you out. I've seen it a hun-

dred times, but I'm not going to be one of those people. I want to
play guitar, sing and make music."

> **Takeaway:** *"I was never going to give up being a musi-
> cian. I'm dedicated and I'm not ashamed to say it."*

1. Be where you are. Rather than just sitting on the bus and
watching TV, I get out to see and do things all around the country
that other people take special vacations for. Like visit Mt. Rush-
more or the Grand Canyon. Or hot springs. Hot springs are everywhere—Wyoming, Idaho, Arkansas! We'll just go rolling right by
one and jump in 'cause we're playing somewhere nearby. Once, in
Hawaii, I discovered a masseur who practiced an obscure school of
massage. He fixed a chronic guitar player's problem I had with my
left hand. Now, when I'm heading someplace, I'm on the lookout
for renowned practitioners that I can go to just because I happen to
be driving by.

2. You are what you eat. You can do better than KFC. There
aren't as many mom-and-pop places for great regional food as there
used to be, but I've always asked the locals, "Where do I find the best
pig barbecue in the South?" "Gator meat in Florida?" "Hatched chil-
ies in New Mexico?" One of my favorites was the Cajun Loser's
Gumbo at Jay's Lounge and Cockpit in Louisiana, made from the
chicken that lost the fight. I look for the places that haven't changed,
'cause chances are if it's around a while it means it's got something
going for it.

3. Get a hobby. Find something on the road that keeps you out
of the smoky bars all night. For me, it's golf. I used to think it was
just a white man's sport, but truth is it's a really Zen-like experience. You can only play in the sunlight, and you better be sober,
'cause if that sun's beating down on you you'll feel like hell and
screw it up. I got hooked about 30 years ago when Willie Nelson

bought a little nine-hole course so he could quit doing cocaine. He let some of us in the band play for free and didn't make us wear the funny clothes. Now, we'll even go out of our way to book a gig near a great course. I seek them out all over—Scotland, Oregon, you name it. I've turned on some of the others in the band, 'cause having someone to be out there with is better than playing alone.

4. Mind your own business. Everybody has to have his or her own space and solitude. A hundred and eighty days a year, 11 people on a 45-foot bus in pressure situations, you're bound to hear stuff you shouldn't. I try to be discreet like the Japanese who lived with paper walls. My motto is, "Just because you can hear it doesn't mean you should listen."

5. Stay connected. For the first ten years I was on the road I couldn't imagine having a family. Didn't want one. On the bus, we used to just play cards or board games or stare out the window. You got to where you were going and maybe you'd make a call using a pay phone, pumping in quarters. Then, I had a family, a wife and two kids. You've got to remember that they exist without you. Which means when you do get home, they have to adjust to you and you to them. So, while you're gone, it's important to stay connected. The two biggest things that came along were the fax machine and the calling card. It was like, whoa! Suddenly, it was a whole lot easier to communicate. Now, there are a hundred ways to stay in touch—email, Skype, cell phones. I'd say it's 90 percent better and 10 percent worse. Before, you could run away from everything and ignore your domestic responsibilities; now you can't hide.

6. Keep your monster on a leash. Got that from Huey Lewis. Drugs, alcohol, sex, fame, money, power, whatever it is that imperils the things that are vital to you—your family, health, career—can take over and ruin you when you're out on the road. You get so drunk or high that you say or do stuff that's really harmful. I've seen people so desperate they snort coke off the floor. But just 'cause everybody else is doing it doesn't mean you can partake without ending up broken.

7. There's got to be a leader. After over forty years on the road, I can say that democracies don't work on a small scale. You can be as nefarious as Jim Jones or as constructive as Gandhi, but you need one decider. A big part of leading has to do with having a vision and enthusiasm. Forming this band, I was like, "Come on, let's have an adventure." As Bonnie Raitt once said, "It's like joining a circus. But there's got to be somebody in charge."

8. Expand the brand. All the money comes from being on the road, so you got to keep going out with new and different products to constantly create new fans. We're putting on a musical play, for instance, where I'm riding on the bus with the ghost of Bob Wills, the King of Western Swing. It's for our older demographic, 'cause they're not interested in going into some loud honky-tonk to hear us play. At the same time, as the saying goes, "Just 'cause you got running water don't mean the outhouse don't work."

9. Find the happy middle. We hit it big early on, and that success has enabled us to keep on keeping on. We're not big time and we're not small time; we're what I call the medium time. Take Willie Nelson. He's big time and he's a prisoner. People become very insistent with him. He can't go anywhere and be left alone. I believe this is a job, and you do owe a part of yourself to the public, but I don't want to walk on the red carpet. I don't want to be a superstar. I don't like limos; I like buses. I enjoy the fact that once we're out of our costumes, we're pretty much able to move around unrecognizable.

10. Keep the dream alive. I've had great heartache and tough times. I once had the bus break down on the side of the road in the middle of nowhere, needing $400 in repairs, already in debt and owing the government $100,000, with no family around and feeling professionally unappreciated. It was the '80s, the low point in our career. Disco was happening. We were not. The ability to push through those times has been my greatest asset. This life's met my expectations, but I tell anyone who asks if it's been worth it, "Can you do anything else? If so, then do that. But, if you can't be happy unless you're a working musician, performing every night, then this is what you got to do." The reward is you get to live your dream and play music all the time.

RAY BENSON FACTS

How the band got its name: Pedal steel player and founding member Lucky Oceans comes running out of the outhouse in West Virginia, crying, "I've got it! Asleep at the Wheel!"

The band: The band plays big-band songs, rockabilly, honky-tonk country, blues, fiddle tunes and Western swing, with 20 charted Billboard singles and 9 Grammys to their name.

On their move to Texas: "In 1973, we came to Austin to drop acid. Now, we drop antacid."

Benson's shoe size: 16EEE.

Weirdest artist to open for: Alice Cooper.

Gigs: Played inaugural balls for Presidents Clinton, G. W. Bush and Obama. Worst venue: Ku Klux Klan hall in Louisiana.

Travel: Benson's road trip mileage is equivalent to six round trips to the moon.

Trial by fire: "It's hard to do 200 dates a year under an ogre like me. If you can play with Asleep at the Wheel for a year and survive, you're going to be a good player." —Benson

TOURING FACTS

Cost of Beatles tickets: 1965, Shea Stadium: $4.65 (including tax).

Most expensive ticket: Miley Cyrus as Hannah Montana with the Jonas Brothers, Atlantic City, 2008: $3,080.

For a song: The Eagles perform their classic "Hotel California" at a private party in New York, 2003, for a fee of $6 million.

Highest-grossing tour: The Rolling Stones, Bigger Bang tour, 2005–7: $558 million.

Backstage demands: LL Cool J, 24 long-stem roses and baby oil; Cher, separate room for her wigs; Madonna, brand-new toilet seats; Van Halen, no brown M&Ms.

Outrageous road antics: 1967, Flint, MI: The Who's drummer, Keith Moon, trashes his Holiday Inn hotel room, strips to his underwear, drives a Lincoln Continental into the hotel swimming pool, and then slips and knocks out his front teeth.

———————

Chapter 24

How to Make Erotica That Turns Women On

•••••••••••••••••••••••••••••••

Candida Royalle

Former adult film actress and founder of the pioneering
female-centric erotic film production company
Femme Productions

"I hated the crude way sex scenes were portrayed. They'd shove cameras way up between your legs," said Candida Royalle, an erotic star during the so-called golden age of porn in the 1970s. Originally drawn to adult films to finance her bohemian San Franciscan lifestyle, Royalle made a name for herself starring in over thirty films, such as *Hot and Saucy Pizza Girls* and *Blue Magic*. But after five years of cavorting for the cameras, she had become disenchanted. Royalle felt there was nothing wrong with consenting adults performing in erotic films, but as a committed feminist, she objected to the fact that women had no voice in those films. They were presented as sex objects to serve male fantasies, but their own needs and desires were not being met. What would erotic films be like, she wondered, if they were made from a woman's perspective? And so, in 1984, Femme Productions was born. Royalle recalls, "None of the major adult film companies took me seriously. They told me, " 'Nice idea, Candida, but women aren't into this sort of thing.' " Royalle proved them wrong by taking advantage of the boom in video and cable and her own porno popularity to become a trailblazer in the field of women's erotica, ushering in a new era of adult filmmaking by women, for women, in which films focus more on explicit sensuality than hard-core sex. "I like to show how we make one another feel good," says Royalle. "You could say we inform people while entertaining them."

> **Takeaway:** *"Our intimate anatomy isn't dirty. It isn't ugly. Women may not be hardwired for hard-core, but I celebrate our true sexuality by including both soft-core and erotically shot explicit sex."*

1. Lose the formula. Traditional porn is really gymnastic. No foreplay, no buildup, no tenderness—it's just brutally direct: We're going to have sex! Male-oriented adult filmmaking is porn by numbers, a menu of certain sex acts, positions, camera angles, ending on the money shot. Women viewers want more than a handful of crude positions. What about the more subtle aspects of lovemaking? Women like to see the seduction. I give my actors a loose idea of how I want an erotic scene to go and let them improvise, so the sex plays out naturalistically, the way a real erotic encounter might unfold. And I constantly remind them: "Please, no over-the-top moaning and groaning for effect. Don't *act* like porn stars."

2. Go heavy on plot. Just look at the popularity of romance novels—heavy on plot and characters. Women are varied in their tastes, so you can't really generalize, but most women watching porn still want to know: Who are the people in this scene? Why are they doing what they're doing? I make sure my actors understand they're playing real characters. Women viewers just don't buy it if the pizza guy appears at the door and the girl immediately drops to her knees.

3. Real women don't do (balloon) implants. Women don't relate to typical trashy porn stars—the perfect-bodied bio-nymphets with balloon implants and no pubes, or bimbettes who sound like Minnie Mouse. They're too porn-y! Women get turned on watching actresses with achievable looks. Of course, some of my actresses have a new set of "girls," but I try to cast only women who have a natural and attainable beauty, women with an innate intelligence and something alive behind the eyes. Porn stars with obvious augmentation convey the negative idea that your natural body just isn't good enough to be lovable and desirable.

4. Cast men for sensuality. My male lead can't just be a hot studsman or a walking hard-on. Women want to be seduced. Women want a guy with personality and sensuality. In my auditions, I have the man caress the woman, and I pay close attention to his hands. If the hands are clunky, awkward, he's not going to work in my films. He has to be someone I'd be attracted to.

5. Put your actors at ease. Just because they're in porn doesn't mean actors can drop into intimate scenes on a dime. Men can have a hard time getting it up. And women, if they're a little anxious, will try to rush through positions to get to the end of the scene. As a director, I try to remove the pressure. If things aren't working in an erotic scene, I don't scream at the actors like I saw some directors do. That creates such awful tension and in the end they have to resort to a stunt cock, and that's an awful thing to go through. Instead, I lean in and gently tell the actors to relax, talk them through it, make suggestions move by move. Just like in real life, you can still have fabulous sex even if the cock takes a hiatus. It's your job as director to put your actors at ease. I've been there, so I have a special feel for what they go through.

6. Beauty *is* skin deep. Skin's the ultimate erogenous zone. Much of the appeal of erotica is about seeing all that flesh, so even though economics dictate I shoot on video, we work very, very hard to get creamy, glowing, beautiful skin. The true test is if the skin looks as if it's been shot on film. Even when the sex is hot, racy and nasty, we'll often light our scenes in amber and rose tones, because it creates that warm, inviting skin that's a real turn-on for women.

7. Do dominance right. Dominance is a quintessential fantasy for women, but it's a challenge to shoot it in an erotic way. It can't be brutal or nonconsensual and yet you don't want to water it down or you'll lose the thrill. In *Eyes of Desire* we had real-life couple Missy and Micky G, who did dominance well together. There is no physical pain. It's all up in the head. But, really, it's so hot. If done right, a dominance scene can illustrate desire without a word of dialogue.

8. Edit for arousal. Women are curious to watch intercourse, but in general they don't get as turned on by the sight of unadulterated screwing, what I call the "piston" shots. In the editing process, we intercut alternate visuals of sensuous arousal with the more graphic elements of a sex scene. I'm talking about the sort of images women want to see—close-ups of the actor's fingers entwined in the woman's hair, his hand gripping her arm, her body convulsing with pleasure, her facial expressions during climax. We'll linger on images of caressing, tenderness and foreplay. And, of course, lots of cunnilingus.

9. Hide the hard-on. On DVD your film can be explicit, but for a film to be broadcast on cable (except for the most X-rated networks) you have to shoot alternate versions of sex scenes to eliminate any glimpse of an erection or the full-screen vagina—what's known in the business as "showing pink." With all the pressures of a shoot it's easy (but costly) to forget this. You better be both creative and very organized or you're going to lose entire scenes. In a sex scene, I let my actors go and then throw in an occasional direction like, "This time when you change positions, bend your legs so we don't see your genitals, please!"

10. Go for afterglow. Just like traditional porno filmmakers, a lot of younger women breaking into the women's adult film markets still treat the cum shot, facial, money shot, whatever you want to call it, as if it's the holy grail. I've ended a scene with it a few times, but with humor—such as a guy asking a woman if she wants to see his "money shot" or a woman in a scene spontaneously asking to see it because it turns her on. This was a clear creative decision when we started Femme Productions. But my actor couples often end a sex scene with the satisfied look of afterglow and affectionate "I love you's." Even when I don't ask for it! It's become a sort of trademark of my work, and the feedback from my viewers is they love it. Is it really what women want? I would never assert that. I think women want a lot of different kinds of sex.

CANDIDA ROYALLE FACTS

Job history: Early '70s, San Francisco: Royalle performs in theater, including with members of San Francisco underground theatrical group, the Cockettes. She is also an artist, a writer, a jazz singer, and an artist's model.

Film career: Royalle is insulted when offered her first adult film role, but when her boyfriend accepts an offer, she visits the set and is so impressed by the professionalism of the cast and crew, she makes her debut in *Hard Soap, Hard Soap,* a spoof on TV's *Mary Hartman, Mary Hartman.*

Partial filmography (actress): *Sizzle, Sissy's Hot Summer, Fascination, Blue Magic, Delicious.*

Partial filmography (director): *Stud Hunters, One Size Fits All, Eyes of Desire* and *The Bridal Shower.*

Sex and business: 2009: *Playboy* names Royalle one of America's sexiest CEOs.

Candida writes book: *How to Tell a Naked Man What to Do: Sex Advice from a Woman Who Knows.*

PORNOGRAPHY FACTS

First pairing of erotic images and text: 1527, Rome: *The Sixteen Pleasures*, combining engravings of sexual positions and erotic sonnets, are circulated. All copies are immediately seized by papacy.

First full-length English-language erotic novel: 1748: *Memoirs of a Woman of Pleasure, or Fanny Hill* covers bisexuality, voyeurism, group sex and masochism.

First erotic film: 1896, France: *Le Coucher de la Marie* (Bedtime for the Bride), a seven-minute silent movie of a couple having sex and a female striptease.

Porno chic: 1972: $25,000 of organized crime money funds first hard-core film to hit mainstream, *Deep Throat*; gross revenues, $30–50 million. Other films such as *Behind the Green Door* and *The Devil in Miss Jones* follow.

Internet porn: Web sites, 4.2 million; searches, 68 million/day; Web users who view porn, 42.7 percent; least popular day for viewing online porn, Thanksgiving; state with highest per capita porn subscriptions, Utah.

Porn economics: 2011: Global porn revenue, $97 billion; U.S. porn revenue, $13 billion; top-grossing porn revenue by country, China, South Korea, Japan and the United States.

Adult films: A new porn film is made in the United States every 30 minutes.

Chapter 25

How to Make It as a Rock Band in the Digital Era

OK Go

A twenty-first-century rock band with a new paradigm
for success

It used to be that bands signed with a major label, cut a record, went on tour, made music videos and promoted the hell out of themselves to sell records—this was the prevailing narrative of the successful late twentieth-century rock band. OK Go, a power pop band that formed in Chicago in 1999, was on track to do exactly that. They signed with EMI/Capitol Records, put out a couple of albums and toured the world maniacally. But the collapse of record sales at the start of the new millennium made the hard-to-attain rock band dream even more elusive. After years of frustration with their label and the music industry, OK Go, which includes front man Damian Kulash, Tim Nordwind, Dan Konopka and Andy Ross, began to question the existing paradigm of music industry success. And in 2006, at a time when most people were still asking, "What's a YouTube?" the upload of a homemade video of the band's hilariously choreographed dance on treadmills, "Here It Goes Again," aka the *treadmill video*, became a sensation on YouTube with millions of hits within its first week. It went on to become the world's first intentionally viral video. OK Go forged ahead to create a hugely popular series of elaborate and antic music videos and myriad collaborative art projects. And, finally, in 2010, after a sharp public disagreement with their label (who shut off the embed feature on the band's videos, causing page views to drop 90 percent), the band took the ultimate step and cut all ties with their record company. They formed Paracadute, their own label, to control all their projects, promotion and distribution. Front man Kulash, interviewed for this chapter, is a tireless proselytizer for how a band can remain vital both creatively and financially in the digital era—by breaking rules and pushing boundaries.

> **Takeaway:** *"The old system doesn't work. We have a new business model. Now, everything we do is up to us."*

1. Quit your day job. I left college thinking, "I want to spend my life making music. But, come on, what's the likelihood of that?" When we started OK Go, I was working two jobs I really liked. But after a while, there was no way I could devote enough time and energy to the band to make it work. It was the first time in my life when I had to deliberately close a door. I was actually going to have to choose paths: either it's the day job or the rock band. You can't do both.

2. Ignore the false line between promotion and art. Some bands think their music is pure and the rest of the chores of being in a band are dirty work. But since I spent most of my youth making visual art I think elevating one type of creativity over another is crazy. You can call making videos, posters and other visuals crass commercial promotion, but all of our creative ideas are connected and promote each other. When we first started playing shows, we'd spend more money making our posters than we were paid to play. We'd go out at night and wheat-paste these incredible four-color silk-screen prints we'd made all over the city. After a year or two, because of our graphics, everyone in town knew our name. We see no line between the music and the work that supports it.

3. Swing for the fences. For the first ten years of our existence, we said yes to every opportunity. Our first offer to appear on TV was a local access show, *Chic-A-Go-Go*. Because of their limited setup, they couldn't record live sound, so we'd have to lip-synch. We didn't want to say no, but we realized if we were going to do it, we had to really *do* it. We thought: Is there an art to lip-synching? Can we do it without irony? We rented the only 'N Sync video we could find and we came up with this silly, joyful, over-the-top dance. I was still working part-time at NPR, so we asked the hosts of the local shows, including Ira Glass and Peter Sagal, to be our backup band and pretend to play instruments. It was an absurd, surreal spectacle. The fourteen people that showed up that day were pretty blown away or, at least, very confused. That's the spirit that has kept us going all these years. Instead of making our "This Too Shall Pass" video that included an intricate 7,000-square-foot Rube Goldberg machine in the couple of days normally allotted to videos, we took six months. Our video with dance troupe Pilobolus might have taken even longer. If we're going to make something, we're going all the way.

4. Question authority. By our second album release, we were very frustrated. It was clear our label wasn't behind us anymore. We decided to try some things on our own. We heard that the brilliant filmmaker Michel Gondry had an idea to make a dance video. To prove we were the rock band he was looking for, we made a little DIY video in the backyard of us doing our new routine that we'd created with my sister Trish, a choreographer. But I don't think it ever even got to him. We thought the video was great, so we brought it to the head of the new digital media department at our label. He said, "It's too geeky, too nerdy; you look like gaywads dancing in the backyard. If this gets out, you're sunk." He was right about the geeky, nerdy gaywads part, but wasn't that its charm? We sent it to our friends anyway, and they started sending it to their friends. Then someone posted it on iFilm (a precursor to YouTube) and we started burning

it to DVDs to give out at our shows. When we noticed the video had
been downloaded over 200,000 times, we were shocked. That was
more than all the records we'd sold combined. We realized, "Something's happening here—this video's as big as we are." Had we listened to our label, none of it would have ever happened.

5. Never mind the metrics. Before Napster and LimeWire,
when recordings were tradable commodities, the economics of the
music industry were straightforward. Recordings were what made
money—concerts, videos and posters were all in the service of selling them. Sales and radio charts were the fickle gods that bands
prayed to. But now that the public's stopped buying recordings in
the same volume, the big machine no longer works. The industry's
yardsticks don't either. Whether or not people care about your art
is no longer directly connected to a specific revenue stream. The
treadmill video has made us almost no money directly, but there's
no question people like it, so it's been fantastic for our career. Simply existing as a band more than five years later is a testament to
that. Our ticket sales and licensing fees have gone up. Our videos
point to our songs, which point to our concerts, which point back
to our videos, and so on. As long as there is an audience out there
interested in our art, we can ignore the old metrics.

6. Don't stereotype yourself. Rock bands sometimes envi-
sion themselves as a bunch of guys standing on stage looking cool.
But that doesn't work for us. Early on, we got a slot at the Reading
Festival. Ten thousand people were going to be at our show, and I
thought, "This is big. We're going to tell our kids about this." But we
were one of 300 bands playing, so how would these people even
remember us? I thought about the ridiculous dance we'd done on
that TV show, and felt like, "It's not very dignified for a rock band
to be doing a ridiculous dance at one of the world's coolest festivals,
but, on the other hand, why not do the most fun thing we can do for
our audience?" So we rehearsed in a field by the stage with the
people staring down at us from a Ferris wheel probably thinking,

"What the fuck is wrong with those dudes?" At the end of our set, we broke into the routine, and the place went crazy. Bananas. And that's how we ended all our shows for the next year or so. The point is, don't stop trying things because they don't fit your own stereotype of yourself. If it feels like fun, it *is* yourself.

7. Listen to your fans. You may have an idea of who you want your fan base to be—throngs in an arena, the hippest kids at school—but they may not be the ones you end up with. When the backyard dance video took off, we realized our hardest-core fans were actually the weirdest, nerdiest ones sitting in their offices and bedrooms, trading videos. It might not have been what we expected, but if that's where the connection was, why not build on it? Let's reach out and give them another gift. We called my sister Trish again and came up with the idea of a dance routine on treadmills. This time we knew better than to ask our label's permission, so we uploaded the video directly to YouTube, which was still very new. The first day, it got 700,000 views. We were like, "There must be a decimal misplaced?!" By the end of the first week, it was up to 2 million. Our manager took it to VH1 and they went nuts. Then, MTV got on it. Next thing you know, we're performing it live on the Video Music Awards and winning a Grammy. Suddenly, we were the poster boys of the Internet and our label kicked in with all of their big-league promotion, but we knew it was our hard-core fans that had started it. It was a fan base we hadn't even known we'd had that changed everything.

8. Cut out the middleman. We used to rely on our label to bankroll us. We used to spend 10 hours a day screaming at them to get what we needed. To make a comparable living since we've left the label, we've had to create a new business model and make our money directly from our fans or through licensing and corporate sponsors. If we want to create a video, we raise the money ourselves. To finance projects, we partner directly with corporate sponsors— State Farm, Samsung, Range Rover, Google Chrome, Chrysler—in such a way that everyone gets what they want; we get to make our art, our fans get to enjoy our work and our corporate Medicis get millions of ears and eyeballs.

9. Control the creativity. Creative control is the ultimate goal. So, in any corporate deal we make to finance a project, it can be a complicated process to figure out exactly where to draw the line. When a sponsor says, "We want you to make a video where you'll be holding this product," we say, "Well, that's not a video—that's a commercial." We negotiate from a very strong position. If they want us to make the stuff that our fans like, they have to let us be in charge.

10. Embrace radical change. It's a challenge to keep falling into places where there's no obvious answer, no *one* way. We do projects with all kinds of artists—dance troupes, marching bands, tech gurus, even rescue dogs. We partnered with Range Rover, using their GPS technology to create an interactive five-hour street parade through downtown LA, and with Google we created a font out of our own bodies for people to send personalized messages online. With the film, music and digital media industries in such flux, the rules are always changing. The money terms are always changing. An idea that seems like a work of art today might seem terrible tomorrow, and vice versa. Not knowing what's around the corner actually helps us to keep chasing our creative ideas. And that's Valhalla. That's the life we all dream about.

OK GO FACTS

Kulash's first record: 1991, Washington, DC: At 15, Kulash gets $2,000 loan from idol, punk rocker Ian MacKaye. Kulash puts out a CD and pays back loan in three weeks.

Kulash's senior project at Brown University: An album of experimental Elvis covers.

Band name: Lifted from art teacher's directive—"Okay, go!"—repeated throughout drawing classes at a summer camp where two band members met as 11-year-olds.

What's a YouTube? When first contacted by a "guy named Chad, starting a thing called YouTube," the band ignored him because no one knew what YouTube was.

Number of OK Go YouTube video views: Over 200 million streams and counting.

Soccer connection: OK Go pens fight song for Major League Soccer team Chicago Fire in 2007.

Videos: 2009, *End Love*: Band appears in a 48-hour time-lapse video in Echo Park in LA. 2010, *Last Leaf*: 2,430 pieces of toast were lasered for the "flip-book style" animation. 2010, *This Too Shall Pass*: Giant Rube Goldberg machine was constructed. 2012, *Needing/Getting*: Chevy Sonic is outfitted with metal appendages on the outside of car to play musical instruments set up along driving course, including a fishing pole attached to driver-side door that strums 288 Gretsch electric guitars plugged into 67 amps for "auto guitar solo."

RECORD INDUSTRY FACTS

First sound recording: 1860, Paris: "Au Clair de la Lune," on a phonautograph.

First jukebox: 1890: Coin Actuated Attachment for Phonograph. Listener turns a crank and listens to music through a tube.

Sheet music sales: 1892: "After the Ball" by Charles K. Harris sells 2 million copies.

Music industry crash of the past: 1921–33: U.S. record sales plummet from $105.6 million to $5.5 million.

Bestselling single: Recorded 1942: "White Christmas," written by Irving Berlin, performed by Bing Crosby, with over 50 million copies sold.

First MTV music video: 1981: "Video Killed the Radio Star," by the Buggles.

Most Billboard Top 10 singles: Madonna, 37; Elvis Presley, 36; the Beatles, 29.

Most weeks with a Billboard Number One single: Elvis Presley, 80 weeks.

Most simultaneous Billboard Top 100 singles: The Beatles, 14.

Top 5 selling artists: The Beatles, Elvis, Michael Jackson, Abba, Madonna.

Biggest record deal in history: 2010: $200–250 million, paid by Sony Music to Estate of Michael Jackson for rights to distribute the late singer's music until 2017.

Chapter 26

How to Negotiate a Hostage Crisis

● ●

Gary Noesner

Former chief of FBI Crisis Negotiation Unit involved in
prison riots, right-wing militia standoffs, plane hijackings
and over 300 hostage incidents and overseas kidnappings

Gary Noesner has spent much of his adult life calmly interacting
with armed militias, murderous cult leaders, cold-blooded killers
and terrorists. At 12, when Noesner saw J. Edgar Hoover in a cameo
appearance on the *Mickey Mouse Club* TV show, he dreamed of joining the FBI. In 1976, 14 years later, he became an FBI agent. Noesner,
who had always been the peacemaker between friends, eagerly signed
up when the FBI established a hostage negotiation training program.
He had the necessary skills of empathy and self-control to communicate coolly with volatile armed men threatening the lives of their hostages. Besides being able to handle perpetrators, his own team and the
media, Noesner was also skilled at "managing up," influencing the
take-out-the-bad-guy tactical teams he partnered with, who at times
regarded the negotiators as "easily manipulated" or "too soft on crim-
inals." First as hostage negotiator and eventually as chief of the Crisis
Negotiation Unit and trainer, in his 30-year career Noesner has responded to incidents or provided training in all 50 states and over 40
countries, including some of the most infamous crimes of recent decades: the hijackings of the *Achille Lauro*, TWA Flight 847 and Pan
Am Flight 103; the standoffs of the Montana Freemen and the Branch

Davidians in Waco, Texas; and the DC Sniper rampage. "It's impossible to calculate the thousands of lives around the world that negotiators have saved," says Noesner. "It is a great source of pride."

> **Takeaway:** *"Find out a hostage taker's emotional needs. Use that knowledge to gain trust and defuse his emotions and you can save the lives of hostages, police and the perpetrator."*

1. Contain and isolate. When you arrive on the scene of a hostage taking, you have to isolate the perpetrator. Control everything he sees or hears. You don't want his brother to call him and say, "Hey, it's crazy out there; those guys want to kill you!" or have him talk to the news media to shop for a better deal. We begin by isolating the phone lines. The hostage taker's only link to the outside world should be with the negotiator. David Koresh's phones at Waco were unsecured at first. He was able to have a farewell conversation with his mother, a sort of last will and testament. If his phones had been isolated from the start we could have used his desire to talk to his mother as bait, saying, "If you come out, we're going to give you a chance to sit down with your mother."

2. Gather intel. Immediately, at the crisis scene you want to find out, who is this guy? Why is he *really* doing what he's doing? Did he lose his job? Get divorced? You're trying to get a sense of his motivation. It may be imprecise, but we go on what we have. You'll probably be interacting with someone who is out of control, angry, frustrated and dealing with the loss of a relationship, job or self-esteem. To know how to proceed, you need to find out as much as you can about what sparked the explosion.

3. Gain trust. When you open a dialogue with a hostage taker you want to defuse the emotion and deescalate the situation. Perpetrators expect the police to be confrontational, so you begin by saying, "We're not here to hurt you. We want to help you. We know that something's really got you upset, and I'd really like to hear about it." There was a case in Louisiana where a cop, Chad Louviere, raped a woman in his police car, went down the street and robbed the bank where his wife worked, then shot someone. Lay out those facts to any experienced police officer and they'll put very high odds on additional loss of life. The perpetrator is going to die and somebody else is probably going to die before we get to him. From a command station across the street fellow officers kept asking him to come out. "I just want to talk to somebody," was all he'd say. When I was called for advice, I recommended a skilled negotiator from the nearby New Orleans office, Gloria Newport. When Gloria arrived, she got Chad on the phone and said, "I've heard you want to talk to someone. I'm here to listen." She heard a loud exhale. Then he began to talk. He was an extremely controlling husband, and he could not bear that his wife had a mind of her own. "I'm worried about you. Tell me what happened. Tell me all about it," Gloria said. Her empathy and sincerity calmed him down. Then she validated his emotions by identifying them: "You sound so angry and frustrated—what do you think your wife would say if you just told her how you feel?" She suggested there might be a chance of repairing his marriage. She was offering him hope. As he let out his pent-up emotions, his rage began to subside. Slowly, by gaining his trust, Gloria was able to convince Chad to surrender.

4. Don't give up something for nothing. If a guy holding hostages wants something, don't give him anything without getting something in return—preferably a hostage. We're going to make him work for everything he gets, and through that process slowly convey to him that he's not as empowered as he thinks. Many years ago a man trying to hijack a plane to Cuba demanded a hot cup of coffee with cream and two sugars. The negotiator said it wouldn't be easy to get coffee out to the plane, but he would try. Intentionally stalling for time, the negotiators waited hours before delivering the coffee—

very cold, black, with no cream or sugar. After the hostage taker surrendered they asked him why he gave up and he said, "If I couldn't even get a decent cup of coffee, I figured you weren't going to let me fly to Cuba."

5. Help them know what they want. A hostage taker can be so angry and frustrated he doesn't know what he wants. To begin the negotiation process you have to help him articulate his concerns. I once came into a hostage situation at an Ohio prison with a history of overcrowding and violence. Three hundred and eighty inmates from three groups—Black Muslims, a nonreligious black gang and the Aryan Brotherhood—had barricaded themselves inside the prison with eight correctional officers as hostages. It's hard enough to negotiate with one person, but we had three factions holding hostages in different areas of the prison who weren't even speaking with each other. We had to help them get organized to figure out what they wanted. To provide structure, we asked each faction to list its concerns and pick a representative. We suggested a meeting away from the greater prison population so the inmate representatives wouldn't feel the need to posture. These sorts of negotiations can take a long time; in this case, it was eleven long days before the meeting happened. With FBI, police and prison officials at a table on one side of a perimeter fence and the inmates at a table on the other side of the fence, the talks began. The prisoners drew up a list of 21 demands that included issues on overcrowding and medical care. It was clear the prisoners wanted to end the siege. They included enough qualifiers in their list to give the authorities all the wiggle room they needed to sign the list. The corrections officers were released and the prisoners surrendered.

6. Manage your emotions. The most important trait of a hostage negotiator is self-control. That also means helping others around you keep their cool. Even when lives are on the line, I have to think clearly so I can project a calm control to the perpetrator I'm dealing with. You can't take anything personally when you're dealing with manipulators and liars. If someone is yelling and screaming at me and I overreact to everything he says, how can I expect to be a positive influence? The point is not to get even—but to get what you want. It's not rocket science, but it's amazing how many people in law enforcement can't or won't do it.

7. Rely on your team. People often ask how does TV get what we do wrong. TV focuses on a single man, a hero, a negotiator jousting with a hostage taker, shooting from the hip—bada-bing! But negotiation works best when there is a team. Depending on the size of the event there could be up to six or more negotiators on the scene. The team listens in on the negotiations, which usually take place over the phone. Then we sit down and use our collective experience to ask, "What did you hear? What is *really* important to this person?" Toward the end of my career, sometimes I would be overly relied on. When younger colleagues said, "Tell us what to do, Gary," I'd tell them, "Not only do I want your take; I *need* your take." I needed to either be challenged or validated to make sure I'd thought of all the angles. I was always more confident with my recommendations when my team came up with consensus conclusions. Every now and then, someone would come up with a different perspective and I'd say, "Wow, I didn't think about it that way!"

8. Coordinate tactics and talk. The best approach is when the tactical or SWAT teams work with the negotiation team. A hostage taker who sees a visible show of force realizes the risks of resisting. That helps us as negotiators. But it doesn't always work that way. The negotiator's ethos is to slow down and stall for time, but that's the antithesis of how a SWAT team is trained. They are action oriented. They've trained their whole lives for a specific purpose. Commanders of these operations are often more in tune with the tactical forces. So when a negotiation takes time, sometimes their viewpoint is, "Why should we let this despicable character control the situation? I've trained my guys. They're ready to go. This guy's a problem. Let's go in and get him." But if the negotiation is not allowed to run its course, there can be tragic and needless loss of life of innocent victims as well as law enforcement officers.

9. Don't take unnecessary risks. An ex-convict, Mario Villabona, fired shots from a machine gun onboard an Amtrak train. He was in a train car with his sister and her four-year-old daughter and nine-month-old son. Amtrak officials decoupled his car from the rest of the train. He was in a heavy-gauged steel car with bulletproof windows. Storming it would probably have led to innocent deaths of Villabona's family. Even worse, they believed Mario's sister was already dead. I arrived on the scene with a Spanish-speaking FBI negotiator, Ray Arras. Mario didn't respond to our offer to deliver water. The clock was ticking. We had two children trapped inside a train under the hot sun, in danger of dehydration next to a decaying corpse. After a stalemate of 72 hours, then the longest incident outside of a prison in U.S. history, talking by phone, Ray finally got Mario to respond. Slowly he developed a rapport, but when Mario said, "The baby is dead," Ray was devastated. He fell to his knees and prayed. Then he stood up and said to Mario, "Will you meet me at the window and give me Julie?" Ray approached the car hiding a pistol under a blanket. I scrambled to follow to give him what meager backup I could. The window opened. Mario reached out to shake Ray's hand. Fortunately, Ray had the pistol in his left hand, so Mario did not see it. Then Mario handed over Julie, the four-year-old. I yelled at Ray afterward, "You stupid son of a bitch, don't ever surprise me like that again!" As concerned as we were about Julie, what Ray and I did was wrong. An agent walking up to an open window where a guy's got a machine gun without advance coordination is unacceptable. Even though he saved the girl, had Ray or I been killed, they'd be talking about the case today.

10. Do what you have to do. There are rare times when a negotiation has run its course. The negotiators are usually the first to know. In 1988, Charlie Leaf was holding his estranged common-law wife Cheryl and young son Charlie Jr. hostage. He had broken into a farmhouse in rural Virginia and was holed up with them in an upstairs bedroom. I had been negotiating outside the bedroom door for 11 hours when I heard Charlie scream, "I have the gun against her head and I am going to pull the fucking trigger." I was out of ideas. The only question was whether we could save the boy before Charlie killed him, too. Just then Cheryl yelled, "Can't you get us out of here?" It broke the stalemate. Charlie demanded a helicopter. I convinced the commander to order one to lure Charlie outside where a sniper could take him out. After the helicopter landed, Charlie left the house, holding Cheryl in front of him and with little Charlie strapped to his back. Agents threw flash-bang diversion grenades, Charlie fell to a knee and a marksman put a bullet through his head. When the medical technicians tried to revive him, Cheryl said, "My God, they're going to bring him back and he's going to do this again." But he was dead. When someone's actions are so desperate he gives you no choice, as a negotiator, you need to do what you have to do for the greater good—which is to save innocent life.

GARY NOESNER FACTS

Beginner's luck: 1976, South Carolina: Weeks after Noesner becomes FBI agent, he tracks down fugitive wanted for murder who is holed up in an apartment. When Noesner enters, fugitive goes for his gun on nightstand. But when he hears "Freeze" and sees Noesner with a gun pointed at him, the fugitive gives up.

Aromatic warfare: 1991, Alabama: During long siege at federal prison, Noesner suggests frying hamburgers just outside of cell block where hungry prisoners have barricaded themselves and their hostages. That night inmate calls: "We want to talk."

Waco: 1993: Noesner's team is responsible for 35 people surrendering in the first 26 days, but after another 26 days and numerous strategic disputes between negotiators and on-site FBI commander, 75 people die at David Koresh's Branch Davidian compound. Noesner remembers it as the "saddest and most painful" day of his career.

Gamble: 1996: On 79th day of Montana Freemen siege, one of the Freemen, who wishes to surrender, asks permission to visit imprisoned leader jailed in Billings. Noesner advocates with commander. Freeman boards FBI plane, meets with jailed leader and with leader's blessing offers to surrender, leading to end of incident.

Book: 2010: *Stalling for Time: My Life as an FBI Hostage Negotiator.*

KIDNAPPING AND HOSTAGE STATS

First: 1874, Philadelphia: Four-year-old Charles Ross is first high-profile American victim of kidnapping for ransom after two men lure him with candy into a carriage. Attempts to deliver $20,000 ransom fail. Ross's family searches for him for half a century, interviewing thousands claiming to be Charley, but he is never found.

Dog Day Afternoon: 1972: Inspired by *The Godfather* movie, John Wojtowicz and two accomplices rob Brooklyn bank to pay for his lover's sex change. They hold bank employees hostage. Wojtowicz is arrested, but one of his accomplices is killed by FBI. Events inspire movie *Dog Day Afternoon*, starring Al Pacino. Wojtowicz receives 1 percent of movie's net profits, which helps finance lover's sex change.

Family disloyalty: 1973, Rome: John Paul Getty III, grandson of oil tycoon John Paul Getty Sr., is kidnapped. Getty Sr. refuses to pay $17 million ransom. After Getty III's ear is delivered, Getty Sr. negotiates a ransom of $2.9 million. Getty III is released and eventually has his ear rebuilt. Nine kidnappers are apprehended.

Highest ransom: 1974, Argentina: 20 members of guerilla group, Montoneros, dress as policemen and kidnap Juan and Jorge Born, scions of multinational business family. Ransom of $60 million and $1.2 million of food and clothing for poor is paid. Brothers are released.

Top 10 kidnapping countries: 2000 to 2009: Colombia, Mexico, Venezuela, Brazil, India, Pakistan, Nigeria, Iraq, Philippines, Argentina.

Chapter 27

How to Open a Great Restaurant (and Stay in Business)

· ·

David Chang

Award-winning chef/owner of Momofuku restaurants in
New York City, Sydney and Toronto

O f all David Chang's struggles his most enduring is with himself.
Working in the high-performance kitchens of New York City's
best fine-dining restaurants, he believed he didn't have what it took
to be a top chef. At 24, he went to Japan on a quest to learn how to
make the perfect bowl of noodles, apprenticing himself in ramen
and soba shops. Back in New York, with a loan from his father, he
opened a low-budget, stripped-down restaurant, Momofuku Noodle
Bar, in a space no bigger than a one-car garage in Manhattan's East
Village. He was deep in debt and had few customers. With his explosive temper and obsessive perfectionism he tortured his employees—
and himself. It was only when he began to apply culinary mash-ups
of extreme flavor combinations and Asian-influenced American
cuisine to his deceptively simple street-food style that Momofuku
gathered a following, first with cadres of after-work chefs, then with
critics and customers. As the restaurant's popularity grew, Chang
became the sort of chef he thought he would never be—the non-

cooking kind. Despite his stubbornly tumultuous approach, within six years, he opened one successful New York City restaurant after another, Momofuku Ssäm Bar, Má Pêche and Ko, which was awarded two Michelin stars in 2009. Multiple Momofuku Milk Bar bakeries, Booker and Dax (a bar), and restaurants in Australia and Toronto followed shortly afterward. Success may have calmed the perpetually dissatisfied Chang—who assumed he would be dead by the age of 35—but only slightly. "In the beginning, our goal was to be better than the Japanese place across the street," says Chang. "Now, there's no fucking excuses, regardless of the location; we're going to try to be the best restaurant in the world."

> **Takeaway:** *"We constantly search for that beautiful ideal, that amazing dish. It's so elusive, it's something you're never going to reach, which is what makes it really hard— but at the same time very rewarding."*

1. Be a kitchen ninja. I was lucky to get a job at Café Boulud with the great chef Andrew Carmellini. The cooks were badass— like Navy Seals. They out-cooked you with their sheer will, technique and insane work ethic. The pressure was unbelievable. It was the hardest job I've ever had, and I had my ass handed to me every night. But I learned about integrity. Now, I tell my cooks, "We may not be the best cooks or the best restaurant, but it doesn't mean we're not going to have the highest standards. Are you willing to sacrifice yourselves for the food? You're a cook—this is what cooks do! If you don't care about the little things—properly cutting scallions or sharpening knives—we're headed toward the middle, and that's not a place I want to be."

2. Find your voice. While working at Café Boulud I knew in my heart of hearts I would never be a great chef like Alex Lee of Daniel. I also knew that if I looked to my left or right I wasn't going to be as good as the people around me. I'd always been obsessed with noodles. The year before, I had even taken a trip to Japan and apprenticed at noodle shops. So, when Alex Lee left Daniel to go work at a country club, I thought, "I'll never be as talented or have the work ethic of that maniac, and even he's calling it quits?" I thought, "Fuck it. I'm 26. Why can't I do something with cooking that I love?" That was the moment I knew I had to find my own voice. I thought, "I'm going to try to open up a noodle shop."

3. Don't fail from lack of hard work. My goal with Momofuku was simply to open a restaurant, arguably one of the hardest things in the world to do. I found a tiny former chicken wingery in the East Village. I asked every cook I knew to come in with me. They didn't want to boil noodles or already had cushy jobs at good restaurants. I couldn't even convince people who had nothing to do with the restaurant business. It was a heartbreaking, lonely process until I found someone as pissed off and frustrated as I was, Joaquin Baca. We were young enough and dumb enough to do stupid things. We spent days and nights trying to scrub the stink out of the place. We did all the shopping, prep, cooking, waiting, bussing and washing dishes ourselves. I would have died for Momofuku. And I thought, "I'm going to give it everything I can. Maybe we'll fail, but it's not going to be from lack of hard work."

4. Cook what you want. Even though Quino and I were killing ourselves at Momofuku we weren't making any money. We wondered what the hell we were doing wrong. We decided, "Screw it!" People were trying to categorize us. But even though we called ourselves a Noodle Bar, we didn't want to be labeled *just* a noodle bar. We developed a very defiant attitude. If you do what everybody expects, you're going to have an exhausted, boring menu, so we were going to just do what we wanted. We started making dishes we thought that the public was going to love or hate. Bowls of tripe, shrimp and grits, a corn with miso butter dish, a Korean-inspired burrito. We thought, let's try to bring customers flavor combinations they've never had. That's when we became more than a shitty little noodle bar. In six months we were packed and finally had the money to pay everybody.

5. Forget the frills. One of my dreams was to open up a crappy Chinese hole-in-the-wall restaurant with fluorescent lighting that served really good Chinese food. You don't need to have a fancy-looking restaurant to have good food. We strip our spaces down to the bare minimum. Why do I need fancy napkins? Silver tableware? Flowers on the table? Fancy servers? I only need what's essential for our restaurants to function. Ko has only 12 counter seats, an open kitchen, it's all plywood and we've got two Michelin stars.

6. Keep it (deceptively) simple. Ask people what's the best thing they've ever eaten and it's usually the simple stuff—like a perfect roast chicken. That's the kind of memory I want my food to create. The idea of Noodle Bar was to take the humblest meal—a bowl of noodles, a pork bun—and turn it into something amazingly delicious with obsessive devotion and four-star technique. Or, offer something that seems simple, like our chicken wings, but what you don't realize when you're eating them is they're so delicious because they took two days and over half a dozen steps to make.

7. Be humble. Say you're cooking eggs. You could literally spend a lifetime learning how to cook eggs. Even the great cooks that I've known have become much more humble than when they were young and cocky. So when I ask a new cook, "How do you rate yourself? How are your knife skills?" and he tells me they're awesome, I know he's not going to work out. That person is not going to embrace failure. He's never going to learn. If you've worked in a kitchen and read about chefs, you know there's always so much more to know. Every once in a while a cook will say, "You know what? I'm okay, but I can get better." That's magic. When I hear that, I'm like, "Holy shit! My mind is fucking blown away."

8. Show the love. I get excited when somebody in the kitchen stops what they're doing to help somebody else out, when somebody who screws up gets so mad at themselves that I don't have to yell at them. They've already held themselves accountable. That becomes infectious. That's our utopian ideal. Family meal, when the whole staff sits down to eat together, is the most important meal of the day. I stop in at our various restaurants to eat the family meals and ask, "Who made this?" If it's a beautiful meal with proteins, starch, vegetables, dessert and a drink, the chef who made it is showing love. Love not just for his peers but love for the food. He's doing that on top of the job that he already has. If cooks care about feeding their coworker, their teammate, they're going to care a hell of a lot more about a paying customer.

9. Keep talent. The hardest thing about running a company is keeping talented people. The guys that were with me from the beginning are all gone. It's a bit lonely. I understand why people leave. It's hard to make a name for yourself in someone else's restaurant. Or, they don't feel they get enough money. It's a touchy subject. We're never going to be an investment bank giving out $5 million bonuses. How do we reward somebody who chooses a profession where they're not going to become an instant millionaire? Working with people in a restaurant setting is almost like being in a marriage. It took me a long time to realize that I actually owe something to somebody who's been with me for years. If I want them to care I have to give something back. Like Christina Tosi. We hired her to work in the office. She started making desserts for the restaurants. Then, when she felt like she could do more, we opened a bakery, Milk Bar. Now she has five Milk Bars around the city. She's a perfect example of someone dreaming big. I want my cooks to think that way. It's unwieldy running multiple restaurants with so many personalities and egos, but we have to grow so we can make enough money to take care of everybody.

10. Stay hungry. When we opened up Seiōbo in Sydney, Australia, we won a bunch of awards. Everybody wanted to celebrate. But I don't like to pat myself on the back, because there's always a place around that corner that's going to be better and faster. We have to keep our heads down and work. Who cares about an award or some stupid magazine that says we're so great? The worst cook at Seiōbo was Little Richard—a young apprentice, a neophyte cook. I said, "Listen guys, it's been a good run so far, but we're not going to know if we're a good restaurant until Little Richard has become a good cook. If we can turn him into a great cook, then we're going to rejoice. Then we're going to celebrate."

DAVID CHANG FACTS

Father's advice: Chang's father, a 30-year veteran of the restaurant business, sends son to best schools so he never has to work in restaurant business.

Junior golf champ: 1980s: Chang occasionally competes in tournaments against Tiger Woods, knows he'll never be as good and burns out at 13.

Nonprofit: 2000, New York City: Chang wants job so badly at Craft restaurant, he works answering phones for free. After pleading, he's admitted into kitchen to chop and clean vegetables for no pay, eventually working his way up to cook.

Noodle dream: 2002, Tokyo: Chang apprentices in unsanitary ramen shop for chef who wears only saggy briefs and chain-smokes in kitchen.

Hands off: 2002, Japan: Chang gets job at 12-seat soba house where expert chef teaches Chang noodle making, but won't let him touch anything. Four months later, Chang is let go when chef hands him a rolling pin and says, "I've taught you everything I know."

Momofuku origin: Name means "Lucky Peach" in Japanese and is also first name of Momofuku Ando, inventor of instant ramen.

Indie: 2006–12: To keep his independence, Chang never takes in investors, financing all projects from loans.

Hater: Chang's pet peeves include truffle oil, tongs, wasabi mashed potatoes, figs as garnish.

Advice for neophytes: "If you want to open up a restaurant, throw a dinner party, tell everyone to bring a thousand dollars, and burn the money on the stove." —Chang

RESTAURANT FACTS

"Restaurant" etymology: Sixteenth century: Derivation of *restaurer*, "food that restores," first referred specifically to rich, highly flavored soup.

Rise of modern restaurant: Eighteenth century, France: After French Revolution, jobless former chefs of aristocrats open first restaurants for the public with private tables, reservations, à la carte menus and tablecloths.

Longest run: 1725–present, Madrid: Restaurant Sobrino di Botín, calle Cuchilleros (Knife Makers' Street). Goya washes dishes there; Hemingway writes about it.

First "fast food": Nineteenth century, United States: Restaurants serve coarse, heavy food, including venison, pigeon, raccoon, elk, turtle and oysters, consumed in what was known at the time in slang as "gobble, gulp and go" style.

Supersized: 2002, Damascus, Syria: Restaurant Bawabet Dimashq opens at a cost of $40 million; seats 6,014, with a staff of up to 1,800, and features waterfalls, fountains and replicas of archaeological ruins.

Priciest: 2007, Bangkok, Thailand: Dome Restaurant, 10-course Valentine's Day meal prepared by world-famous chefs from

France, Germany and Italy and paired with rare wines. Dinner for two costs $60,000. Tax and tip not included.

Restauronomics: 2012, United States: 970,000 restaurants, 12.9 million employees, $632 billion in sales; share of food dollar, 48 percent.

Chapter 28

How to Optimize Your Brain

Richard Restak

Neurologist, neuropsychiatrist, and author of 18 books on
the brain, called "one of the world's most important
scientific thinkers" by *Scientific American* magazine

Dr. Richard Restak tells a cautionary tale about a British bus
driver. Reassigned to a double-decker bus from his usual
standard-size vehicle, out of habit the driver takes his usual route
back to the depot. When he unwittingly drives under a low railway
bridge he shears off the top half of the bus. "Activities we repeat on
a regular basis become habits that we tend to perform almost uncon-
sciously," explains Restak. "If you talk to people about improving
their health or getting rich they're all ears, but they don't always
realize how much we can do to enhance our brains." Restak believes
that just as athletes train their bodies with focus and exercise, we
can train our brains. When Restak began his career in the early
1970s, it was unusual to practice both psychiatry and neurology. "If
you had a migraine you went to your neurologist and if you were
bipolar you went to your psychiatrist," said Restak. "It would never
occur to anybody to try to find someone who could treat both symp-
toms." Restak is the ultimate generalist in a brain science community populated by highly specialized researchers, academics and
practitioners. Synthesizing psychology, cutting-edge neuroscience,
the humanities, academic research, and his own observations of his
patients and strangers he comes across in daily life, Restak is fasci-

nated to unravel the interconnection of the disciplines. His 18 books on the brain chronicle the history of man and his relationship to his mind from Socrates and Salvador Dali to tai chi and the most recent revolutionary brain research. His books also offer exercises, parables, tips and personal anecdotes on how we can unleash the brain's full potential. He is optimistic that one day what he knows about the brain will be common knowledge. "I foresee a future," he says, "when children will be taking courses on the brain between classes in American history and math."

Takeaway: *"The more we challenge the brain, the more it improves."*

1. Remember this! On a very basic level, you are what you remember—your very identity depends on all of the events, people and places you can recall. Improving your memory will help you develop a quicker, more accurate retrieval of information that will increase your intelligence. Sharpening your short-term or "working" memory requires concentration. For instance, study four unrelated words for 15 seconds, then set an alarm for five minutes. Pay attention to another activity until the alarm sounds. Then try to remember the words. As you get better, change and add to the number of words and increase the amount of time. You can do similar exercises with numbers, visual designs, spoken words or even try to recount the scenes of a television show you just watched. When you do these exercises your brain will require extra oxygen, blood and glucose. Just as with physical exercise this can tire you out. But with practice it will get easier. Many "tricks" to sharpen your recall use memory pegs, systems to attach an association or meaning to what you desire to remember. There are visual and story memory systems, some dating back to Ancient Rome. One of these systems is called "the memory palace," in which you associate the things you want to remember with vivid mental pictures, which you then imaginatively place in a familiar setting such as your living room. Later, you can "tour" in your mind the living room to observe the remembered objects in their familiar places. This technique can be so effective it is often used by memory contest champions.

2. Feel what you felt. Another aspect of recall is emotional memory, when we relive how we felt at moments in the past—elated, sad, depressed or angry. When we lose emotional memory of our own youth, we find that we no longer understand young people. If this forgetting progresses, we begin to lose touch with ourselves. And if we allow our emotional memories to disappear, as happens with Alzheimer's patients, we will find a stranger staring back at us from the mirror. There are many exercises to reacquaint yourself with your emotional memory. Find a picture of yourself in which you are half of your present age. Stare at the picture for a while. Then write a letter to your older self from the perspective of the younger you in the photo, expressing all of the younger self's hopes and concerns about the future. Follow this with a letter back from the present self to the younger you, telling that younger self about all the things they will do in their future and who they will grow into. Hopefully you will uncover feelings and memories of things you haven't experienced for years. The olfactory nerve links directly to the emotional centers of the limbic system, so the scents of your past—such as mowed grass, crayons or perfumes—can also bring back emotionally charged memories. Think of Proust and his madeleine.

3. Focus the brain. Our technological culture overwhelms us with information, creating short-term, powerful excitement. Television, video games and our multitasking on several devices are actually causing a complete change in our cognitive geography: an inability to focus and an explosion in ADD. In order to think logically, explore things in greater depth and see different possibilities, we need the ability to concentrate. There are many exercises to sharpen concentration. One is a very simple Hindu exercise. Take a flower. And look at it. Then, close your eyes and try to imagine the flower. When you think you see it as clearly as you can in your mind, open your eyes and look at the flower again. You might be surprised how much you've missed. Keep doing it until you have it etched in your mind. I can perform a similar focusing exercise sitting right here, just by looking at the objects on my rather cluttered desk. Then I close my eyes and try to re-create those objects in my mind, seeing which ones I can remember. I might miss an awful lot. But if you keep practicing you can get to the point where you're not missing anything. That's enhancing visual stimuli, and you can do the same with auditory stimuli, or touch. Thinking of one thing at a time is a very unified way of being in terms of your identity, as opposed to scattered thinking in which your identity is scattered as well.

4. Brain, meet the hand. As man evolved into an upright species and began to use his hands to manipulate objects, his brain had to change. Now, a very large proportion of the sensory and motor cortices are dedicated to the hands. Brain performance and hand dexterity have become intimately coupled. But today, with mass production, most jobs no longer require fine motor control of the hands. If you allow your hands to become redundant a large part of your brain will experience a form of disuse atrophy. The good news is that anyone can take up a skill that involves sustained fine finger control. And whatever that skill may be—carpentry, knitting, drawing, painting, playing a musical instrument or bike repair—practicing even just a little each week will enhance your brain's performance. You'll develop new circuits in your brain and those areas will communicate with even more brain areas. Think of manual and mental skills as a continuum.

5. Brain, meet the body. If you feel at your best in the morning and lose energy at night, you are a "lark." If you're best at night but tired in the morning, you're an "owl." The timing of our energy levels is based on these lark or owl cycles. According to psychologist Robert Thayer there are four basic moods. CALM-ENERGY is an almost ideal state in which we feel aroused and energetic. CALM-TIREDNESS is a state in which we feel calm and relaxed after accomplishing a goal, a physical workout or a good meal. TENSE-ENERGY is a wired, exhilarating, adrenaline-fueled feeling that can be pleasant and edgy at the same time. And TENSE-TIREDNESS is a stressed-out, irritable mood. Knowing if you are a lark or an owl will help you schedule your day to take advantage of your natural cycles. Try to synchronize your work to your energy levels. Take on the tasks that require the most brainpower when you are experiencing calm-energy or tense-energy. Routine tasks can be handled during the early stages of calm-tiredness. Once you are aware of these cycles you can regulate them to a certain extent. Nothing much will be accomplished during periods of tense-tiredness, but a nap, if possible, can move you to calm-tiredness or even calm-energy. A brisk walk can convert you from calm-tiredness to calm-energy. When you maximize your energy levels, you'll find you can take on bigger life challenges.

6. Think outside the box. The brain is connected to itself at every level, and each neuron can potentially connect with every other neuron. When we learn, new information is stored in associative links in this network, and this expands the brain circuitry by creating even more linkages. Any piece of information we learn can potentially connect with any other. In fact there is no knowledge until these connections are made. So enhancing intelligence requires us to create many neuronal connections. But to do this we have to break out of the confining idea that knowledge can be broken into specific "disciplines." If you think outside the box, playfully altering your perceptions, and try to look beyond the obvious, you will improve your imagination, thinking, and other cognitive processes by creating new linkages and new networks. Being open to and experiencing art or music can help us with this. Keep a journal in which you jot down your random thoughts and associations. Or speak them into a tape recorder. Every day take some time to interpret images, objects or events in the world according to your own personal and sometimes even seemingly irrational associations.

7. Observe the brain. Every event we experience is accompanied by what psychiatrists call an "emotional valance," a positive or a negative reaction based on that event, which occurs in the brain's limbic system. Usually this valence is weak and doesn't affect our actions. But in extreme cases, such as when we become very angry at someone, our limbic system can override the rational alternatives suggested in our prefrontal lobes, and we do or say something that we will later regret. Our emotions have interfered with our performance. Even though it is hard to detect, we can train ourselves to observe our emotional valence changes as they are happening. As you get better you develop what is known as the "observing ego." Eventually you will recognize the first stirrings of emotion and be able to not only recognize your emotions but to use them as personal inquiry, asking yourself, "Why am I responding with such anger to this situation?" And then you can begin to determine if there are actions you can take to clear up situations. Your ability to observe your emotions objectively puts you at a tremendous advantage in emotionally charged situations.

8. Relax the brain. Stress can cause brain damage, resulting in a loss of cells and the shrinking of the hippocampus. This can lead to memory disorders. Not surprisingly, stress can be particularly acute in situations that we feel we have little control over—causing a powerful sense of futility and helplessness. But the solution is to change the things that we *do* have control over—our breathing and attitude. We breathe shallower and faster when feeling stress. This rapid breathing tricks the brain into responding as if an emergency exists, triggering the fight-or-flight response, which provokes the person into breathing even faster and so on. The first step is to slow down your breath and breathe not so much with your chest but with the lower part of the abdomen expanding with each inhalation. It's the way a baby breathes—the natural method of breathing. And that in itself is relaxing and can break the cycle of your stressful thoughts. And as far as your attitude, when you're under stress, pay careful attention to your thinking. Try to slow down frantic thoughts. Put everything into perspective. Remind yourself of your goals. Think positively and remind yourself that no matter how you perform, the world will not end.

9. Let the brain be the brain. Most of the brain's operations do not require consciousness. Trying to control everything that happens in your brain can actually be an impediment. When you try to control thoughts by suppressing them, you create a painful mental duality. The thought, "I want to suppress that thought," exists at the same time as the thought itself that we are trying to suppress. It's not the thought that creates the problem, but the attempt at suppressing the thought. The way out of this is to allow the thoughts to occur freely: Don't fight them; observe them and even embrace them. When we trust our brain, we sometimes find that our thoughts and feelings will lead us to explore some aspect of our lives that might yield a sudden insight from outside of conscious awareness. Don't hurry the process. Remain confident that your brain will provide you with answers you may not even know you are seeking.

10. Remember the future. Humans are the only creatures capable of projecting themselves into the future. We not only have visions of our future, but the capability to remember those visions, set them as goals and pursue them. This effort of following through on a goal is spurred on by "remembering" a vision of an earlier self, and of course, it can take many years and require overcoming many obstacles. Much of this mental activity of planning, choice, volition and memory takes place in the frontal and prefrontal cortex. PET scan studies have shown that thinking about something brings changes in the brain's patterning, and that in the case of musicians or athletes, imagining themselves going through the motions improves their performance. What happens during this rehearsal or training is that the prefrontal cortex draws up a plan of action and the motor cortex practices it. It then takes several hours for your brain to remember it. Lewis Carroll captured the essence of this when he wrote, "It's a poor sort of memory that only works backwards."

RICHARD RESTAK FACTS

Speed-reader: Growing up, Restak is inspired to write by his mother, who reads a book every day.

Near miss: Age 15: Restak and his mother have tickets to meet one of his heroes, William Faulkner, at the Princeton Club, but miss out because of a blizzard.

Writing routine: Before seeing patients, Restak gets up early in the morning and writes 500–1,000 words, putting in the back of his mind what he will write about tomorrow. He quotes author E. L. Doctorow: "Writing is like driving a car at night. You only see as far as your headlights go, but you can make the whole trip that way."

Epiphany: Because of his interest in behavior, Restak studies psychiatry in school; but when a bipolar person who has been frequently institutionalized talks to students about how he hasn't been back to the hospital in a decade after lithium treatments, Restak is inspired to study neuroscience as well.

Restak's books: *Mozart's Brain and the Fighter Pilot, The Secret Life of the Brain, Mysteries of the Mind, The Self Seekers, The Infant Mind, BrainScapes, Poe's Heart and the Mountain Climber, Receptors, The Longevity Strategy, The Naked Brain, The Modular Brain, The Brain Has a Mind of Its Own.*

BRAIN STATS

Early neuroscience: Some medical historians believe brain surgery is earliest operation ever performed, dating back to Stone Age. Tibetan Tripitaka, a 2,900-year-old collection of Buddhist texts passed down orally, describes a successful craniotomy on a man with headaches so severe that he bangs his head on hard objects.

A billion billions: The brain has 100 billion neurons; each neuron is connected to about 10,000 others, for a total 1 million billion connections.

Brain weight: Average adult, about 3 lbs.; Albert Einstein, 2.71 lbs.

Blood flow: 750–1,000 ml of blood (about three cans of soda) flow through the brain every minute.

Stream of consciousness: It is estimated that a human brain has 70,000 thoughts in a day.

Energy hog: Although the human brain represents only 2 percent of the body weight of an average person, it receives 15 percent of the cardiac output, 20 percent of total body oxygen consumption, 25 percent of total body glucose utilization, and consumes more energy than any other organ.

Synapses: If you counted one synapse every second, it would take 32 million years to count every synapse in the brain.

Yawns: It is thought that a yawn sends more oxygen to the brain, therefore working to cool it down and wake it up.

Short-circuited: Since the left hemisphere specializes in language, calculation and logic, and the right hemisphere specializes in spatial abilities, music, visual imagery and synthesis, when asked to perform two competing tasks that use the same areas of the brain—such as being interrupted by someone talking when you're on the phone—most people experience cognitive dissonance.

Chapter 29

How to Produce a Smash Hit on Broadway

• •

Marc Routh

Tony Award–winning Broadway producer of many hit
shows, including *The Producers* and *Hairspray*

As a child actor in Ohio, Marc Routh played all the charming little
boy roles in summer stock and dinner theater. "When I was 16
and cast as a 10-year-old in *Bye Bye Birdie*, trying to sing the harmo-
nies with my voice changing all over the place, it hit me that rather
than be on stage, I actually wanted to be behind the scenes," says
Routh. After majoring in dramatic arts in college, Routh went to New
York City and worked as an off-Broadway press agent. A year later, in
1985, he joined the Richard Frankel production company, one of the
biggest producers on Broadway. Routh's track record has been phe-
nomenal, producing a series of Broadway hits including *The Producers*, *Hairspray*, *Little Shop of Horrors*, *Smokey Joe's Cafe* and *Sweeney
Todd*, that have been produced in over 40 countries. Routh measures
a show's success by four criteria—audience reaction, how the show
fares financially, critical acclaim and his own role in the production.
"With every show I'm involved in I ask, 'Did I have artistic input that
led to something great on stage? Did I find a unique way to market or
position the show?'" says Routh. "When the four key elements come
together, for me, that's a hit."

Takeaway: *"Producing on Broadway really is like they say in* The Producers: *'We got the wrong play, the wrong director, the wrong cast. Where did we go right?'"*

1. Fall in love. You have a long road ahead of you when you produce a show. If it's successful, you'll see it hundreds of times in previews, premieres, cast replacements on Broadway, then all the permutations of its national and international tours. If it's hugely successful, one day you may even have to see a high school production of it—either the ultimate achievement or disappointment—so you'd better love watching that show or be prepared to wear a poker face through all its phases.

2. Be tenacious. Shows take so long to develop, as long as eight years or more, so we always have at least a dozen projects in the pipeline. We search everywhere for books that can be developed into plays, online properties. We brainstorm about revivals and how movies can be adapted for Broadway. We scout regional theater for productions, and if someone calls me and says there's a show playing in Madrid, Moscow or Shanghai that I should know about, I jump on a plane and go see it. We just keep developing, because you never know what's going to be a hit.

3. Be a team player. Recently, when *The Norman Conquests* won a Tony, I was embarrassed to get up on stage amid such a gaggle of producers. But it's a sign of the times. Putting on a show has become wildly expensive, so these days you've got to be willing to partner with even *more* investors than before. For *Hairspray*, 230 investors put up at least $10,000 each. It's like a pyramid scheme— you find a few people to invest and they find a few more people to invest and so on and so on. But investors who have contributed, say, upwards of a million dollars may consider themselves producers. And, though the best decisions aren't made by committee, we have to solicit their opinions and invite them to meetings. Somehow the design of the show's logo always generates a lot of debate—suddenly everyone on the team has an opinion. Because they're the only graphics everyone agreed upon, some logos are just the stupidest things I've ever seen.

4. Plays don't pay the bills. There's a saying on Broadway that musicals are a business and plays are a hobby. We produced *Marvin's Room*, a wonderful play about a woman dying of leukemia that became a movie, but it was too personal to be a successful commercial show. It was a noble effort, but it wasn't a Saturday night out and never made money back for the investors. Whereas, if you take a show like *Hairspray*, it's the perfect balance—a lively personal tale with universal appeal.

5. If it ain't broke . . . American musical comedy continues in the tradition of vaudeville, a formula that engages and satisfies the audience. The hero/heroine follows an arc. He or she voices a specific desire at the beginning of the show, what we call the "I want" song. There's a romantic ballad that establishes the hero or heroine's love interest, and a "charm song," usually from a secondary character, that provides comic relief or contrast to the desires of the main character. Then, the hero or heroine must face obstacles, triumph over the odds and go through a transformation that comes near the end. It's revealed in what's called the "11 o'clock number." Shortly thereafter, everything turns out all right.

6. Don't always wish upon a star. Celebrity sells Broadway tickets, but what happens when the star leaves? We sold *A Little Night Music* on Catherine Zeta-Jones, but when she left, we couldn't recast. We made the announcement that we were going to close, but at the 11th hour, Elaine Stritch and Bernadette Peters told Steve Sondheim they wanted to do the show together. We closed for three weeks to rehearse the new leads, resumed ticket sales and the show continued selling profitably. In a less happy scenario, after Hugh Jackman left *Boy from Oz*, his shoes were too big to fill and the show closed. Sometimes a lesser-known but fine actor may not sell tickets based on his or her name, but could deliver a great performance. And, when he or she departs, the show can still go on.

7. Timing's everything. We had the rights to do a revival of *Hair* a few years ago, and we couldn't get anyone interested in partnering with us. But we stuck with it and did a short run in Toronto. A year later the Public Theater wanted to do it in the park. It was the summer of the primaries before the presidential election and people were pumped for political change. That *exact* moment was the perfect time. The show was a sensation. Then it moved to Broadway, and the rest is history.

8. All buzz is good buzz. Critics used to be able to make or break a show. Now, an audience is less likely to read a review, so you have to rely on advertising, television appearances, awards and word-of-mouth. It's a massive undertaking. A typical play's marketing budget is $1 million before the show even opens and another $4 million per year. We hire advertising, press, online and marketing agencies. There's a street team to persuade TKTS patrons to choose your show. We shell out for barter advertisements, email blasts, social networking campaigns, a show Web site, search engine optimization— all to promote awareness and hopefully convert that to ticket sales.

9. Take the show on the road. The more global our shows go, the more successful they become, but you have to be culturally sensitive. English musical comedy has its roots in opera. It's a different formula from the American musical, and English audiences require different elements. We thought a lot of our hit shows, such as *Driving Miss Daisy* or *Frankie and Johnny in the Clare de Lune*, would do well over there. But the reviews came back calling them claptrap or overly sentimental. On the other hand, when we brought *The Producers* to Tokyo an American company first performed the show and the crowd enjoyed it as a cultural experience as much as entertainment. Then a month later, using the exact same sets, costumes, staging and choreography, a Japanese cast with a couple of home-grown pop stars took over. The audience laughed at different jokes and responded to different themes, but it was a huge hit. We bridged the gap and it was extraordinary.

10. No one has a crystal ball. When Rocco Landesman and his partners took over Jujamcyn Theaters in the '80s, they met with an old Broadway producer, Arthur Cantor. They kept asking Cantor questions, and he kept saying, "I don't know. I don't know." And Rocco and the others said, "Either that's the dumbest man in show business or the smartest." And, after a few years in the business, they realized Cantor was the smartest, because you can think you've done everything and that you have a hit on your hands, but in the end, you just don't know.

MARC ROUTH FACTS

First brush with fame: 1974, Ohio: Vincent Price played Fagin when Routh was understudy of Oliver in summer stock production of *Oliver!*

First Broadway show attended: 1974: *Magic Show*, starring Doug Henning.

First Broadway show coproduced: 1997: *Forever Tango*.

Broadway runs: Shortest run: 10 days, 1994, *What's Wrong with This Picture?* Longest run: 6 years, 2001, *The Producers*, and 2002, *Hairspray*.

Most profitable show: *The Producers*, with over $27 million profit.

Most produced show on the road: *Hairspray*, including productions in Argentina, Australia, Brazil, Canada, China, Denmark, Dubai, England, Finland, France, Germany, Iceland, Israel, Italy, Japan, Mexico, Norway, South Africa, South Korea, Switzerland and the Philippines.

Awards: Four-time Tony winner, nine-time Tony nominee.

On the wall: 2004: Routh's caricature joins hundreds of other Broadway greats, including Noel Coward, Jerome Robbins, Tommy Tune and Jessica Tandy, at Sardi's Times Square theater restaurant.

BROADWAY FACTS

Broadway break-in: 1849: 20,000 working-class men break into an opera house playing *Macbeth* and start a riot. Police fire guns into the crowd, killing over twenty and wounding more than 150. Rioters do not disperse until cannons are brought in.

First modern musical: 1866: *The Black Crook*, a five-and-a-half-hour-long musical featuring a scantily clad female dancing chorus of 100 ballerinas in skin-colored tights, opens at the 3,200-seat Niblo's Garden and runs for a record 474 performances with proceeds of over $1 million.

Times Square: 1900: Theaters move to Longacre Square (now Times Square), where unemployed vaudevillians congregate on the concrete island nicknamed "the Beach," between Seventh Avenue and Broadway.

Broadway peaks: 1927–28: Broadway has more than 70 legitimate theaters with over 250 shows. Soon after, the Depression and talking films take their toll and business plummets.

Broadway economics: 2011: Nightly attendance, 25,000; audience share: tourists, 63 percent, and women, 66 percent; annual gross, $1.02 billion; local jobs created, 84,400.

Recoup: 15–20 percent of the Broadway shows recoup their investment.

Chapter 30

How to Rehabilitate a Bad Reputation

. . . .

Michael Sitrick

CEO of Sitrick and Company, one of the world's top crisis
management firms, representing entertainers, athletes and
other high-profile clients

What happens when a celebrity is arrested for soliciting prostitutes? Or for going on a drunken rampage? What happens
when a frenzied pack of reporters descends on the scene and the media unleashes a torrent of sensational nonstop coverage? What happens when, as a result, the celebrity's career is on the brink of
annihilation? Who are they going to call? A crisis manager. And, hopefully, one of the best—someone like Michael Sitrick, whom the *Los
Angeles Times* called "the Wizard of Spin." Brought up on the South
Side of Chicago, Sitrick has risen through the ranks of the public relations industry to become one of the go-to guys (if not *the* guy) for VIPs
embroiled in scandal. A journalism major who only briefly worked for
the press—he chose a PR job because it paid $35 a week more than a
reporter's job—Sitrick has educated himself in the ways of the media,
with an ability to assess and understand the intricacies of how the
media behaves as a herd and what makes an individual journalist tick.
"This is not a game for beginners," says Sitrick, whose firm has defended and rebuilt the reputations of scores of celebrities caught in the
media glare, including Paris Hilton, Halle Berry, Rush Limbaugh, Michael Vick, Chris Brown and Tommy Lee, as well as embattled com-

panies and high-profile executives, many of whom he can only discuss off the record, if at all. "This job is a serious commitment and there are no shortcuts. If I don't do the work and make the sacrifices that I owe to my clients, I'm sure they'll find someone else who will," says Sitrick.

> **Takeaway:** *"If you don't tell your story, someone else will tell it for you."*

1. Strike fast. When a high-profile client calls and says, "CBS Evening News is outside my door. What should I do?" we have to get the facts, assess the situation and establish a strategy in a matter of minutes. We have to know immediately who to contact and how. Many of the people at my firm are ex-journalists (with five Pulitzer Prizes among them), so we can get the facts quickly. Some people worry about having the *last* word; my concern is getting the *first* and *last* word. Get your story out first so you can set the tone for the coverage that follows.

2. Prepare the client. Powerful people don't like being challenged, but a crucial part of my job is telling the emperor or empress they have no clothes. CEOs wield incredible power, but I often have to explain to them that they can't control the press. A celebrity might be able to act, but what if they don't come across sympathetically in front of a camera after being accused of shoplifting or trashing a hotel room? Before we put a client in front of reporters or cameras we rehearse them very carefully, the way a lawyer would. To prepare Paris Hilton, who'd just been released from jail, for *Larry King*, we brought in a videographer. Paris could field the type of questions she would get on the air and see her body language. Tiger Woods isn't a client of mine, but before his apologia press conference I would have rehearsed him, shot a video, and if it had come off the way it aired, I'd have done it differently.

3. Know when to do nothing. A journalist is taught to ask who, what, where, when, why and how. In my business, we add "So what?" Does anybody care? About 20 percent of the time, I tell a client, "Do nothing." You can take a small matter and turn it into a major crisis if it's handled wrong. I had a famous person who was going through a divorce. He thought his ex-wife would come after him in the press because he was marrying a much, much younger woman. I told him, "Just have your lawyer tell your ex-wife's lawyer you've retained us. And if her lawyer wants to get in the ring, I guarantee his client is going to get bloodied." My client was skeptical at first, but we were able to preempt the crisis and keep the nastiness of the divorce outside the public eye.

4. Identify your audience. When a client comes to us, one of our first questions is, "Who is the audience you're aiming your message at?" For an actor in a crisis, that audience could be his fans, the movie studios or sponsors. For a CEO, it could be his company's investors or government officials. The former wife of a hugely successful rock star came to us. She had been drugged and beaten by her ex-husband. She was suing the star for damages, but his lawyers wouldn't even return her lawyers' phone calls. Her audience, we determined, was three parties: her former husband, his record company and his lawyers. She was reluctant to go public with her story, but we convinced her that because of the nature of the physical abuse she'd suffered, we could use the media to reach her intended audience. We decided *People* magazine was the right venue. They put her on the cover. The impact was predictably huge. Her story generated enormous media interest, and of course, the record company put immediate pressure on her ex-husband's lawyers to avoid further damage to the rock star's reputation. Not only did the lawyers take her calls; they settled the suit shortly after.

5. Tell a story. Almost all newspeople believe in the power of the "story." Regardless of how actual events occur, journalists believe that the best way to recount these events is in the form of a story with a beginning, a middle and an end, with drama, conflict and surprising twists. This might be a highly stylized—even sensationalized—way of reporting on events, but this way of thinking is so internalized by members of the media that to get your message across to them you have to present that message in the form of a story, sometimes with clearly drawn heroes and villains.

6. Put yourself inside the reporter's head. The media is not a pack of jackals or an impersonal machine. They're a group of individuals with their own attitudes, anxieties and aspirations. To be successful in my business you have to be able to put yourself inside a reporter's head, influencing how he or she covers your client. Newspeople tend to be skeptical, idealistic, naïve and sometimes relentless, with egos larger and more fragile than the average person's. For example, journalists love to scoop their rivals, so give a reporter exclusive access to your high-profile client and you might have just made a grateful ally for life. It might seem obvious, but you'll often get more sympathetic coverage for your client if you treat reporters with respect. Journalists believe their most important mission is to uncover the truth, so if you can persuade them with facts, or steer them to where they can find the facts themselves, reporting will follow.

7. Engage the media. It is a critical mistake for a client to brush off a crisis with a "no comment." To a journalist, "no comment" usually means "guilty as charged." Refuse to talk? Reporters will find someone who will. And *that* version of the story may not be one you like. My firm's first client was a Disney-backed investment firm. They didn't engage and were getting slammed with inaccurate coverage about their intentions for acquiring Polaroid. Polaroid's hometown press, the Boston media, was tough. I called the reporter from the *Boston Globe*, cleared the air and arranged an exclusive interview with the firm's CEO. The result was a very favorable and accurate in-depth story. It was far better than any paid advertisement would have been. Sometimes by working *with* instead of *against* the media you can turn an unmitigated disaster into a success story.

8. Correct every mistake. Today, stories pop up 24/7 and create media frenzies. No matter how outrageous the claim, many people believe what they read. If you leave an incorrect statement unchallenged it will spread through the media and live on in Google searches. Journalists and bloggers covering the individual will repeat the uncorrected mistake so many times that it will become conventional wisdom. When a media outlet gets the facts wrong, we go after them right away to correct it. To persuade a reporter to back off an erroneous story can require meticulous research. If they still won't back off, we go higher up, contacting the editor or even the outlet's lawyers to point out how much of the story is in question. We deploy truth squads that scour the media for every mention of a client-in-conflict to knock down inaccuracies on the spot.

9. Find a lead steer. For all its iconoclasm and competitiveness, the media has a herd mentality. Finding a lead steer, a well-regarded reporter from a reputable institution willing to question conventional wisdom, can initiate a positive media stampede or reverse the direction of a negative one. We recommended this tactic to a well-known actress who came to us after having been involved in a bad investment and a bankruptcy. Her story was complicated. It couldn't be told in short news items. She was being vilified in the press. And her career was suffering. We knew she would need to sit down and open up with an experienced reporter who had the ear of Hollywood. We suggested someone from the *Los Angeles Times*, Hollywood's hometown paper, and warned the actress that it would not be an easy interview, no puff piece like those she'd been used to. But, because of the reporter's reputation, we could guarantee she would have a fair interview. The reporter spent hours with the actress and her husband, as well as thoroughly reporting the other side of the story. For the first time since her troubles began, the actress came across as the vulnerable, hardworking professional she was. The story by this lead steer reporter changed the media's attitude toward the embattled actress and drove news about her in a new direction.

10. Never lie. Public relations is about persuasion and persuasion depends on credibility, so you can't lie. It's the cardinal rule of PR. A lie may get a client out of an awkward situation temporarily, but they'll always be found out, especially now with the scrutiny of the digital media and the accelerated news cycle. When high-profile clients get into situations, such as drugs, sex addiction or domestic violence, we advise them to admit the truth quickly, let the public know they're seeking treatment for their behavior, and move on. Anthony Weiner might have survived in office if he'd immediately said, "I don't know why I did it, but I have to get well. I've sought professional help and I am asking for a leave of absence." Credibility is a crisis manager's ultimate resource. We deliver it. We expect it. We walk away from any client that lies to us.

MICHAEL SITRICK FACTS

First media lesson learned: 1968: Sitrick submits an exposé on the fraternity system for his college paper that his editor praises, then tosses in the trashcan because Sitrick missed his deadline by five minutes.

On how to get high-profile clients: "An overwhelming number of our clients come through word-of-mouth; we don't even have a brochure."

Hourly fee: $895 per hour.

Number of active clients in any given year: 250.

On hiring journalists: "It's easier to teach a journalist what PR is than to teach a PR person what news is."

On his clients' adversaries: "I'm not afraid to put my adversaries under the wheel of pain by shedding light on details about them."

Favorite quote: "Keep your head when all about you are losing theirs." —Rudyard Kipling

BAD REPUTATION FACTS

Misunderstood? Considered Jesus' betrayer by most Christians and vilified in art and literature for millennia, Judas Iscariot, some scholars theorize, was the negotiator in a prisoner exchange or he may have acted with Jesus' foreknowledge of his own Crucifixion.

Ruined: "Reputation, reputation, reputation! O! I have lost my reputation. I have lost the immortal part of myself, and what remains is bestial. My reputation, Iago, my reputation!" —Cassio in Shakespeare's *Othello*

Backfiring smear: 1828: In presidential election, surrogates of sitting president John Quincy Adams accuse challenger Andrew Jackson of murder, and his wife, Rachel, of being an "American Jezebel" and adulterer for marrying Jackson before a divorce from a previous husband was finalized. Adams is seen as humiliating a woman who has been a devoted wife of 40 years. Jackson wins in a landslide.

Hollywood blacklist: 1947: 10 Hollywood writers and directors refuse to give testimony to the HUAC (House Un-American Activities Committee), created to investigate Communist sympathizers in America, and are cited in contempt of Congress. Many in the film industry are accused of Communist Party connections. Those who do not name names are "blacklisted," harassed by FBI, called traitors and have their careers destroyed. Blacklist peters out by early '60s.

(Un)saved: 1988: Photos of TV evangelist Jimmy Swaggart leaving motel frequented by prostitutes are taken by son of fellow minister (whom Swaggart accused of adultery) and given to Assembly of God authorities. Swaggart makes infamous tearful "I Have Sinned" speech to TV audience. After Swaggart is defrocked he becomes independent Pentecostal minister and, in 1991, is caught with a prostitute by a cop after driving on wrong side of road.

Articles of adultery: Monica Lewinsky's blue Gap dress, Eliot Spitzer's black dress socks, Anthony Weiner's gray briefs.

Chapter 31

How to Sail Around the World

· ·

Jessica Watson

Australian teen who sailed solo, nonstop, around the world
in 2010

Sixteen-year-old Australian Jessica Watson was off the coast of
Sydney for a trial run on the Sparkman & Stephens 34-foot sailboat, *Ella's Pink Lady*. While catnapping in the cockpit at 2:00 A.M.,
Watson was jolted awake by the sound of screeching metal. Rushing
to the deck, Watson discovered that the tiny boat she planned to sail
around the world in the coming days had been rammed and dis-
masted by a 63,000-ton bulk carrier, the *Silver Yang*. Five years earlier, when Watson was 11, her mother had read her the story of
young teenage solo sailor Jesse Martin, who had circumnavigated
the globe in 1999. Watson wasn't much of a sailor and not even
particularly adventurous, but the tale inspired her. She wondered,
"If he could do it, could I?" Telling her parents of her plan was the
hardest part, but her determination to improve her sailing skills and
focus on safety and survival skills turned her free-spirited parents'
tepid support to cautious enthusiasm. "When people heard about
my plans," says Watson, "many doubted that it could be pulled off
by a *scrawny little girl*. But I knew what I could do and I wasn't going to let other people knock my confidence." And, while most teens
mark adolescence in more predictable ways, Watson methodically
prepared for her voyage. She logged thousands of nautical miles,

enlisted the help of countless experts and volunteers, secured funding for a boat, plotted the course and found sponsorship for everything from cans of Spam to Panasonic video equipment that would allow her to run a live video blog from her boat. As the journey drew near, Watson had one last nagging doubt—whether she actually had the mental toughness to survive an eight-month, 20,000-nautical-mile voyage alone. But in the aftermath of the collision with the *Silver Yang*, as she cut the rigging and tied down the mast to head back to land to repair her crippled boat after the trial run, she had a realization. She had not panicked. She had known exactly what to do. "After living through that," said Watson, "I knew I could handle anything that an around-the-world trip might bring."

Takeaway: *"Everyone thinks I'm a great sailor, but I'm not. I'm just a kid. The success of my trip was not about being incredibly talented at sailing, but being incredibly well prepared."*

1. Commit to the dream. After my mum read me the story of solo circumnavigator Jesse Martin, something clicked inside of me. Jesse was just a normal teenager that I could relate to. I began reading everything on solo sailing I could, including a book by Joshua Slocum, who was the first person to circumnavigate the globe single-handedly in 1895. I didn't tell anyone about my plan, but I made lists of what I'd need. I researched boats, rigging and long-lasting food. I posted pictures of the wild seas and storms of the Southern Ocean on my wall, and visualized myself dealing with them. And I kept asking myself whether I could do it—whether I really wanted to do it. I didn't have the strength of a fully grown man. I'd have to work out ways to do things that suited me. But sailing is not about strength. It's about knowledge. If I had the right boat, prepared myself mentally and physically and developed my sailing skills, I'd have as much chance as anyone. The hardest part, the scariest part, was actually telling people. First I told my parents and family. And I was so jazzed that I'd actually told them that I kept talking about it. Eventually they realized, "Okay, I guess she's going to do it."

2. Find your power. When I was 13, I used to go on sailing adventures along the Sunshine Coast with my sister Emily, who is a year older, and a friend, Nick, who is two years older. I was the quiet one. I was afraid of heights and crowds, and people thought of me as a scared little girl. One time we sailed 35 nautical miles out to Moreton Bay in Nick's sailboat to spend the night and return the next day. Nick got sick that night. In the morning the wind started rising and shifted from the north. By midafternoon we'd made no progress back. Emily was seasick, the sea was steep, the wind picked up and it was getting dark. Normally I would have just fallen to pieces, but since I'd been put in a situation where I had to pull my own weight, I thought to myself, "If you're really serious about sailing around the world, you're going to have to toughen up and pretend you know what you're doing." I jumped into it. I was drenched and exhausted and wrestling with the tiller and it was fun. All of a sudden Nick was letting me take the lead. We spent another night dragging anchor and sailed home the next day. It was an amazing feeling to think, "Oh! I'm not a kid anymore. I actually *can* do this. I can influence how things turn out."

3. Get a little help from your friends. You can't just hop into a boat and circumnavigate the globe. You need a lot of help. You need a boat, mentors, sponsors. It might be scary at first to ask people you don't know for assistance, but you never know what's going to happen until you put yourself out there. I contacted newspapers and anyone I could think of to build up contacts and get the word out about my trip. Don McIntyre, one of Australia's greatest sailors, became a mentor and generously offered to buy me a boat. When my family didn't have money to pay wages for the refit, volunteers came from all over the country. Not only did they help with the sanding, grinding and painting, but many of them had years of sailing experience and gave me invaluable advice on sailing and equipment. Ella

Baché, the skin care company, and other corporations helped with expenses and equipment. Throughout the actual voyage, I communicated by satellite phone with my support crew—my project manager; my communication equipment adviser; a meteorologist; my mum, who'd keep me up with news back home; and my dad, who I talked to about everything else. Although I was physically out there by myself, I felt that all the people who helped me get the *Pink Lady* ready were part of the team, too. And all of their goodwill made a difference.

4. Provision well. I made list after list before my trip. It was hard to get my head around all the food I'd need. Food for over eight months isn't something you see every day. I had no idea how much there should be. I just had to trust that Mum had got it right! A partial list included 24 cans of Spam, 200 liters of powdered milk, 64 cans of potatoes, 32 cans of pineapple, 36 cans of tuna, 250 juice drinks, 5 crates of candy, powdered eggs, canned veggies, canned mangoes, custard, hot chocolate, popcorn, cereal, porridge, Pringles, chocolate cookies, muffins and bread-baking supplies. And a partial list of equipment, gear and personal items included 2 autopilots, remote commander, passive and active radar reflector, 4 ship detection systems, AIS alarm, distress radio beacon, high-frequency radio, computer, wind generator and solar panels for power, navigation equipment, sextant, gel batteries, engine for charging batteries, battery monitor, 2 satellite phones, satellite dome for Internet connection, GPS tracker, life raft, diesel heater, cabin fans, freshwater tanks, hand desalinator, needle and thread to mend sails, wet-weather gear, life jacket, tool kit, wrench set, knife, first-aid kit, hair dryer, iPod, still camera, video camera, stereo, trashy novels, adventure books, chick flick DVDs, 2 alarm clocks, handheld vacuum packer, teakettle, pressure cooker, good-luck charms and half a dozen stuffed animals.

5. Survive sleep deprivation. There's no such thing as a full night's sleep when you're circumnavigating the globe. I had to be awake to deal with squalls, choppy seas, unstable weather, islands, reefs and passing boats. I woke up when the wind picked up or the boat changed direction. Sleep deprivation and learning how to survive on little sleep is one of the toughest things about solo sailing. The first leg of my trip was the hardest. I was on constant alert. I had two different alarm clocks to wake me, and one was so loud it made me jump out of my skin. Fortunately, before my trip, I did a lot of research on fatigue management. I learned that you could survive on catnaps—20 minutes here, 40 minutes there—for quite some time. But every two or three nights you'll need a couple full hours of sleep. When I was in the Southern Ocean I did something I hadn't done since I left Sydney. I slept for five hours straight. It was Christmas. And the wind changed while I slept, so we were sailing in the opposite direction and I lost six nautical miles.

6. Bond with your boat. *Ella's Pink Lady* was definitely a she. And very pretty. She was slow, steady and easy to handle. And small, one of the reasons I chose her, because I wouldn't have had the strength to sail a larger boat. There was something special about her. I would have been incredibly proud of her even if she were ugly, which she definitely wasn't. I had put all this time and effort into her, and it was only the two of us out there for a very long time. We had our good days and our bad days, and when I felt nervous before a gale or bumpy seas, I gave her pep talks. About 100 days into my voyage, I hit a gale in the Atlantic with 65 knot winds and waves like giant black mountains. As a wave came at us, I'd yell, "Okay, girl, here's a big one! Get ready!" and when the wave knocked us sideways, I'd keep yelling, "Hold it! You can do this!" After a few hours it got even worse. I battened down everything, went down to the cockpit and belted myself in. There was one knockdown after another. It went on for hours. Just before the third knockdown, I heard a roar like an airplane engine. The *Pink Lady* was picked right up and thrown violently upside down. As we turned over 180 degrees, everything that wasn't tied down flew around the cabin. I was clinging to the handholds and my feet were touching the roof. I kept yelling out, "Hang in there! You'll be okay!" I was bluffing myself into thinking if I *acted* confident, I'd *feel* more confident. Eventually we came out of it. The cockpit was a disaster and I was full of bruises. I felt like I'd aged 10 years. But on deck there was surprisingly little damage—a bent stanchion and a few rips in the mainsail. The way the *Pink Lady* came through those knockdowns was incredible. It showed what a great boat she is, and I probably got a lot more out of our conversations than she did.

7. Take one day at a time. Circumnavigators I met had advised me to think of the trip as a one-day sail followed by another one-day sail, and so on. And it really helped to think of the trip like that. I also broke the entire journey down into six stages with notes on what to expect at each stage. And if things weren't going well, I could focus on counting the miles to the next stage. It gave me something to focus on and look forward to. I was mentally checking off oceans and whole stages of the trip. And if things were going very badly—if I was in the middle of a storm—I could think about just getting through the next few hours.

8. Do it yourself. Out in the middle of the ocean you are very much on your own. I had to know how to fix every system on board—electrical and engine repair, plumbing and rigging. I had to do constant maintenance, tightening fan belts, re-taping chafe joints and stitching torn sails. I depended so much on my Fleming Windvane—an autopilot that helped steer *Ella's Pink Lady*, that I had even given him a name: Parker. When only three weeks into the voyage Parker stopped steering, I thought about a fellow circumnavigator whose trip ended when his autopilot malfunctioned. Parker was one of the few things on board I couldn't replace. After searching for the problem I discovered that the circlips that fastened the blade to the main shaft had come off. When I rummaged through my wind vane spare parts, the circlip was of course the one thing that I hadn't brought. There was no manual for me to look at. No mechanic to help me. Certainly no hardware store to stop at. As a short-term fix, I strapped it together with twine and a bit of trusty duct tape. I imagined the worst, but the repair held up—all the way through the Southern Ocean.

9. Don't overthink. The success of your trip is as dependent on your mood as it is on your rigging. You're down there in the middle of the ocean weeks from land or help. You can't just say, "Okay, I've had enough." Occasionally I cried. But if you start thinking, "Ohh, it's wet and it's cold," that little thing turns into a bigger thing. And then you get more upset about that. And that makes you more upset about the next thing. And it snowballs. And soon you're saying, "Ohhh, there's a whole ocean to go." One of the big tricks when you're out there is to not overthink things. I'd stop myself and say, "Hey, it's cold and I'm in a bad mood, but I'm going to get through the day, and eventually I'm going to warm up and feel better." You can't change the conditions, but you can change the way that you deal with them. I learned to accept it when I was in a bad mood or lonely. I learned to accept it when I was tired or cold. I knew the trip would be very tough, and I always thought I was a crybaby. But I ended up being a lot better at coping with my emotions than I'd expected. And anyway, chocolate always helped!

10. Enjoy it. The most important advice I got from experienced sailors was to remember that you're only going to do it once, so take a moment to enjoy it. And I'm very glad that I took that advice. I had read and reread books about solo sailing around the world, but once I set off on my voyage, I began to understand their stories in a whole new way. The feeling of solitude, when all I could see in any direction was endless ocean and endless sky, made me feel connected to them, even to Joshua Slocum, who'd done the sail more than a century before me. On the *Pink Lady* there was only the moment. Looking out at the horizon, I felt alive and exhilarated.

JESSICA WATSON FACTS

Homeschooled: Australia: Watson and her three siblings are homeschooled on the 52-foot motorboat they live on with their parents.

Readiness training: 2004–9: Apart from thousands of nautical miles logged while volunteering or working on paid crews for yachts, Watson studied navigation, passage planning, weather chart interpretation, sea survival, first aid and boat maintenance.

***Pink Lady*:** 2009: Watson's mentor, sailor Don McIntyre, buys her a Sparkman & Stephens 34-foot sailboat for $68,000. Watson names boat *Ella's Pink Lady* ("Ella" after sponsor Ella Baché) and, upon her return, donates boat to Australian National Maritime Museum.

New Year's Eve: 2010, Cape Horn: Coming through treacherous ocean, Watson is deeply touched by satellite phone conversation with Dilip Donde, the first-ever Indian solo circumnavigator, who is on his own voyage only 200 nautical miles away.

Sighted: Albatross, hundreds of dolphins, blue whale.

Homecoming: On May 15, 2010, after Watson sails into Sydney Harbor and while a customs officer stamps her passport to officiate her return, she eats first fresh food in seven months and devours whipped cream from its nozzle. In a ceremony that follows she meets Australian Prime Minister Kevin Rudd.

Homecoming wish: To get her driver's license.

CIRCUMNAVIGATION FACTS

The first: 1519, Spain: Ferdinand Magellan sets off with five ships and a crew of about 270 men in search of a route to the Spice Islands (in present-day Indonesia). Magellan is killed by bamboo spear in a tribal war on the Philippines, and only one ship, the *Victoria*, arrives back in Spain three years later having gone around the globe, with just 18 of the original crew still aboard.

First woman: 1766: Naturalist Philibert Commerçon takes his servant (and lover) Jeanne Baret on a French-backed circumnavigation of the world. Since women are not allowed aboard, Baret dresses like a man. When her female identity is revealed she must leave the ship, staying on Mauritius off the coast of Africa with Commerçon, who dies in 1773. Baret marries and finally sails back to France, completing her circumnavigation in 1775.

Solo: 1895: After repairing and refitting an old rotting oyster sloop, the 36-foot *Spray*, Joshua Slocum sets out from Rhode Island to sail around the world. Three years and 46,000 miles later he returns almost unnoticed. In 1899 he publishes story of his voyage, *Sailing Alone Around the World*, becomes famous and continues to sail until he is lost at sea at the age of 65.

Rescue: 2010, United States: Abby Sutherland, 16, in an attempt to circumnavigate at the same time as Watson, is caught in high winds in a remote area of the Indian Ocean. Her boat suffers multiple knockdowns. Her satellite phone loses contact, her emergency radio beacons are activated and a search plane is sent to find Sutherland, who is unharmed but whose boat cannot complete the trip. 2012: Sutherland takes flying lessons to be able to fly around the world.

The fastest: 2011: Designed by architects to break oceanic speed records, the 130-foot racing trimaran, *Banque Populaire V*, skippered by Loïke Peyron, circumnavigated in 45 days, 13 hours and 43 minutes at an average speed of 26.51 knots.

Chapter 32

How to Shoot a Great War Shot Without Getting Shot

Lynsey Addario

Pulitzer Prize–winning photojournalist

Taking photos in war-ravaged areas and crisis zones might not have seemed a likely career for a five-foot-one-inch woman with no professional photographic training, but Lynsey Addario has not only photographed conflict in Afghanistan, Iraq, Pakistan, the Congo, Darfur, Haiti and Libya for *National Geographic*, the *New York Times* and other publications; she has brought a unique sensibility to her work. Addario's photography goes beyond the gore of war to demystify foreign cultures and expose the tragic consequences of human conflict. Combining keen journalistic skills with an artist's eye, Addario draws attention to the lives of people in conflict zones, earning her critical acclaim, a Pulitzer Prize in 2009 and a MacArthur fellowship in 2010. She has never shied from putting her life on the line. She has embedded with troops, endured firefights and military ambushes and entered communities closed to outsiders. Despite her kidnapping in Iraq, a car crash that killed her driver in Pakistan and a harrowing capture in Libya in the days of civil war, Addario remains undaunted. "Raising the camera to my eye and taking a picture is only a tiny fraction of what's involved in actually getting a photograph. It has to do with having good sources, anticipating events, getting there, sometimes taking hours in a car or on foot, and then hoping that people allow me to shoot when I arrive."

> **Takeaway:** *"If someone is injured or killed near me, I try to keep my emotions in check and focus on whether I might be able to help. And if there is nothing I can do, I document the scene."*

1. Pack smart. Burqa, chador and headscarves for the Middle East. Linens, loose-fitting, button-down shirts for the Congo and Darfur. Raincoat, hiking boots, flip-flops, running shoes and two pairs of sunglasses. (I always lose one.) French press, good coffee, sugar, protein bars and soup packets. Twenty passport photographs, 10 passport copies. (Most countries are incredibly bureaucratic.) Three cameras, 5 lenses, 10 flash cards, pocket drives, hard drives, backup, a satellite dish for transmitting images, a bag of cables, more cables and backup cables. A satellite phone, spare handset for local SIM card, iPod, earbuds and a loaded Kindle. Clinique SPF30 sunblock and copious quantities of Cipro, which cures almost any infection.

2. Go where the action is. The more calculated the risks you take, the better the chance you'll get to the heart of the story. When embedding with the military, the most remote bases are the best. No porta-potties, running water or beds, and none of the higher-ups around, means you're in the right place. In 2004, getting into Darfur was nearly impossible. You couldn't get a visa and attacks against villages and killing of civilians were in full force, so we left most of our gear behind in Chad and walked across the border into Sudan. We trudged two kilometers across the desert, then we went neck-deep in water through wadis, the impromptu rivers that fill up during the rainy season. Finally we met some rebels who drove us around on the back of their truck for a week. It wasn't easy, but if I hadn't done it I would have never gotten the shots that landed on the front page of the *Times*.

3. When in Kabul . . . I've been shooting in foreign countries for over 10 years now, so I'm very comfortable outside of the U.S. bubble. I do love being with locals, but you have to be aware of how to conduct yourself as a woman. An Afghan official once told me, "You better be careful; your eyes look Afghan. If you don't wear a burqa you could be beaten on the street." When I'm in those situations, I keep my head, face and body covered, my mouth shut and wait for permission to shoot. Once when I was on assignment to photograph a Taliban meeting, the commander kept saying, "No women. No women." The reporter introduced me as his wife saying that he didn't want to leave me at the hotel in Peshawar. I sat in a corner totally veiled. I didn't make eye contact with anyone. After a while, the reporter asked if I could take some pictures. I was terrified. I had to shoot through my veil, calculating my shots and shooting sparingly.

4. Rely on local intel. You can't always rely on your editor who is sitting at a desk at least a continent away. The most important information in a conflict zone comes from local sources—a good driver and translator. And, of course, the town and village people. I realized just how important these locals were in 2003 at the beginning of the Iraq War. When we arrived in the Kurdish area, the U.S. was raining down cruise missiles on the terrorist group Al-Ansar. Locals were fleeing with all their belongings piled on top of their cars. They pulled up alongside us, warning, "Get out! Get out!" We listened and turned back, and just then, a car bomb exploded in the very spot where we'd been. On the other hand, there was a time in Iraq when we'd heard insurgents had downed a helicopter and killed many U.S. soldiers near Fallujah. All roads had been closed off to the city. We asked truck drivers and journalists who had been along a smugglers' route that circumvented the blockade, but no one would say whether it was safe or not. We chanced it anyway. As we got deeper in, we should have stopped to ask locals. We were scared, though, that they might give us up to the insurgents. We continued. Finally we turned a corner right into an insurgent-occupied village. It was too late. We were abducted and held at gunpoint. I wasn't sure if we'd get out alive. In the end, it was our driver and translator and our Iraqi support staff back in Baghdad who engineered our release. We hadn't paid attention and almost paid for it with our lives.

5. Gain trust. People think photography is about photographing, but it's really about relationships, making the people you're photographing comfortable enough to open up their lives to you. There are advantages to being a woman. In the Muslim world, for example, I can enter private homes, whereas most of my male colleagues can't. It's not easy getting the right to photograph in a home in many of these cultures closed to foreigners, but being a woman, at least I have one foot in the door.

6. Never waste good light. Wake up before sunrise and start to shoot at dawn when the light is at its best.

7. Be still. It's miserable when I have to get a shot in a limited time. The best images are usually shot with patience. I like to spend a great deal of time in one place, letting the people around me get comfortable with my presence and watching a scene evolve. I'm selective about what I shoot, which character or scene to follow. And then I keep shooting and shooting as the scene changes, because you never know what's going to happen.

8. Deal with fear. Gun battles are incredibly surreal—the adrenaline, the amount of firepower, the helicopter gunships that swoop in and fire artillery at "the enemy" or whoever is shooting at us. Even though fear can be paralyzing, you can't let it overwhelm you. You have to stay calm and focused. I can't remember the last time I've kneeled down to pray, but inevitably my Catholic roots kick in. Hail Marys come out nonstop. Often in a firefight I have to remind myself to take pictures. If someone is injured or killed near me, I try to keep my emotions in check and focus on whether I might be able to help. And if there is nothing I can do, I document the scene.

9. Dead people don't take photographs. If and when you feel like your life is actually in imminent danger, concentrate on staying alive. I'm small—five foot one—and with a flak jacket and a helmet, my ability to run and jump or quickly climb up a mountain is limited. It doesn't matter how much I work out; I'm not a man. I have to run where the soldiers are telling me to go without falling down. If there are no soldiers, I try to find any cover that can protect me from bullets—a large rock, a thick tree, a divot or canal in the earth I can dig myself into. It can be terrifying.

10. Make an impact. Going into a conflict zone takes a great toll on your personal life. It's lonely. It's physically demanding. It's emotionally taxing. You see and document things that take a lot to process, both mentally and physically. It's hard to put your loved ones through it. But, as a photojournalist, you have a responsibility. You have unique access to what unfolds on the ground, and it's important to show people, policy-makers, what's happening.

LYNSEY ADDARIO FACTS

First camera: Nikon FG at 12 years old.

Photographic influences: Diane Arbus, Nan Goldin, Mary Ellen Mark, Sebastião Salgado, James Nachtwey.

First assignment: 1996: *Buenos Aires Herald*, photo of Madonna as Evita.

Most frames per shoot: 30,000 for a *National Geographic* photo essay.

On assignment: 275 days per year.

On embedding with American soldiers: "I regress about 15 years when I'm with them. It's like hanging out with all the guys I grew up with. At the end of the day, we're all Americans and have the same cultural references."

On Broadway: 2010: Tony-nominated play *Time Stands Still*, written by Donald Margulies and starring Laura Linney, loosely based on Addario's life.

Most precarious moment: 2011: Covering Libyan conflict, Addario and three colleagues are abducted and abused by government forces and threatened with death. After tense negotiations with the U.S. State Department, they are released six days later.

PHOTOJOURNALISM FACTS

First identified war photographer: 1848–49: John McCosh, a Scottish surgeon and amateur photographer, takes calotypes of the Second Sikh War in Punjab.

Civil War photos: 1861–65: Mathew Brady and over 20 assistants spend more than $100,000 to create 10,000 photo plates documenting the war. Brady goes bankrupt and dies penniless and blind in 1896.

Controversial photo: 1936, Spain: Robert Capa's photo "Falling Soldier" depicts a fatally wounded soldier in the Spanish Civil War, but its authenticity is disputed. After a long career, Capa is killed by a land mine in Indochina in 1954.

First female war photographer: During WWII, Margaret Bourke-White, aka "Maggie the Indestructible," is torpedoed in the Mediterranean, strafed by the Luftwaffe, and bombarded in Moscow and on the ground at Buchenwald.

Iwo Jima near miss: 1945: Piling rocks for a better vantage point, photojournalist Joe Rosenthal suddenly notices flag-raising, grabs camera and without using viewfinder snaps iconic image.

Media workers killed: First Iraq war, 4; second Iraq war, 203.

Deadliest countries for media workers: 2012: Somalia and Syria.

Chapter 33

How to Start a Start-up

• •

Bill Gross

Founder and CEO of Idealab, a business incubator that has
fostered the creation of nearly 100 businesses

It was 1973 during the energy crisis when Bill Gross dropped his
high school English literature class to tinker in the school's machine shop. Some of his fellow students believed he was building a
newfangled marijuana bong, but what he was designing was a parabolic concentrator and an engine that converted solar power to electrical power. Gross went to the library to learn everything he could
about the mail-order business and formed the company Solar Devices. He sold 10,000 plans of his invention for $4 each. It was the
first of nearly a hundred businesses started by Gross, who shares
with his hero Thomas Edison a passion for tinkering and a hardheaded business savvy to turn his inventions into profit. Before he
turned 30, Gross had created several other idea-based businesses,
including an audio store that sold a lead-lined speaker he designed
at Cal Tech, accounting software he developed at the dawn of the PC
age, and educational software he was inspired to create for his five-year-old son. These companies would go on to be sold for $90 million. But Gross's greatest idea was *having* ideas. Frustrated by the
limitations of being one man with too many ideas and too little time,
in 1996 he created an incubator, Idealab, in which ideas would be
developed, companies would be nurtured and those that found a

market would leave the incubator to thrive on their own. Gross's head-spinning history of company creation includes wild successes, spectacular failures and concepts that were too far ahead of their time. "The mad scientist with the soul of an entrepreneur," as *Fortune* magazine calls him, says the most satisfying part of his job is "seeing an idea go from nothing to something."

> **Takeaway:** *"There are so many problems in the world that beg for solutions. Find the ones that you are passionate about and devote yourself to them."*

1. Solve a problem. My ideas arise from an internal need, something I want that I can't get. When I use a product or drive in traffic and experience something that irks me I want to fix it. It doesn't matter who had the idea. Whether it's creating an app to organize the chaos of Twitter or an electric car, we take a good look at these ideas and if we decide to go to the next step, we'll mock them up at Idealab. If we find a CEO who's interested, we often form a company. If not, it becomes a piece of technology we may use someday in the future.

2. Build a team with complementary skills. Of the 100 companies I have started, every single one that succeeded had people with complementary skills. According to a management coach I worked with, Ichak Adizes, there are four types of management skills. And you need people with each one of the four skills to complement each other. The *Entrepreneur* is ahead of his time, sees the future and invents things. The *Producer* takes the new product and executes. The *Administrator* is the organizer who puts systems in place, makes sure the orders are filled and the bills are paid. The *Integrator* is a people person who understands the other three types and helps them get along, because they often hate each other's guts. A team with complementary skills can take a mediocre idea and create an incredible result, but a great idea without these complementary skills will fizzle. It's the most important lesson for a start-up, and I wish I had known about it earlier in my career.

3. Reward risk taking. All across America, businesses pay lip service to risk taking, but as long as people are punished for failing, they'll be more focused on keeping their jobs than taking risks. At Idealab everyone knows that if they take a wild risk on an idea and it doesn't work, we'll stand behind them. They won't get fired. We'll put them on another job. And that job might be the one that pays off.

4. Go against the flow. Going against conventional wisdom with a new idea can be risky if you're doing it just to buck the trends. But if you have a solid business plan for that idea, it can be a high-reward opportunity. If everyone else thinks your idea is heresy, they won't compete with you. In 1998, you had to buy online traffic by signing multiyear homepage portal deals that could cost as much as $5 million to become a featured site. But there was no way to tell whether that cost was worth it. This spurred me to create a model where companies could pay for traffic on a pay-per-click basis. I was confident that companies would want to buy traffic that way, but when we developed the model for it, the *Wall Street Journal* panned us. Companies said they would never cooperate. We launched the model as GoTo.com and signed deals with AOL, Microsoft and Yahoo, who had originally opposed the idea. Five years later, Yahoo bought the company, renamed Overture, for $1.6 billion. The pay-per-click model completely changed the way sites buy traffic. At first the idea was ridiculed, then violently opposed, then finally accepted as the new conventional wisdom.

5. Stealth is overrated. I used to be very guarded about discussing new ideas, but I've learned that if you openly discuss an idea, you'll get feedback that can actually improve it. You'll excite people about the product, and most important, you'll recruit quality people to your cause. Having said that, you do want to protect your ideas if you can. By the time we thought of patenting our pay-per-click

model we were five days past the one-year patent deadline. We had
no idea the model would one day have a market cap of $200 billion.
We lost out on the fundamental patent, but we rushed to patent a lot
of the smaller things and later sold many of these to Google for $350
million, which at the time was the largest patent sale in tech industry history.

6. Test before you invest. Test your ideas against the reality
of the market. You're biased toward your company's ideas and success, so test your idea as soon as you possibly can—before you invest
too much time or money to find out if people will open their wallets
and give you their cash. In 1998, back when people were still nervous about giving credit card information to Web sites, I had an idea
to sell cars online. When I started a site called CarsDirect people
said, "You're crazy! Who's going to buy a car online?" I knew *I*
would buy a car online, because I hated going to the dealer and haggling and I wanted a vehicle delivered to my home. But would anyone else? We had to find out. I told the entrepreneur running the
start-up, "Let's put up a site and see what happens." He was unsure,
saying, "What if somebody buys one?" I said, "We'll go down to the
Auto Mall, buy a car at retail and ship it to the guy's house. They
don't need to know where we got it!" The entrepreneur finally put
the site online. The next morning he called me in a panic: "We sold
four cars last night!" I told him, "Turn the site off! Now!" But we
knew the idea would work. We had done the minimum to test if the
premise was right. We now had the confidence to go ahead and build
the whole infrastructure—the site and the relationships with the
vendors and dealers. CarsDirect had its ups and downs, but it went
on to become a huge success and grew to become Internet Brands,
one of the largest online retailers.

7. Be 10 times better than your competition. Customers
don't want to switch to a new product or service that's 10 percent
better. They'll only switch to something that is radically better than
what's already out there. Our rule of thumb is that we have to be 10

times better than the competition to beat them. Before you start a new company be harsh and ask yourself, "Is my fundamental idea really a significant improvement on what's out there?" Or, "Is my idea something that cannot be replicated?" You can beat your competition if you have a patent, or if like Apple with the iPad, by the time you get to market you have such critical mass that you have a prohibitive head start. Another route to dominance is if your idea requires your competitors to change their structure so drastically that they can no longer compete—for example, if someone introduced a new form of online auction that was so radically different from eBay's model that eBay would have to change their entire methodology.

8. Survive until the world catches up to you. If you have a breakthrough idea that is far ahead of its time, you'll still need to survive until the market catches up to you. That means conserving your cash, growing slowly and sacrificing some upside so you don't go out of business before you become profitable. We learned this painful lesson with several start-ups after the Internet bubble burst in 1999. For example, in 1997, our first year of eToys, an online toy store, we did nearly $1 million in Christmas business. And $35 million two years later. We were the hottest thing out there and going like gangbusters. We were projecting a $300 million Christmas the next year. We sank money into building warehouses to support those expected sales. And then the crash hit. We only made half of the projected $300 million. By any measure, that was incredible—a 400 percent increase over the year before—but we had used up all the cash in building the warehouses. The company went bust not because the idea was flawed but because we had overspent and run out of cash. Markets change faster than you can imagine. Instead of judging your success by the size of your office, your marketing budget or the number of employees, sometimes you have to immediately scale your company to last as long as it's going to take until people are ready for it.

9. Don't think of investors as an ATM. When I was younger I was reluctant to give away equity to investors, but now I realize I'm buying their connections and expertise. In one of our latest ventures, UberMedia, a series of Twitter apps, we have a group of very accomplished and well-connected investors. Because of their vast experience they've advised us on difficult strategic questions. They've given us high-level introductions to celebrities, retail stores, media companies and even other strategic investors that we couldn't have gotten to on our own. I'll happily give away equity to get an investor who is passionate about our company and has professional experiences and contacts they can bring to us.

10. Share the wealth. Magic occurs when you give your employees equity. Once they have a significant stake in the company you'll find that human potential is unlocked, teamwork is fostered and performance increases. In 2010 when a company we started was acquired, we decided to pay a dividend to our Idealab employees, who were all shareholders. We met in a restaurant across the street from our office. People had no idea what they would get. When they opened the envelopes we handed out and saw how big their payouts were, they were overwhelmed. A few started crying. Then a whole bunch of people started crying. Then the whole company was crying. The dividend allowed people to buy cars, houses, rethink their kids' college plans, really improve their lives. It was the most incredible moment, one of Idealab's high points, because every single person was in it together. It brought us together like a family. You can't overestimate the power of giving everyone a stake in the company and spreading the equity around.

BILL GROSS FACTS

Gross's boyhood nickname: Alva, in honor of his boyhood hero, Thomas Alva Edison.

Candy arbitrage: At age 12, Gross takes advantage of the "3 Snickers Bars for a quarter" deal at his local drugstore and resells the bars individually at the school bus stop for 9¢ each. Profit: 2/3¢ per bar. Business boomed.

Payday: 1985: Business software CPA+ sells to Lotus for $10 million; educational software company Knowledge Adventures also sells for $90 million. 2003: Overture sold to Yahoo for $1.6 billion.

Not to the moon: 1999: Idealab company, Blastoff!, is year and a half from sending robotic rover to moon. Users will pick landing site, name rovers and "push" the launch button on their computer screens at moment of firing. Participants include James Cameron, NASA and Jet Propulsion Laboratory veterans, but when the dot-com crash hits, Blastoff! is shut down.

Funding: Idealab invests hundreds of millions of dollars in their companies and has helped them raise $2.8 billion. Idealab companies have had 8 IPOs and 35 acquisitions.

Idealab companies (partial list): Answers.com, CarsDirect, Citysearch, eSolar, eToys.com, Insider Page, Internet Brands, Intranets.com, NetZero, Overture, PetSmart.com, Picasa, Swap.com, Tickets.com, UberMedia.com.

START-UP FACTS

Explosive growth: 1867: Alfred Nobel, Swedish chemist, develops dynamite, first explosive that can be safely handled. He builds global empire, with explosive plants in 14 countries, absorbing all competition and creating world's first international holding company. He leaves fortune to create the Nobel Prizes.

Ideas into dollars: 1876: Prolific inventor Thomas Alva Edison creates first industrial research lab to apply principles of mass production to process of invention. He creates successful companies based on his lab's inventions in industries including automobile, battery, cement, electric light, electrical utility, mining, motion picture, office machinery, phonograph, railway, telegraph and telephone industries.

Ford has a better idea: 1903: Henry Ford founds Ford Motor company. After being able to produce only three cars a day, he pioneers automobile assembly line and by 1920 produces a million cars a year.

Start it up: 2011, United States: 12 percent of adults between ages 18 and 64 are actively involved in setting up a new business or currently own and manage a new business.

Chapter 34

How to Win Friends and Influence People (in the Twenty-First Century)

· ·

Guy Kawasaki

The business guru's guru, entrepreneur, one-time Apple
evangelizer and author of several bestselling books,
including *Enchantment*

Guy Kawasaki's journey to become the Dale Carnegie of the digital age began in 1983, when a former college roommate who worked for a little-known company called Apple gave Kawasaki a sneak preview of a prototype computer called the "Macintosh." At the time, the closest most people had come to a personal computer was an IBM Selectric typewriter. Kawasaki's Mac encounter was a revelation. It was the moment, he says, "when the clouds parted and I heard angels singing." Eventually Kawasaki went to work at Apple as an "evangelizer," someone who promoted the cult of the Mac. Because of his passion for the product, it was the perfect job for Kawasaki. When he felt his work at Apple was done, he wrote his first book, *The Macintosh Way*, because he was "bursting with idealistic and pure notions about how a company can change the world." Since then, Kawasaki has not only founded several successful companies, but preaches what he practices, as he continues to evangelize the gospel of salesmanship, workplace skills and interpersonal relations. An eclectic sage, Kawasaki has become the Dale

Carnegie of the twenty-first century. He has written books on subjects as diverse as getting through painful times, beating the competition, innovation, evangelizing a product or service and changing hearts and minds. Part handbook, part manifesto, Kawasaki's books are peppered with earthy insider advice on everything from the perfect length of a YouTube video to how to get a standing ovation to how to get your boss to love you.

> **Takeaway:** *"Winning friends and influencing people isn't rocket science. It's about being likable and trustworthy and having a good product or service—which may just be yourself."*

1. Be likable. Think about this: Have you ever been enchanted by a person you didn't like? You cannot influence people unless they actually find you likable. When I first met Richard Branson, he asked me if I flew on Virgin. When I told him that I didn't, he got on his knees and started to polish my shoes with his jacket. That's likability. And now whenever I can, I fly Virgin Airways.

2. Develop trust. You can be liked but not trusted—for example, celebrities are often liked but not trusted. You develop trust by first trusting others—before they have trusted you. Then you need to think like a baker, not an eater. A baker believes she can bake more and bigger pies. An eater believes that life is a zero-sum game: What others eat, he cannot eat. Bakers are trusted. Eaters are not.

3. Keep it simple. It's hard to influence people if they don't understand what you're saying. Or if they think you're talking down to them by using hoity-toity words. The more complex people make something, the less you should trust it. It's that simple. Whether you're interviewing for a job, pitching an idea, creating a slogan or just meeting someone for the first time, simplicity is best. Find a simple message that expresses the core of your idea. Keep it short;

use simple words, the active voice, more verbs and fewer adjectives. Everyone remembers "Got milk?" and "Just do it."

4. Align your goals. Whether you are representing yourself or your company, it's a lot easier to persuade people if your goals are aligned. Then people enter into a kind of natural, unforced state of agreement. First of all, don't impose your own values. Then try to find something in common. If you're not making progress, try to harmonize objections. Saying "Not yet" or "Tell me more" as opposed to "No!" will buy you time to look for more options and build rapport. In business, it's not just about what *you* want. If you are driven by the desires of your customers you will be focused on delivering what *they* want. A win-win situation for everyone.

5. Nobodies are the new somebodies. Marketing 1.0 was hierarchical: You sucked up to the powerful, hoped they liked what you did and would tell the masses what to do. Marketing 1.0 is dead. Marketing 2.0 is horizontal because of blogging, Google +, Facebook and Twitter. Now a bunch of Lonelyboy15s with a few dozen followers, fans or friends can make your product tip. Seven years ago, did you see the *Wall Street Journal*, *Fortune*, *Forbes* or *BusinessWeek* predict the success of Twitter? It was the Nobodies who made Twitter successful, because "nobodies" are the new "somebodies."

6. Tweet like Dale. Dale Carnegie would love Twitter. He would be able to reach people anywhere in the world, and teach his clients to use Twitter to win friends and influence even *more* people. The rules of engagement of digital communication are: fast, flat and frequent. You win over people by responding to tweets, posts, updates and comments within a few hours and by responding to email within a few days. Flat means that whether the person has one million followers or fifteen, you respond to him. You never know—he might become your most valuable supporter or a good friend. By frequent I don't mean you communicate when everything else is done—you do it all the time. Winning people over is a process, not an event.

7. Create an ecosystem. Where would Apple's and Google's phones and tablets be without Apple's iOS developers and Google's Android developers? An ecosystem is a community of people—partners, friends, allies, evangelists—who work with you and align themselves with your cause's success. You can apply this to a rock band, a muffin store, or a billion-dollar start-up. First you have to create something worthy of an ecosystem. Then pick your evangelists. Give people something meaningful to do. And create a dialogue with blogs, Web sites or social media. The Grateful Dead provide a wonderful example. They set aside an area for people to record their concerts. Instead of fighting against "piracy" they encouraged it. These "tapers" then spread the word of the Grateful Dead to a larger community that helped to support the band.

8. What goes around comes around. Asking people for favors can bring them closer to you. In his autobiography, Ben Franklin tells a story about a member of the Pennsylvania Provincial Assembly who opposed Franklin's appointment to a post he wanted. Franklin won him over by first writing him a note requesting that the man lend him a "very scarce and curious" book from his library. After the loan, Franklin returned the book with a note, "expressing strongly" his "sense of the favor." The man then spoke to Franklin for the first time and they became great friends for the rest of their lives. And it goes both ways. Always be generous. The most powerful favor is the one given with no clear link between the favor and what you want back.

9. Make your boss love you. The first key to getting your boss to love you is to drop everything when she asks you to do something. This might not sound optimal or fair—life's tough. (Incidentally, this is good advice for husbands, too.) The second key is: Prototype fast. If your boss asks you to do a PowerPoint presentation, show up with a text-only version in a few hours. This proves you dropped everything. It also increases the likelihood that you do a good job because there's more time to revise things. The third key is: Deliver bad news early rather than praying for a last-minute miracle. That way there's more time to prevent the bad news from occurring.

10. Get close and personal. Show up. Pressing the flesh is the best way to create relationships, so get out of your chair and jump into the analog world. But when that's not possible get close to people through digital means. That's why social media are called "social" media. The good news is that most people aren't willing to make the effort. So separate yourself from the pack and set a goal that's higher than just closing a deal. Get close enough to people that they become your fans and they love what you do so much that they camp overnight in front of your store to be the first person to buy your iPhone.

GUY KAWASAKI STATS

Presidential rival: Honolulu, 1972: Kawasaki graduates from Iolani School, rival of Punahou School, where at the same time Barack Obama is enrolled in sixth grade.

Contempt of court: Attempting to please parents, Kawasaki attends law school at UC Davis, but hates it so much he quits after a week.

Diamonds are forever: 1979, Van Nuys, CA: Kawasaki, working for fine-jewelry manufacturer, learns not only how to count diamonds and speak Yiddish but, most importantly, how to sell.

Jobbed: 1983–87 and 1995–97: Working for Apple, Kawasaki is terrified when boss Steve Jobs tells him his work, ideas and even existence are worthless, and he is in ecstasy the few times Jobs tells him he's great.

Missed opportunity: Mid-'90s: Yahoo, a start-up company, asks Kawasaki to be CEO. Not believing their business model is viable, Kawasaki declines offer. Now, he estimates it was a $3 billion mistake.

Crowdsourced: 2010: Kawasaki sets off online design competition offering $1,000 for best cover for his book *Enchantment*; 250 people enter 760 designs. Indonesian electrical engineering student wins with design of stock photo of butterfly on red background, but publisher hates design. Kawasaki perseveres and commissions origami butterfly that ends up on cover.

Kawasaki's books: *Reality Check, The Art of the Start, Rules for Revolutionaries, How to Drive Your Competition Crazy, Selling the Dream.*

Favorite business maxim: "If an entrepreneur's lips are moving, he's probably lying."

DALE CARNEGIE FACTS

Got milk? Missouri: Born Dale Carnagey in 1888 to poor farming family, Carnagey grows up waking every day at 4 A.M. to milk family cow.

Meat sales: After college, Carnagey works for large national meatpacker and sells so much bacon, soap and lard his sales territory leads all others.

Thespian: 1911: With $500 in savings, Carnagey moves to New York to become an actor, appears in a traveling production of *Polly of the Circus*, decides he hates theater and quits.

Success: 1912, New York City: Teaches first course on public speaking at YMCA and runs out of material before 90-minute class is over. By 1916, his course in "effective speaking" sells out Carnegie Hall.

Name change: 1920s: Trading on cache of well-known Carnegie family, Carnagey changes last name to "Carnegie."

Self-help: 1936: After reading hundreds of biographies of great leaders and works of philosophers and psychologists, and interviewing luminaries such as Thomas Edison, President Franklin Roosevelt and Clark Gable, Carnegie publishes *How to Win Friends and Influence People* with print run of 5,000 copies that sell for $2 apiece. Since then, book has sold 15 million copies worldwide.

Dangerous advice: 1950s: Carnegie's book is translated into Russian for sole use of Communist Party leaders and KGB. 1990: After perestroika reforms, book becomes available to general public.

Foundation of Carnegie's advice: "Forget yourself; do things for others," and, "Cooperate with the inevitable."

Chapter 35

How to Win the Indy 500

. . . .

Helio Castroneves

Racing superstar and three-time winner of the Indy 500

R ace car driving is a sport based on failure—for every race, there can be only one winner, to say nothing of the potentially devastating consequences of careening around a crowded track at speeds close to 200 mph. Expenses can run into the millions for race cars, repairs, mechanics, engineers and transportation before you ever rise to a level where somebody actually pays *you*. Most aspiring drivers fall by the wayside, but even though Brazilian-born Helio Castroneves experienced financial meltdowns, unscrupulous managers and crises of confidence, he persevered. Inheriting a passion for racing from his father, Castroneves received his first go-kart on his 11th birthday. By 14, he had won his first Brazilian go-kart state championship. Rising steadily through the ranks of racing from kart to car—Formula Chevrolet, Formula Three South America, British Formula Three—at 21, he ascended to the Indy Lights in the United States. Just three years later, Castroneves had no team, no sponsors, and his family, who had invested their entire fortune in his career, had gone bankrupt. It seemed the dream was over. But after a tragic accident involving Greg Moore, one of the most promising drivers on the celebrated Team Penske, a replacement was needed. Roger Penske turned to Castroneves, and the heavyhearted young driver reluctantly stepped in. Against all odds, in 2001, his rookie season,

Castroneves finished first in the Indy 500. The next year, he won again. Another big win in 2009 made him a racing superstar. "All of life is a race," he wrote in a letter to his unborn daughter, Mikella. "But you have to pace yourself. Sometimes you have to change your strategy. Sometimes you have to go maximum speed."

Takeaway: *"Racing isn't just a sport; it's a quest."*

1. You can't do it alone. I've been very lucky to have a family that backed me every step of the way. My father was my friend and mentor, and was crazy enough to support me in my racing obsession. My sister gave up her dreams of being a dancer to manage my career. My mother instilled a faith in me and supported me no matter how nervous my racing made her. During one of my lowest points, when I was ready to give it all up, she told me, "Don't quit." She read to me from the Bible, "Blessed is the man who perseveres under trial, because he has stood the test. . . ." I have depended on them for my entire life. As a member of the great Penske race team, I found a new family. Just like my own family, they practice the values of loyalty, dedication and hard work.

2. Devote yourself. Very few drivers get the opportunity to be on a team that races at Indy, and every year only 33 of those drivers qualify. Only one of them is going to win, so you have to put dedication into your work. At 14, when I came in second at the Brazilian Karting Championships, I made it my mission to one day be at the top of the podium. Besides countless hours of practice at the track, I started serious physical training, running wind sprints every day before or after school on the days I wasn't out of school traveling all over Brazil to races. I took up an intense program of weightlifting. I let everything else go so that I could just drive. As one of my trainers told me, the girls and the parties will always be there, but once you lose a race you cannot get it back.

3. Wait for the right moment to make your move. When I was young I wanted to go full throttle and lead every single lap of every single race with the fastest time. But sometimes that obsession led to mistakes. My father tried to break me of that habit, telling me, "You don't have to win on the first lap." At a go-kart race when I was 14 years old, I stayed in the middle of the pack and waited until the final laps. When I saw an opening, I went for it, going top speed to pass the three cars in front of me. It was the first time I'd actually followed my father's advice. And I won. To become a champion you need more than sheer speed. It's not about pushing harder; it's about knowing *when* to push harder.

4. Keep your head. During my early races, my father stood on the side of the track with his index fingers on his temples to tell me, "Keep your head. Trust yourself. You are only as good as you believe." Many years later when I was 21, I was driving with broken ribs. I was trying to get the hang of IndyCars on oval circuits and I kept crashing into the walls. It was killing my ribs. Self-doubt had taken hold. I wondered, "What the heck is going on? Is my career over?" Racing is half physical and half mental, and my head was a mess. I went to a performance psychologist who helped me realize I was not just negative about my chances of winning in a race; I was *very* negative. Later that summer, at a race in Quebec, as soon as I began the first lap, a switch went off in my head. I blocked out my negative thoughts. I remembered my father's words and focused on the race. I was back. I won that race. And the focus and trust in myself carried me through the next race, the next year, and into so many other areas of my life. It was a turning point in my career.

5. It's you *and* the car. Racing is 30 percent driver, 70 percent car. My first mechanic, Rubio, told me that. I was only 13, but he taught me that to win I'd need to know everything about the car. The more I knew, the better I could communicate with the mechanics. As I rose through the racing classes, I had to understand each new type of car from Brazilian go-karts to the more powerful Euro go-karts, from the open-wheel Formula Chevrolet cars to the even more sophisticated Formula Three cars. At that point, I had to learn to deal with technology. I had never had anything in the car and all of a sudden there's a radio, a computer and an antenna right in the middle of the windshield. I was racing half as hard and going twice as fast. Inside the cockpit of my first Penske car, the ride was so smooth. I realized, "I'm not holding my breath. I'm breathing!" To win championship races you need a great car, but only the driver who masters the car will win.

6. Let the race come to you. Even if I've been on a track before, every time I race, it's a whole new track. The walls might appear to be the same, the corners might appear to be the same, but they're not the same. They're a new challenge. There are so many factors you can't control—the wind is different, the temperature is different, the car is different, the tires might be a little bit different. When it rains *everything* changes. You need to pay close attention and let the race reveal itself to you and adjust your strategy to the conditions.

7. Don't stop learning till you're six feet in the ground. Some people think that when they achieve a certain amount of success they know more than anyone else. But you're always picking up new information. Take driving strategy. At first, riding go-karts, I only knew to accelerate and brake. I had to learn to ease into turns and to use the pedals with finesse. I had to learn about competition, that the race isn't a game, it's a contest. With each style of racing there was so much to learn. Years later, when I joined Penske, the team was much more experienced than I was. They had won Indy races and challenged for championships. I hadn't done that yet. I had to start from the ground up. When I made a mistake I said, "OK, guys, I screwed up. Help me figure out what I did wrong."

8. It's not you or me—it's *we*. Everyone on Team Penske has the same attitude. When we win, *we* win; when we lose, *we* lose. I depend on the pit crew, engineers, spotters and strategists. In the

2002 Indy 500, there were problems with our car and I was a lap down, but the team never gave up. I heard our race strategist, Tim Cindric, telling me through my headset, "We have to take a chance." We skipped refueling at the last pit stop. When everyone else pitted, I took the lead. But we only had enough fuel for 30 laps and we needed to stretch it to 40. Cindric kept saying, "Save fuel!" So I ran at half throttle and let some lap cars pass me to draft behind them. At lap 195 out of 200, Cindric said, "Paul Tracy's gaining on you!" I went flat out with whatever fuel I had left. Tracy passed me, but it was just after the yellow caution flags came out when drivers can't pass each other. Cindric said, "Slow down to save fuel. Just make sure you get to the finish line." There were four-tenths of a gallon of fuel left as I crossed the line. Skipping the last pit stop was something no one had ever done. People paid attention to it. Now, it's become a very common strategy. It was a great team decision that won that race.

9. Go with your gut. Your team prepares you, and your strategist and spotter advise you during the race, but ultimately, you're the only one in the cockpit of the car. You're the only one who can make that split-second decision that can decide the fate of a race. At Indy in 2009, Scott Dixon, the defending champ, was in front of me. After a late restart, as soon as the green flag dropped, I went for it. Our guys on the radio were saying it was too early to pass, but I felt the adrenaline. That was the moment. The whole thing came to me: Boom! This is it! It was a feeling. An instinct. It was lap 142 when I just made my path. I passed Scott and held the lead the rest of the way.

10. Have fun. When you arrive at Indy and see the 500,000 fans in the stands, it's an incredible feeling. That's why they call it the "Greatest Spectacle in Racing." To get there, you have to work so hard and face so much frustration that you can forget why you even got into racing. But when you stop enjoying yourself, what's the point? When I won my first Indy 500 in 2001, I could hear the crowd going crazy and I was so excited that I unbuckled myself and leapt out of the car. I kept my helmet on because I was crying and thanking God. I ran toward the crowds and scaled the safety fence between the track and the stands. I looked behind me. My crew was coming. I called for them to join me. And they did. Now, I always climb the barrier when I win, because I'm so happy to be racing that I'm going to celebrate as hard as I can.

HELIO CASTRONEVES FACTS

Brazilian birthplace: Ribeirão Preto, or "black stream." "It's redneck country," says Castroneves.

Castroneves' parents' advice: Father: "Act like a champion." Mother: "God has a plan."

First accident: Age 11. Driving on an abandoned track, Castroneves hits a wall and flips go-kart. Father rushes him to hospital and then straight back to track to ride some more.

First serious girlfriend: Age 18. She: "You never have any time for me. Make a choice: the track or me." He: "I'm sorry, but I choose the track."

Nickname: Spiderman, because he climbs the fence after each win.

Occupation if not a race car driver: Chauffeur. "I'd get lost most of the time, but I like to be behind the wheel."

Dancing with the Stars: 2007: Castroneves wins reality TV show with partner Julianne Hough.

Legal trouble: 2009: Castroneves almost misses entire racing season when he's prosecuted for tax evasion. Exonerated and acquitted of all charges, he rushes to Indy months behind schedule and wins race.

Favorite saying: "Sometimes you're the windshield and sometimes you're the bug."

INDY 500 FACTS

Size: Interior oval is larger than Yankee Stadium, the Coliseum, Vatican City, the Rose Bowl, Wimbledon and Churchill Downs combined.

First Indy auto race: 1909: Track disintegrates, contributing to multiple crashes and fatalities.

First Indy 500: 1911: Winner Ray Harroun drives a Marmon Wasp, averaging 74.6 mph. 80,200 attend.

A French twist: 1913: Winner Jules Goux, driving a Peugeot, chugs champagne at each pit stop.

"Got milk?" tradition: 1936: Winner Louis Meyer is first to drink milk in winner's circle.

Women in Indy: 1977: First woman to qualify, Janet Guthrie. 2005: First woman to lead, Danica Patrick finishes fourth and attracts more media attention than the winner, Dan Weldon.

Closest finish: 1992: Al Unser Jr. beats Scott Goodyear by 0.043 seconds.

Fatalities: 60 total, including 38 drivers, 12 riding mechanics, 5 spectators, 2 pit crew, 2 firemen, and a 12-year-old boy in 1932 who is killed in his front yard when detached wheel bounces out of speedway and across street.

Most victories by owner: Roger Penske, 15.

Annual consumption at Indy 500: Beer, 14,000 gallons; fries, 12 tons; hot dogs, 5 miles if laid end to end.

———————

Chapter 36

How to Write a Runaway Bestseller

•••••••••••••••••••••••••••••••

Stephen J. Dubner

Coauthor of the books *Freakonomics* and *Super-
Freakonomics*, with total sales of over 5 million copies;
host of *Freakonomics Radio*

Stephen Dubner learned the rules of competitive journalism at a tender age. "We had a family newspaper when I was a kid, called the *Quaker Street Quacker*," recalls Dubner. For a story to be published in the *Quacker*, it had to be both newsy and good. And since Dubner was the youngest of eight children, the competition was stiff. "I snuck one in once in a while," he says. After getting an MFA in writing from Columbia University, Dubner was drawn to dynamic long-form, literary journalism. Supporting himself as a magazine editor, he wrote features as time allowed and authored a pair of nonfiction books. In 2003, while hard at work on a third book, a *New York Times Magazine* editor asked him for a profile of Steven Levitt, an iconoclastic University of Chicago economist. Three times, Dubner passed—until one night, out of curiosity, Dubner downloaded the economist's research and discovered that "Levitt's brain was a beautiful mirror image of what I wished my brain could be." Dubner's inspired profile of Levitt received so much attention that the "two Steves" (as they came to be called) agreed to collaborate on a book. The result was *Freakonomics*. Dubner's abilities as a master storyteller and interpreter of complex material coupled with

Levitt's provocative subject matter made *Freakonomics* a cultural phenomenon and publishing sensation. The critically acclaimed book has been translated into 35 languages, with sales (including a sequel) of over 5 million copies, as well as spin-off radio and TV projects, a documentary, a foundation and a popular blog. "Sure, we've both worked hard," says Dubner. "But let's not underestimate how lucky we've been as well."

> **Takeaway:** *"The best way to write a bestseller is not to try to write a bestseller. Write the book that you want to read."*

1. Begin with good material. I'm not a person who was put on this earth to make high art. Or, to declare, "this is what I have to say." What I am all about as a writer is finding out about stuff. I tend to go to the smartest, most interesting people I can find and say, "I don't understand what you do exactly. I don't know how it works. I'd love for you to explain it for me."

2. Write what you like. I'm convinced that the worst way to write a bestseller is to *try* to write a bestseller. I got lucky because I got a contract for a book that I wanted to write. Levitt was lucky to get a contract for a book he was happy to have this other guy write with him. Once we started the work, we felt like we'd already won. We said, "Let's write a book we both want to read." Whenever I've read a book or article I've written, it's a horrible experience. *Freakonomics* was the first thing I'd written that I was still engaged and tickled by afterward.

3. Imitation gets you nowhere. The reason things work in life, whether in love or art, is because someone or something is appealing. There's a woman that people want to get to know. There's a singer that people like to hear. There's a politician that people want to vote for. There's a book that people want to read. Trying to manufacture that appeal never works. In the arts especially—film, publishing, even theater—so much energy is put into copying the latest success. The publishing industry keeps making the same mistake, thinking if they can sell a $20 million Harry Potter, then even a B-minus Harry Potter rip-off could sell $1 million. But, no, it won't. People don't like Harry Potter simply because it has elements A, B, C, D, E and F that can be replicated in another book. They like it because they *like* it. It has some ineffable alchemy of attractive elements that is impossible to imitate.

4. Every topic needs an idea. As a magazine editor, I learned a topic is nothing without an idea. If you can't wring out the idea from a topic, then don't do the story. For example, one episode of our *Freakonomics* radio show is about prediction. Well, what about prediction? We need an idea; we need a thesis. So we came up with the following: Human beings are terrible at predicting the future and yet we can't stop—why? And, furthermore, what's to be done about it? So there's our topic turned into an idea. Another topic we worked on was quitting. We all know the bromide that winners never quit and quitters never win. But the question we asked was, Is that really true? What about the upside to quitting? When we began writing *Freakonomics* we realized that Levitt's research covered many topics but there was no unifying idea, as in Malcolm Gladwell's *Tipping Point*. We had a big pile of case studies with a lot of data. The challenge, then, was to find the ideas that all those stories illustrated.

5. Let the reader experience the experience. In *Freakonomics*, whenever possible, we featured characters. Take Sudhir Venkatesh. He's a remarkable person, who at the time was a sociology grad student in Chicago who basically embedded himself with a crack gang. I thought it'd be much more interesting to read about his research if we also knew how Sudhir is kidnapped by this gang on the day he meets them. So, let's make Sudhir a character. Levitt and I wanted the book to be interactive in the sense that, as the reader encounters these data and case studies, she's also imagining herself in the moment. I am quite fond of stories that simply go, "This happened and then this happened and then, surprisingly, this happened, and what do you think happened next?"

6. Keep it simple. One mistake that smart people often make is trying to remind everyone else how smart they are. I have perhaps a slightly above-average IQ, and Levitt is really quite smart. But I believe it's always better to tell a story simply than to show off. I've encountered a lot of brilliant people and asked them to explain what they do and they can't. They don't have to know how to explain what they do. Explaining is my job. I like to do a ton of reporting and synthesizing and thinking and then write one simple sentence that says something like, "If you want to get rid of violence, get rid of young men." Simplicity allows you to connect with your readers. They trust plain language.

7. Listen to your writing. Writing was originally a way to preserve oral speech, and I've never forgotten that. When I was very young, my mother would sit me down at the kitchen table with my writing and say, "Well, let's read this out loud, and see how it sounds." At home, we were all musical, so we thought of music and writing as twins. I use alliteration, repetition, and call-and-response. Reading is boring if the writing lacks variation; if all the sentences are roughly the same length, have the same Latinate/non-Latinate blend, have the same blend of long and short words. After writing every sentence, I read the words aloud so I can hear all of that. What's now accepted as quality literature is very different from the original form of storytelling, but I prefer to write in a way that draws on that oral tradition.

8. Keep the reader's eye engaged. People forget that reading is a visual experience. The most beautiful page should look like a painting. When you open a book, your eye travels down the page. You can immediately see if it's a page that someone has written while keeping in mind variety and pacing and tone. For *Freakonomics* I did a lot of interviews so we'd have a lot of quotes. In a musical sense, quotes are like a different instrument coming in to change the rhythm and the feel and the way the sentences flow. A beautiful page contains variety and different points for jumping in. You think, "Oh, there's a numeral." Or, "There's a dollar sign." When I'm reading a book and turn the page, I always scan the new page. Sometimes I'll just jump to the middle of a paragraph where there's a capital letter: "Oooh, whose name is that?"

9. Keep it short. We intentionally kept *Freakonomics* quite short. When the book became popular, some people complained: "I paid $26 and finished it in 4 hours." Personally, I finish about one out of 30 books, so I take that as a compliment. If people finish a book, they're much more likely to tell other people about it. When Saul Bellow wrote a novella late in his life people said, "You're Saul Bellow—why aren't you writing an 800-page novel?" And he said, "The world has changed. People don't have time to read anymore, and if I want to be read, I'm going to write in a format that they can read." And I thought, "Wow, if Saul Bellow can write a novella because that's what people want, then who am I to say that we're going to write some huge thing?" I always think of how Michelangelo is said to have described sculpting as the simple process of removing the pieces of stone that don't look good.

10. You're not done when the book is done. *Freakonomics* didn't become that big a deal until well after we published. There had been a very good review in the *Wall Street Journal*, and we entered the *Times* bestseller list at number five. At that point, I would have happily died—to have a *New York Times* bestseller! We were doing promotion, but the publicist said, "We're having trouble getting you booked on TV." Everyone asked, "*Freakonomics?* What the hell is that?" When they told the *Today* show what was in the book, they said, "Sorry, we don't do the Klan, we don't do sumo wrestling, we don't do black baby names, we don't do abortion and crime." So about two or three weeks after the book was out, Levitt and I wrote an op-ed for *USA Today*, which most "classy" writers won't even

admit to reading. The op-ed was about parenting, a point-by-point
thing about what matters and what doesn't matter as a parent. It
had nothing to do with anything, but TV producers read *USA Today*, so suddenly we got on the *Today* show. Matt Lauer said, "Oh,
man, this is really cool—what else is in your book? Why don't you
come back every week?" Then ABC came to us and said, "Why
don't you come back every week on all our shows—*Good Morning
America, World News Tonight*, etc.?" So, we started to have a cumu-
lative advantage—once something becomes big, it's a lot easier for
it to get bigger. We went from being grateful for any exposure at all
to this bizarre, amazingly fun Freakonomics enterprise.

STEPHEN DUBNER FACTS

First writing gig: Age 11: A poem, "The Opossum," in *High-
lights for Children*.

On religion: Dubner's Jewish parents convert to Catholicism.
He converts back.

Rock band: 1986, CBGB's, New York: After gig, Dubner's
band, the Right Profile, is signed by Clive Davis. Dubner quits
band a year later.

Other books: *Turbulent Souls, Choosing My Religion, Confessions of a Hero-Worshiper* and the children's book *The Boy with
Two Belly Buttons*.

On coauthoring *Freakonomics*: Magazine editor's advice to
Dubner: "You're a known writer. Why do you want to coauthor a
book? It'll be a disaster."

Dubner/Levitt $plit: Before agreeing to write book, the pair
write down nonnegotiable percentages they'd be willing to
work for. Both write 60/40, offering to give the other 60 percent.
So, they split the difference, 50/50.

On Levitt's work: "It's about what most people in the world find so interesting—cause and effect. Things happen in the world and people try to explain them, and half the time they're making it up. Levitt not only has curious thoughts; he knows how to work with data to prove his explanations."

On writing: "I've got a family; I've got to feed them. I've always had the good luck to write what I wanted and get paid. But, if I couldn't write what I wanted, I wouldn't write. I'd do something else, 'cause I've got to get paid."

Favorite joke about writing: From sportswriter Red Smith: "There's nothing to writing. All you do is sit down at the typewriter and open a vein."

BESTSELLER FACTS

First American bestseller: 1662: *The Day of Doom* by Rev. Michael Wigglesworth, a doggerel verse of Calvinist theology.

First fiction bestseller (in English): 1740: *Pamela; or, Virtue Rewarded* by Samuel Richardson, the story of a servant girl climbing the social ladder. Pamela motifs were reproduced on teacups, fans, prints, paintings, waxworks and playing cards.

Revolutionary bestseller: 1776: *Common Sense* by Thomas Paine. The 48-page pamphlet had higher per-capita sales than any other book in American history, with first-year sales of 500,000 copies. (Paine donated his royalties to the Continental Army.)

Political bestseller: 1852: *Uncle Tom's Cabin* by Harriet Beecher Stowe, the bestselling novel of the nineteenth century. An antislavery novel, it helped lay the groundwork for the Civil War. First year's sales: Unites States, 310,000 copies; Britain, 1 million copies. In addition to the novel, there were children's versions, sheet music, dramatizations, figurines, games and handkerchiefs.

First bestseller list: 1895: Appeared in *The Bookman*, a literary magazine.

First book to sell a million copies in a year: 1936: *Gone with the Wind* by Margaret Mitchell.

Bestsellers of all time: Book: *A Tale of Two Cities*, Charles Dickens (over 200 million copies). Series: *Harry Potter* (450 million copies). Authors: William Shakespeare and Agatha Christie (over 2 billion copies each).

Best bestseller quote: "There's many a bestseller that could have been prevented by a good teacher." —Flannery O'Connor

———————

Acknowledgments

We'd first like to thank the extraordinary people included in these pages. They are the book and the book is them. And we are grateful. We also want to thank our agent and consigliere, David Patterson of the Foundry Literary + Media agency, who helped us march our idea out the door, and Becky Cole, our Book Whisperer, who helped us realize a long-held dream. Any writer would benefit from her intelligent, genial editor's advice. We'd like to thank our parents; Rita Sweeney for coparenting; Harry Sweeney, editor emeritus, for being the most overqualified intern on the planet; cheerleader in chief Phyllis Gosfield; and the late Eugene "Stranger Than Nonfiction" Gosfield. And we couldn't have done it without our crew of cowranglers, readers, researchers, transcribers, supporters and opinionators: Earl Adams; Brooke Ashforth; Henry Astor; Alex Bertman; Carol Ann Blinken; Diane Cardwell; Elaine D'Farley; Kate Dries; Mila Drumke; Joey Fortuna; Kevin Fortuna; Philip Gefter; Annie, Avery and Reuben Gosfield; Jenna Kagel; Selma Kalousek; Alan Light; Svend Lindbaek; Caroline Marks; Kate Napolitano; Robert Newman; Catriona Ni Aolain; Richard Press; Stacey Pressman; Valentina Rice; Celeste Richardson; Linda Rubes; Hilary Shanahan; Larry Smith; Naomi Starobin; Perry van de Meer; Jonathan Van Meter; and David Wallis. Many thanks to Gigi Gaston for being our inspiration. And last, but really first, we want to thank Roxana Fortuna Gosfield, for being the coolest kid on Barrow Street. May you all pursue your art of doing and do it well.